Macmilla

Macmillan Professional Masters

Titles in the series

Company Accounts Roger Oldcorn
Constitutional and Administrative Law John Alder
Contract Law Ewan McKendrick
Cost and Management Accounting Roger Hussey
Criminal Law Marise Cremona
Data Processing John Bingham
Employee Relations Chris Brewster
Land Law Kate Green
Landlord and Tenant Law Margaret Wilkie and Godfrey Cole
Law of Trusts Patrick McLoughlin and Catherine Rendell
Management Roger Oldcorn
Marketing Robert G. I. Maxwell
Marketing for the Non-Profit Sector Tim Hannagan
Office Administration E. C. Eyre
Operations Management Howard Barnett
Personnel Management Margaret Attwood
Study Skills Kate Williams
Supervision Mike Savedra and John Hawthorn
Systems Analysis John Bingham and Garth Davies

Systems Analysis

John Bingham

and

Garth Davies

MACMILLAN

First edition 1972
Reprinted three times
Second edition 1978
Professional Masters edition 1992

Published 1992 by
THE MACMILLAN PRESS LTD
Houndmills, Basingstoke, Hampshire RG21 2XS
and London
Companies and representatives
throughout the world

ISBN 0–333–56984–9

Copy-edited and typeset by Povey–Edmondson
Okehampton and Rochdale, England

Printed in China

Contents

Preface

This book has been written with the aim of enabling the reader to attain a good working knowledge of the principles and practice of systems analysis. With the aid of *Self-Checks* and *Activities*, the book has been designed to serve those readers studying the subject on their own. Naturally, some interaction with persons experienced in the field can only be advantageous, and readers are encouraged – in the text – to relate studies wherever possible to the world around them.

The book owes its origins to a handbook on the subject written by the authors over twenty years ago. Advances in methods and technology have changed much of what was known as *systems analysis*, though the fundamental concept that improvements can always be achieved through a systematic approach is as valid today as it was then. Above all, systems analysis has become established as a core profession in the development of modern decision-making and information systems.

While systems analysis continues to be an exciting profession, the practitioner carries greater responsibilities than ever before. Large and small organisations alike depend on the quality of their information systems. This places a heavy burden on the systems analyst to understand the needs of the organisation and to deliver correspondingly effective and reliable information systems.

The only sure way consistently to perform to a high standard is to follow well-established guidelines, avoiding the mistakes of others and using proven techniques. In this book, the reader will find a comprehensive guide to systems analysis, drawing on the experience of the authors and others, but also opening doors for self-discovery – which lies at the heart of every healthy business discipline.

JOHN BINGHAM
GARTH DAVIES

Part I

The Nine Steps of Systems Analysis

1 Systems Structure, Strategy and Planning

1.1 The Structure of Systems Analysis

If you ask the average systems analyst to describe and define the work that he or she does, you will probably receive a very vague answer. This is not because the work is too complex or difficult to describe (it is not, as this book attempts to show), but simply because most systems analysts themselves do not have a very clear idea of how the way they do their work is structured. In most organisations it is the backlog and urgency of outstanding tasks which tend to define what the systems analyst does next. So systems development often becomes a matter of achieving a series of purely short-term goals, and the methodology of systems analysis is overlooked.

An important theme of this book is that a **systematic approach** to systems analysis brings major advantages: in terms of **quality, management control** and **user satisfaction**. These and other benefits depend on the fact that systems analysis itself can be analysed into clearly definable steps.

In Part I, the nine broad steps of systems analysis are described:

* 1 System project selection
* 2 Feasibility study
* 3 Project planning
* 4 Definition phase
* 5 Design phase
* 6 Build/buy analysis
* 7 Implementation phase
* 8 Post-implementation review and evaluation
* 9 Maintenance and enhancement

Together, these steps form an ordered approach to systems analysis. Other aspects (such as cost-benefit analysis), described in Chapter 16, complement the nine broad steps and define the range of skills needed by a systems analyst.

1.2 Systems Strategy and Planning

This book is concerned primarily with the analysis and design of individual information systems. Any information system must, however, be placed in the context of the organisation's **systems development as a whole**: if this is not done, there is a danger of duplication, over-stretching of resources and incompatibility between data. The development of an information system should therefore take place within the framework of an overall systems strategy and should form part of a broader plan for systems development.

(a) Systems Strategy

The essence of good systems strategy is to bring together the following three elements:

* user priorities
* systems integration
* resource availability.

(i) User priorities – balancing these is perhaps the most difficult task in all systems development. The only rational approach is to relate user requirements to the **goals** of the organisation as a whole and to reach agreement on **priorities** jointly among the various users. Failing this, it is essential at least to obtain senior management involvement, in order to avoid setting priorities which reflect skilful **user pressures** rather than the **real needs** of the organisation.

Self-check

How do you think the priorities would compare between information systems for (i) a personnel pension scheme, (ii) stock control, (iii) sales statistics?

(ii) Systems integration – this is concerned with different information systems which use **common data**. This concept appears in a variety of forms, such as data sharing, applications convergence

and common data bases. The more awareness there is of this concept during the development stages of individual information systems, the greater the payoff later when systems are integrated or when new systems are designed using data which already exists. In practical terms, the essential points are:

* use of consistent data **definitions**
* consideration of **other possible uses** for data (for example, field sizes should take this into account)
* mandatory checks during analysis and design to see if 'local' data has implications for **other information systems**.

Systems integration can be achieved, however, only if the **technical environment** is capable of sustaining it. Hardware, software (in particular, data base management systems) and data communications facilities have all to allow the process of system integration to take place. For this reason, it is essential for systems integration to incorporate the concept of **systems architecture**, whereby the evolution of the technical environment is planned in relation to that of the applications. The dominating concept that is emerging is that of 'open systems', which enable interconnections between different types of hardware and software, based on standard interfaces and functions – in particular, those at the level of the **operating system**.

(iii) Resource availability – this determines what can be done to meet established user priorities and the need for systems integration. Development and integration of several information systems in parallel can be very costly, and the complexity of the task increases greatly with the number of dependencies between information systems; project management becomes correspondingly more difficult. Nevertheless, urgent needs may call for short-term developments and even here a **strategic framework** brings benefits, by giving guidance in design decisions which have to be made under user pressure.

Self-check

What will be the main types of resource needed to develop an information system?

Systems strategy is concerned with ensuring that separate developments today will jointly bring additional long-term **advantages** – and not **problems** – to the organisation. This strategic approach must be expressed in concrete terms in the form of **long- and medium-term plans**.

(b) Systems planning

The creation of a long-term plan has three major benefits:

* it forces systems developers and users alike to project their needs **beyond immediate actions and priorities**
* it provides a rational basis for **budgeting and human resource planning**
* it acts as a reference framework for **progress** and for new **proposals.**

These benefits should not be underestimated. A frequently encountered failing of systems development is the lack of a structured approach which relates individual developments and facilitates the **convergence** of systems, where desirable.

The time-scale for a long-term plan for systems development is 3 to 5 years. Beyond 5 years the needs and environment are likely to be too uncertain to allow realistic planning; systems development in the period up to 3 years belongs to operational planning. Whatever the timeframe chosen, the principle of a 'rolling plan' should be used, namely that the plan is **updated** on a regular (normally annual) **basis**.

The contents of a 3–5 year plan will typically set out:

* An executive summary
* A review of current status and progress
* Objectives to be achieved in the coming 5 years
* Strategic principles to be followed
* The main lines of action, identifying main projects and activities.

An essential complement to the long-term plan is an **operational plan**, which translates the first projected actions of the 5-year plan into a blueprint for the actions immediately ahead. In most cases, it is practical to do this on an annual basis – i.e. create a 12-month operational plan.

The operational plan should primarily show:

* how it relates to the 5-year plan
* combined plan of projects
* project-by-project summaries
* resource allocation required.

The operational plan is the basis for **management control** of ongoing and new systems development in the year ahead.

Activity

Obtain a copy of the systems plan for an organisation you know well. Compare this plan with that outlined in Section (**b**) above. In what respects do they differ? What are the reasons for the differences?

---

2 Structured and Data Driven Approaches to Analysis and Design

2.1 System Methodology

The objective of the systems development process is the resolution of a business problem, the achievement of a business goal or the improvement of a business process by the creation of a series of interdependent procedures which may be regarded as a functional set or system. The approach to the analysis and design of the system is today codified in what has come to be known as a methodology. Formally, a methodology is an ordered set of ideas or procedures; a set of guides, standards and procedures.

2.2 Systems Techniques

In data processing, a methodology is generally implemented by the application of specific techniques which may be described as an explicitly stated procedure for doing something technical.

2.3 Importance of the Distinction Between Methodology and Techniques

In practice the terms 'methodology' and 'technology' have both been used fairly loosely and often as if they were interchangeable. It is, however, useful to try and maintain the distinction which has a methodology as an overarching **concept** or **approach** which is **implemented** by using individual techniques. This distinction makes two important points. Firstly, it assumes that there is a requirement for an overall concept and, secondly, it makes it clear that a technique is not of itself sufficient to constitute a systems development approach. An analogy might be taken from the field of engineering design. Stress calculations are essential to the process of designing a bridge but they are not a complete approach to bridge design. In this example, stress calculations are a technique, not a methodology.

2.4 Systems Engineering and Information Engineering

In recent years the terms 'systems engineering' and 'information engineering' have entered the vocabulary of data processing. As with many other terms, they have come to mean different things to different people. As generally used, however, they are virtually interchangeable with 'methodology', although in many cases they have a built-in bias towards a particular methodology rather than to methodology as a general concept, and they imply the use of **control techniques** derived from the mainstream engineering disciplines.

Self-check

Can a collection of techniques be called a 'methodology'?

2.5 Formalised Methodologies for Computer Systems Development

At least since the early 1960s there have been attempts to develop formalised methodologies for computer systems development. A number of approaches have been tried. Among those which found favour during the 1960s and early 1970s were:

* Accurately Defined Systems (ADS), which started by defining the output of a system, and was promoted by the NCR company;
* Study Organisation Plan (SOP), a documentation intensive, risk minimising approach developed by IBM;
* Business Information Systems Analysis and Design (BISAD), an early top down approach to the study of the information needs of an organisation advocated by Honeywell, an approach which had conceptual similarities to IBM's Business Study Plan which became popular in the mid 1970s.

In addition to these computer manufacturer sponsored approaches (which in some cases were conceived as dealing with the information requirements of the entire organisation whilst others confined themselves to addressing specific application systems), the UK's National Computing Centre (NCC), many consultancies and a significant number of the larger computer-using companies, acting either singly or in cooperation, developed their own methodologies. Some of these, such as the Philips ARDI approach, became the subject of textbooks or could be purchased from their developers and so came to be used in a variety of environments.

(a) Multi-phased approach

For the most part, these early methodologies followed a **multi-phased** approach in which a formalised checklist of tasks had to be completed for each phase before moving on to the next. Each phase made use of one or more techniques (flow charting was probably the most widely used) and the phases were frequently separated by formal reviews. They also required extensive documentation and nearly all the documentation was prepared separately after the work to which it related (or exogenous).

Much of this general approach survives, although the design approach is now typically **top down** rather than sequential and the techniques used are more sophisticated and varied. Indeed, the approach which forms the core of this book follows the same general outline, enhanced by elements from both of the main families of systems development approaches used in the 1980s.

(b) Structured analysis

Chronologically, the next general development was that termed 'structured analysis' which owed its genesis to ideas from the engineering disciplines and its translation to the field of data processing to Constantine, Yourdon and others. Initially applied only to programming aspects, the structured approach was soon extended to the whole field of systems development. The characteristics of the structured approaches are **top down functional decomposition** (whereby analysis and design takes place from the macro to the micro level in a series of iterations (called explosions) which progressively study ever smaller parts of the whole in increasing detail) and the separation of the **logical** aspects of the system from its **physical** implementation. One of the big advantages of the structured approaches was that much of the necessary documentation became an integral part of the systems development process (or endogenous). This not only meant that its preparation immediately became much less of a chore but also that the documentation was kept up-to-date much more rigorously.

Both the first group of methodologies discussed above (which may be termed the traditional methodologies) and the structured methodologies fall into the category which some observers have labelled 'process centred approaches', i.e. they are primarily addressing what the system being studied has to **accomplish**.

(c) Data centred approaches

The third general family of systems development approaches started from a different point of departure. This school (which came to be known as the data centred approach and of which James Martin has become the principal advocate) started from the premise that within any organisation the basic **data** (here meaning the things about which the organisation will keep information and usually called 'entities') is stable, whereas the **procedures** to which it is subjected are not. Thus in the data centred approaches, **data and the relationships between data** are given central importance. This has given rise to a range of techniques promoting the understanding of data and its relationships within the context of the particular organisation being studied. In this approach data is a **separate resource** within the organisation, and processes become merely means of transforming data. The design of the data base becomes the most important aspect of information systems development – and one, moreover, that should be considered in terms of the complete organisation, not merely for a single application.

(d) Prototyping approach

Other approaches to systems development include the 'prototyping approach', which foreshortens the traditional or structured development process by the construction of a **prototype system**. In prototype systems development the user and systems designer develop a system using interactive computing. The underlying assumption is that most users do not know what they want from a system and, even if they do, are not very effective in describing their requirements to the systems developer. With a prototype system the users can see it grow, use it and recommend changes which can be incorporated with minimum fuss or formality.

When the user and analyst are satisfied with the prototype, it may be used as working specification for the definitive system, or in some cases upgraded to production status (although the main difficulties experienced with the prototyping approach have been encountered when this has been attempted). Prototyping was not possible until very high level programming languages and development aids became available and works best in an environment where the underlying data bases have already been created.

Self-check

Why is prototyping so important in modern systems development?

Whilst it can be argued that only the traditional approach fully meets the definition of a methodology, it is convenient to think of all the 3 approaches considered here as methodologies.

Self-check

Describe briefly the evolution of methodologies for systems development, from the 1960s to the present day.

2.6 Strengths and Weaknesses of Methodologies

Given that there are differing methodologies, the question arises: 'Which one should be used?'

It is now necessary to look at the respective strengths and weaknesses of the methodologies we have considered.

(a) Traditional methodologies

The major problems associated with the traditional methodologies resulted from their rigidity and the fact that documentation was exogenous. Both of these facts tended to make these approaches laborious and time consuming – and helped create the paradox that automation is labour intensive!

Nevertheless, if followed correctly, these approaches were capable of delivering systems with relatively low risk – at least when these were within the state of the art and not pioneering efforts.

(b) Structured approaches

With endogenous documentation and more rigorous techniques, the structured approaches overcame many of these problems and, moreover, their nature enabled them to be included in the same, or a similar, application oriented project structure as adopted for the traditional approach. (Structured techniques can also be used across a complete organisation.)

The weaknesses of structured approaches tend to lie in the problems of portraying temporal relationships, defining enquiry based systems and indicating the relative importance of major and minor processes which are often given the same apparent emphasis.

(c) Data centred approaches

By contrast the major problems with the data centred approaches is that they usually incur a heavy front end loading both in terms of cost and time before results are produced. They normally require a relatively long period of study and significant investment before it is possible to develop new applications. Once this front end investment has been made, their adherents claim, systems can be developed more rapidly than with the structured approach. Data centred approaches also tend to have a centralist, big computer orientation to them.

The strengths and weaknesses of the various approaches strongly suggest that no single approach should be used to the total exclusion of the others. Indeed all the current approaches may be regarded as **complementary** (the traditional approach may be regarded as superseded except insofar as it provides a formal, phased, project oriented framework which is also applicable to other approaches). Linking the structured, data centred and prototyping approaches into one coherent framework is not easy: it is necessary to modify some of the conventions usually employed in the first, to rethink the scope of the second and regard the third as a particular technique for use in the system definition phase (see Chapter 6).

2.7 **Optimum Use of Methodologies**

Where the scope of a structured approach includes the complete organisation, the data which supports the systems derived through that structure is the same data which is obtained through the application of a data centred approach. Similarly, where a data centred approach is used for a sub-set of the complete organisation then the data from that approach will be the data required to support the complete range of systems within that same sub-set of the organisation. More generally where data centred and structured approaches are used on similar applications then the data content and ultimately the data base design, should be the same.

To apply this concept in practice requires, as stated above, the modification of some of the conventions of the structured approaches. In particular the content of **data stores** (data at rest) in data flow diagrams (DFDs, see Chapter 13) must be treated *en masse* for the purpose of data base design and the data flows out of each data store may then be regarded as logical sub-schemas (see also Chapter 18).

Similarly, if the intention is to use a data centred approach first, a structured approach may still be used for design. In this case a single data store may be used to represent each defined data base – the data flows out of which again represent logical sub-schemas.

The two approaches can readily thus be used in conjunction with one another and are not mutually exclusive, as some writers have tried to suggest. Moreover, neither is naturally subordinate to the other and either may be used first depending on circumstances.

With the ability to control the situation fully, a luxury usually denied the analyst in real life, the optimum use of the various approaches would be as shown in Figure 2.1.

In this book we advocate the use of a data centred approach in support of systems strategy and planning while in the approach to systems development which is explained in the remaining chapters of Part I, we adopt a structured approach which fits within the framework of a traditional, multi-phase methodology. Moreover, this approach embraces prototyping as one of the possible techniques to use in the systems definition phase.

Type of development	*Development approach*
High volume routine data processing applications (batch or on-line) in well studied business functions – including redevelopment of existing applications	Structured
Overall development of centralised suite of integrated applications	Data driven
Development of data retrieval-type applications	Data driven
Preliminary development in business functions which have not previously been subject to computerisation or where user requirements are very unclear	Prototype development

Fig 2.1 *Use of systems development approaches*

Self-check

Can structured and data driven approaches be considered as complementary to one another?

2.8 Case Tools and the Analyst's Workbench

Recent developments in powerful and relatively inexpensive personal computers (PCs) – and, in particular, their graphics capabilities – have led to the emergence of so called Computer Aided Systems Engineering (CASE) tools and the Analyst's Workbench. Both terms are used to describe PC based software which seeks to improve the productivity and the work quality of the systems developer.

As is so often the case, there is no agreed definition of either term. Some of the tools available focus on the analysis and design aspects while others concentrate on supporting the programming aspects – the ultimate aim, of course, being a tool which automates systems development from analysis through to computer code generation.

An Analyst's Workbench would typically provide a graphics package to assist in the development of DFDs and help apply other graphically based techniques such as entity analysis, a data modelling package, a data dictionary and, perhaps more importantly, **logic** which enables the various diagrams and their contents to be checked for internal consistency. This is a fast developing field and extensive research work has been funded under the European ESPRIT programme. It undoubtedly offers the opportunity for both quantitative and qualitative improvements in systems development.

Activity

Find out the methodology in use within your own organisation or in a company with which you are familiar. Is it a structured, data-driven, prototyping or hybrid approach? How was the methodology developed (i.e. was it developed in-house or is it a proprietary technique)? Is the methodology used consistently throughout the organisation?

Activity

Examine the 'Situations Vacant' pages of 'Computing', 'Computer Weekly', 'Computerworld' or any other data processing magazines to which you have access. Make a list of the methodologies referred to in the advertisements and group them under one or more of the approaches listed in the text.

Activity

Obtain a description of a commercial CASE tool (details may be obtained directly from the vendors of such products who periodically advertise, or by reading one of the review articles in the data processing press). Make a list of the major facilities provided by this CASE tool.

---

3 Step 1: System Project Selection

Every system must at some stage have been the object of a **selection process**. Sometimes the systems analyst does not take a significant part in this and in many cases first becomes involved when the decision has already been made. Nevertheless, the systems analysis function begins when an area is identified for study.

3.1 Reasons for initiating systems projects

(a) Requests from user departments

The primary sources for project proposals are requests or suggestions from **user departments**. These are normally the best possible sources, since they are the people for whom one wants to provide a service. But the systems analyst has to be constantly aware that what is convenient for one department may not be the best solution for the organisation as whole. For example, the cost accounting department may like to receive special weekly statistics of costs of materials used at each cost centre throught the factory. In itself, this may be a goood idea, but to implement such a system may involve creating special sets of codes to identify the materials in the way that the cost accounting department wants. This may **conflict** with, and partially **duplicate**, the existing codes which are in standard use by the production and purchasing departments. To introduce an additional set of material codes would certainly cause confusion and very probably extra work for the personnel who have to collect the data for processing. In such a case, therefore, the systems department should do its utmost to try and satisfy the accounting department's requirements with the existing set of codes.

(b) Results from previous systems projects

At the end of any project, the systems analyst is usually left with a host of ideas for better ways to have done the job just completed and for possibilities for other information systems that were not evident before the project in hand was started. It is important to document these ideas **at the time**, so that they are available when systems development plans are being reviewed. For example, perhaps the systems analyst has been working on a system designed to help production personnel schedule jobs to run on different machines. Although the scope of the system may have been limited by this objective, the analyst may well have recognised that the information generated by this system could also provide the machine maintenance department with vital information for their work. So it would be sensible for the systems analyst to note this idea at the time, so that when resources become available a deeper investigation could be made.

(c) Possibilities for linking or integrating with other systems

During a systems project it can often be seen that a linkage exists with another existing system. Sometimes these logical linkages are so many that the separate systems can be considered as a single integrated system. In the example described in Section (b) above, the machine scheduling system can be seen as just part of a much wider system ranging from the initiation of each customer order through production planning to final despatch of the goods. In such a case, it may be decided to link these different elements together to form an order entry, processing and despatch system. This viewpoint may emerge from development work in **apparently isolated areas**, such as the machine scheduling system.

(d) Opportunities created by new hardware, software or techniques

Sometimes a new technical development makes possible a new approach to a problem. Examples of this are optical storage, digital voice systems, etc. Genuine advances may be made in this way, but the analyst should take care not to take a **solution** and look for a **problem**. This may lead to clever systems, but they will not satisfy the users – who will be left to work with the system long after the systems department has moved on to other interesting technical advances.

(e) Outside sources

Many systems analysts base systems projects almost exclusively on their experience within their own organisation. This is a mistake;

the requirements of one organisation are rarely unique and an exchange of ideas with other concerns usually leads to new ideas and solutions.

Through one, some or all of the sources listed above, a set of **desired projects** is maintained. Within the framework of systems strategy and planning, the task then arises of **selecting** those projects which are of priority interest to the organisation.

Activity

Make a list of computer projects which you think would be valuable in your workplace or educational institute, or in a sports/social organisation with which you are familiar. State what the major justification for each project will be.

3.2 Criteria for selecting systems projects

The factors listed here are all dependent on the judgement of one or more experienced personnel in the systems department. It is to be hoped that their judgement will be confirmed where possible (for projects initiated), but it should be recognised that the selection of systems projects consists of only a very preliminary investigation into the five key factors:

(a) Potential return on investment

This is the most important criterion for selecting a project. Even a very broad estimate of the potential benefits and costs to the company can give a strong guide to the desirability of implementing a system. During the Feasibility Study (Step 2), this aspect is developed more fully and for deeper analysis of this subject the reader is referred to Chapter 16 (Cost-Benefit Analysis).

(b) Critical company need

Sometimes an organisation finds itself in the position of urgently needing an information system in a particular area, even though the financial justification is unclear. If the need is felt strongly, then the benefit will be ultimately measurable in financial terms, but the major justification for the project at the time will be expressed simply in terms of urgent need. For example, when a new production plant is planned, it is very difficult to isolate the financial justification of any integrated computerised information systems involved. Similar situations frequently arise when a company is forced to react to a competitive move and has rapidly to develop a new information system on a specific market segment.

Occasionally, senior management become very enthusiastic about a project, even though it does not seem to offer measurable financial gains. But implementing the system successfully enhances senior management's involvement in systems work generally. As discussed in Part III, management involvement is a key factor for the success of systems development and **promoting this involvement** is an important task of the systems analyst.

(c) Technical feasibility

Although a project may appear useful and desirable from a user point of view, there may be technical reasons which preclude even a feasibility study. Such a decision not even to examine a potential project, on technical grounds, will depend completely on the experience available in the systems department. An example of this would be a project involving optical character reading of handwritten text produced by personnel in different countries, as may happen in the case of a multinational company. On a local or more limited scale such a system may be feasible, but the practical problems of machine-identification of the scripts of different nationalities are likely to be beyond the capabilities of most available systems. It is therefore valuable for some **technical screening** to take place before projects are launched with full-scale feasibility studies.

(d) Consistency with systems development strategy

Each systems development project must fall within the organisation's strategy for systems development as a whole. This strategy is the basis for the **overall systems planning** which relates the different projects to each other. It is sometimes necessary to undertake a project simply because other projects cannot start, or be completed, unless the project in question is accomplished. For example, a quality control information system may be urgently needed by a company, but may well depend on a lower priority production control system that in itself may not be considered as a worthwhile investment.

(e) Capability of the systems department to do the project

Many apparently desirable projects are allocated to – or accepted by – the systems department without sufficient consideration being given as to whether or not the systems department is in fact **capable of doing the job required**. Sometimes the difficulty may be fitting a project into an already overloaded workload, but is also sometimes due to lack of technical knowhow. If the systems department is fully aware of the technical requirements, even if it cannot itself fulfil them, then the option exists to have the system supplied by an **external supplier**, as described in Chapter 8 (Build/Buy Analysis).

For each project selected, there should be a clear **statement of objective**. This is essential for starting the following phase: the Feasibility Study.

Self-check

What key factors must considered when deciding on a data processing project?

---

4 Step 2: The Feasibility Study

4.1 Objective of the Feasibility Study

The objective of this phase is to establish the **overall feasibility** of the systems development being considered and to explore the possible general approaches which may be adopted.

'Feasibility' in this context basically means answering three fundamental questions:

* Can it be done? Is the planned development **technically** possible?
* Can we do it? Is the planned development within the qualitative and quantitative **resource capabilities** of the organisation?
* Is it worth doing? Is it **commercially sensible** to make the investment in systems development? (This is generally expressed in terms of a cost-benefit analysis in which the costs are balanced against the quantified benefits, see Chapter 16.)

Conducting a feasibility study is in some ways rather a 'Catch 22' activity. To address many of the issues you need answers to questions which have not yet been finalised! For example, to establish reliable cost information the analyst needs to know a considerable amount about the planned system. Yet in the feasibility study he or she is only just beginning to consider what the various options are and making only the most preliminary assessment of which alternative is likely to be the best. Nevertheless, the attempt has to be made to establish some basis for deciding whether or not it is worthwhile to undertake the development.

There is an important caveat to be entered at this point. It is clear that any assessment (economic or technical) can only be preliminary and the **methodology** in use (and the **corporate culture**) must allow for significant changes of direction and emphasis at later stages without loss of face for the staff concerned (this is the major reason for the formal **decision points** included in the approach to systems development which forms the core of this book). Parenthetically it may be remarked that one of the authors' main criticisms of much systems development is that the project team becomes 'locked in' to one approach to the system solution far too early in the development cycle and fails to consider alternative solutions seriously.

Self-check

What are the three key points that must be addressed by a feasibility study?

4.2 Activities Included in the Feasibility Study

The twelve major activities included in the feasibility study are:

* Determining the main **user requirements**, including timing requirements
* Determining the **data** to be used, their sources and volumes
* Analysing the **organisation chart**, **geographical distribution**, etc. of the department(s) and users concerned
* Identifying the main **characteristics** of the system
* Examining **other systems** meeting similar requirements
* Determining that the requirements of the **system** are consistent with the objectives of the **organisation**
* Considering **alternative design** scenarios
* Considering **alternative development** scenarios
* Determining that the proposed system is consistent with the organisation's systems **architecture** and **strategy**
* Preparing gross estimates of probable overall direct and indirect **benefits** for each practical alternative
* Preparing gross estimates of probable overall implementation and operating **costs** for each practical alternative
* Documenting the feasibility study in a **report** for user and systems management.

(a) Determining the main user requirements, including timing requirements

What the users **need** must, of course, be the major determinant of what systems are **developed**. It is, therefore, a major concern of the feasibility study to determine what those needs are. Note, however, that we have used the word 'needs' rather than 'wants' because there will be many occasions where the users are not well placed to identify what their true needs are. Frequently, the analyst will encounter the situation where the immediate users are so close to the trees that they are unable to see the wood!

Under these circumstances the analyst has to look behind the **symptoms** of the problem and try and identify the **underlying cause**. The analyst cannot stop there, however, since he or she must have the active support of the users if the final outcome of the systems development process is to be a success. It follows, therefore, that the analyst must 'sell' a more extensive view of the needs if his or her investigation shows that to be necessary. In practice this will mean extensive discussions with user staff at all levels, possibly reinforced by exposing key users to a wider systems environment by visiting other analogous organisations or arranging demonstrations of commercially available systems.

During this task the analyst should also determine the users' **timing requirements**. Is a batch system (with or without on-line data capture and/or enquiry) adequate? If so, what should the frequency of operation be? If an on-line system or facility is required what response times should be aimed for, and for how long each day must the system be on-line?

(b) Determining the data to be used, their sources and estimated volumes

Data **volumes** are a key factor in determining the nature and scale of any system and it is, therefore, important to make an early start in estimating the types of data, their **sources** and **volumes**. For systems which are being developed to replace or automate existing procedures, most of this information will be readily available or may be rapidly obtained from departmental statistics, reports and/or existing files. Examination of **historic** volume information is also essential so that any growth (or decline) trends can be identified, e.g. in a credit card system it may be discovered that not only is the number of card holders growing but also that the average card holder is using his or her card more frequently with the passage of time.

Where the organisation does not already have a comprehensive data dictionary (see Chapter 18), the data volume exercise should also identify and document the key **data elements** (also discussed in Chapter 18) for the proposed system.

More problematical from the point of view of ascertaining likely data volumes are systems which are genuinely **new** or introduce completely **new features**, e.g. on-line enquiry via data terminals. Estimating volumes in such cases is notoriously difficult and the analyst is well advised to **cross check** any estimates made with the actual experience of analogous systems both within and outside the organisation.

Activity

For one of the projects you identified in the activity in Chapter 3, find out the main user requirements and data to be used. Sketch out at least two alternative design scenarios and list the advantages and disadvantages of each.

(c) Analysing the organisation chart, geographical distribution, etc. of the department(s) and users oncerned

The **organisation** and **geographical dispersion** (or **concentration**) of the users of a system can have a major impact on systems design and economics. In many cases these are not absolute factors (organisations can and do reorganise and reallocate office space) but in the short run – and, in some instances, even in the long run – they are fixed. Between them organisation and geographical dispersion will determine such factors as the need for data communication facilities and the number of terminals required, thus having a major impact on the hardware cost of the system. Furthermore, the **responsibilities** for the various tasks involved in the subsequent operational information system will need to be analysed at this stage, e.g. data input, security requirements, etc.

Activity

Draw up an organisation chart for a company with which you are familiar. Indicate how this organisation reflects its geographical features.

(d) Identifying the main characteristics of the system

With the above three tasks complete, the analyst will be ready to specify the main **characteristics** of the system. This can be done effectively using data flow diagrams (DFDs). The data flow diagramming technique is described in Chapter 13. In the feasibility study, DFDs should be used to define the logical system, i.e. **what** has to be done, not **how** it is to be done. It is important that this step is taken at an early stage of the systems development cycle, before ideas about how the system will be delivered have begun to form. Once identified, these characteristics should be **formally ratified** with the user management concerned.

(e) Examining other systems meeting similar requirements

Systems development is, in part, a creative activity and since no one person ever has a monopoly on creative ideas and since almost by definition most analysts will have had little or any direct experience of state of the art systems for the application on which they are currently working, it is always worthwhile examining what has been done elsewhere in similar circumstances. In large organisations this may include what has been done in **other parts** of the organisation (other countries, divisions, subsidiaries or associated companies). Where this is not possible, a study of the trade press, discussions with other members of computer user groups, conversations with hardware and software vendors and investigations as to what **similar** and **competing** organisations are attempting may all be useful sources of ideas.

(f) Determining that the requirements of the system are consistent with the objectives of the organisation

It may seem obvious that systems development should be consistent with an organisation's objectives – why else should the feasibility study be mooted? Occasionally, however, circumstances conspire to prevent this happening and the authors are aware of some cases where time and money have been expended on a system which not only did not support the objectives of the organisation concerned but was actively opposed to them. For example, a project to integrate a subsidiary's accounting system into that of the parent organisation will be harmful as well as pointless if the medium-term corporate strategy is to divest the company of that subsidiary. The analyst is, therefore, well advised to ensure that the requirements expressed are consistent with the objectives of the organisation, **whether or not these are formally published**.

(g) Considering alternative design scenarios

Now that the analyst is familiar with the requirement and has studied what is being done in other organisations to address similar problems, he or she is in a position to start developing thoughts about alternative ways of **meeting the user requirements**. Not that this should be an individual activity – 'brain storming' sessions with a small group of analysts and users, most of whom are familiar with the problem or opportunity being discussed but some of whom have only an outline of the situation (so that they may raise the 'idiot boy' questions) – is often the best approach.

The objective is to create a series of design scenarios, each of which is supported by a rough list of its major advantages and disadvantages. The scenarios may include options for simple (quick/cheap) and very sophisticated (and necessarily more expensive and longer-term) solutions. They may also include manual, personal computer (PC), mini or mainframe computer based systems and stand alone or fully integrated approaches. Other options may include a prototyping approach (particularly useful where the requirements are not especially clear and/or the proposed system is breaking new ground). As discussed in Chapter 2, prototype systems rely on high level systems development techniques which enable a 'mock up' or prototype of the proposed system to be created rapidly and relatively inexpensively . The user(s) can then 'experiment' with the system and suggest changes until such time as they are happy with the results – at which time the prototype (which is, *de facto*, a 'live' design specification) may be upgraded to production status or used as the specification for the **definitive system**.

(h) Considering alternative development scenarios

The design scenarios will usually determine the development scenarios, i.e. which of the systems development approaches described in Chapter 2 will be used to develop the new system: for example, if a pilot system is to be developed it is clear that a prototyping approach must be used. In normal circumstances, the approach to be used in the other design scenarios is equally obvious – using the approach usually adopted by the organisation for that type of development, e.g. the use of a structured methodology for mainframe system development. From time to time, however, there will be a requirement to recommend a **new methodology**, either because of the need to keep abreast of developments in systems design technology or because of the unique features of the system under study.

(i) Determining that the proposed system is consistent with the organisation's systems architecture and strategy

This task presupposes that there is a systems architecture for the organisation! Many organisations have a systems architecture, or at least a clear policy on systems development. This may be clear and explicit (i.e. there is a master plan for systems development into which all developments are expected to fit), or it may be unarticulated but nevertheless real (e.g. all developments will be on IBM or compatible mainframes using the DB2 DBMS and the Cobol programming language, the use of stand alone PCs will be restricted, networking will be based on the X25 protocol, etc). Whichever is the case the analyst should **check** the proposals against the explicit or *de facto* standards. Of course there will be occasions where there is no fit and, in these circumstances, the analyst must consider whether the facts of the situation justify 'tilting at windmills' like a latter-day Don Quixote, or whether that particular design scenario should be discarded.

(j) Preparing gross estimates of probable overall direct and indirect benefits for each practical alternative

Estimating benefits is one of the more difficult tasks facing the analyst. It must, however, be attempted. **Cost displacement**, i.e. the introduction of automated systems to improve the productivity of clerical or other operational staff, can be estimated with reasonable precision. For example, it may be that with the proposed system a clerk will be able to deal with (say) fifty enquiries per day rather than (say) twenty with manual methods. Similarly, improvements in such quantifiable things as inventory levels can be calculated or simulated. Benefits from better information or faster decision making are, however, much harder to quantify. Where these are considered to be a major justification of the new system, the analyst is obligated to make an honest attempt to quantify them. Several approaches assist in this aim.

First, the analyst can use the 'bracketing' technique. Broadly, this seeks to ascertain the value of benefits by an **iterative approach** which initially ascribes an arbitrary value to the benefit then refines it on the basis of the response of one or more user managers. A typical dialogue would be:

Analyst: 'What would the new system be worth to the organisation in terms of benefits?'
User: 'I consider it to be impossible to quantify – but I do know that it would be very valuable.'
Analyst: 'Would it be worth as much as £50,000 a year?'
User: 'Oh, much more than that!'
Analyst: 'As much as £250,000?'
User: 'I wouldn't go that high but it's probably nearer that figure than £50,000.'
Analyst: 'Would you be happy with a figure of £200,000?'
User: 'In round figures, yes.'
Analyst: 'Now, I'd like to identify the reasons you had in mind when you said that......................'

Although the results are necessarily imprecise, they do give a working basis for cost-benefit analysis and, with experience, it is possible to obtain reasonable estimates.

Secondly, there is the use of the **calculated, inferred savings approach**. In this approach the analyst quantifies (in money terms) the value of such statements as: 'We could reduce stock by 10%' or, 'We could increase sales by 5%'.

Whilst it is true that the answers produced by these techniques are by no means exact, they are, however, an attempt by the users to **place a value** on the proposed system and may legitimately be used as part of the cost-benefit analysis used to justify it (or otherwise). Appropriate qualifiers must be added to all numbers based on such estimates: as a general rule, the less precise the basis of benefit estimation the higher the internal rate of return (IRR) that should be expected of the system development. The question of quantifying benefits will be discussed further in Chapter 16.

Activity

What is the current interest rate which organisations in your country must pay if they borrow money to make a new investment? Is the trend upwards or downwards? What policy would you recommend with regard to borrowing money at fixed or variable rates for an investment requiring money over the next 3 years?

(k) Preparing gross estimates of probable overall implementation and operations costs for each practical alternative

Clearly, at this stage of the investigation, costing is going to be an imprecise science. Nevertheless, as with benefits, it is important to get some kind of handle on the likely costs associated with each practical design scenario for the purpose of deciding which of the alternatives is **economically the most attractive**. Note that the concept of 'cost' used here extends beyond the basic cost of systems development to include running and maintenance costs, since these can often, over the lifetime of the system, radically change the apparent costs and benefits of the alternatives considered.

(l) Documenting the feasibility study in a report for user and systems management

The final stage in the feasibility study is to document the findings in a single report in a manner which facilitates the decision as to whether to proceed with the project or not and, if so, which of the design scenarios should be the **preferred option** during the definition phase. A main ingredient of the feasibility report is the cost-benefit analyses of the various design scenarios. This is a fundamental set of information for the management of both the systems and user departments. In addition to the cost-benefit analyses and the recommendations about subsequent actions, the report should document the work **done during the study** and the **user requirements**.

Self-check

What should go into the feasibility study report? What will the contents page contain – set out a specimen page.

Clearly the feasibility study is a **microcosm of the complete systems development process** and if unconstrained could easily become the entire project. For practical reasons, therefore, this phase of the systems development cycle should be constrained both in **elapsed time** and in terms of **manpower employed**. For most commercial applications, target levels of 6 to 8 weeks and 13 weeks respectively should be adequate to conduct a feasibility study of sufficient rigour to determine whether or not to proceed to the next stage of the systems development cycle.

5 Step 3: Project Planning

When the decision has been taken to go ahead with a systems project, the immediate tasks are to form a **project team** and to start **project planning**. The activities which then follow are subject to project management and control.

5.1 The Project Team

The basic elements on which it is essential for clear decisions to be taken, when setting up a project team, are:

* clear allocation of **responsibility** for the team, and in particular for its project manager, notably with regard to:

  budget
  role of user departments and the systems department
  reporting to senior management

* informing all **relevant parties**, notably:

  other departments affected
  staff representatives
  auditing department

* **administrative** support for the project team, particularly:

  budget spending procedures
  hiring of external experts
  office space and equipment.

These and other aspects will need to be documented in a **project file**, which will grow and become the **permanent record of the project**. Its contents will typically be:

* project **specification**
* budget breakdown and **expenditure** analysis
* **correspondence file**
* name and address list of **contacts**
* **security rules** for the project
* **contracts**
* **work schedules** and **progress reports**
* minutes of **steering committee meetings**.

Having established the formal and procedural aspects of the work, the first main task for the project team is to produce a **project plan**.

5.2 The Project Plan

The **project plan** is created as the **master document** for the project team itself. In addition, this plan serves as a source for providing senior management with **summary information**. The detailed project plan should contain:

* project **scope** and **objectives**
* analysis of user needs, including **quality** and **security**
* breakdown of project into **component activities**
* **resource allocation** for each major group of activities
* main **milestones** and dates
* project team **responsibilities**
* references to relevant **documentation**.

The 'milestones' should be definite events (for example, written agreement on the system definition) and should be not more than 2 months apart. The value of such milestones is that they show up **problems** sufficiently early to enable delays to be avoided or lost time recovered.

5.3 Planning Techniques

The first stage in the application of a good planning technique is identification of all the **activities** which collectively form the project. This analysis of the tasks to be undertaken, completed in narrative form, is in itself an aid to understanding project needs and enables the next, vital step to be undertaken: estimating the **time** needed for each activity.

Activity

For the same project used in the activity in Chapter 4, make a list of the tasks that will be necessary to realise the project and make a provisional estimate of the time and resources required for each.

Having completed this work, the project planner can prepare the project plan in narrative form with the aid of visual representation techniques or by the use of one of the many personal computer (PC) based project planning and management tools.

(a) GANTT charts

The simplest of these techniques is the familiar bar or **GANTT chart** (see Figure 5.1) which consists of a horizontal bar to represent each activity in the project. The length of each bar is proportional to the time that it will take and the horizontal axis of such a chart serves as a time scale. If shading is used to show completed activities (either in full or in part), then the use of a vertical cursor will quickly show which activities are behind schedule and which are ahead. The major advantage of GANTT charts is their simplicity, especially the fact that they show the activities on a **direct time base**. The main disadvantage is that the **interdependence** between activities is not shown. Thus, although a visual inspection will give the current status of each activity, it does not reveal what effect a delay on one activity will have on the total project.

(b) Network diagrams

It was to overcome this fundamental disadvantage that **network diagram techniques** were developed. A simple network diagram (see Figure 5.2) illustrates this point. In this case, activities are represented by the arrows joining the nodes; events are represented by the nodes themselves. Events are the start or completion of a particular action, for example 'computer delivered', whereas activities are the elements of the project, such as 'write program A'.

(i) Interdependence of activities

Network diagrams overcome the major disadvantage of GANTT charts, by showing the **interdependence** of activities: for example, Figure 5.2 indicates that event 4 (the start of activity G) cannot take place until activities F and B have been completed. They also have a major advantage in that adding the times of the activities on each route or path between the start and finish of the project will

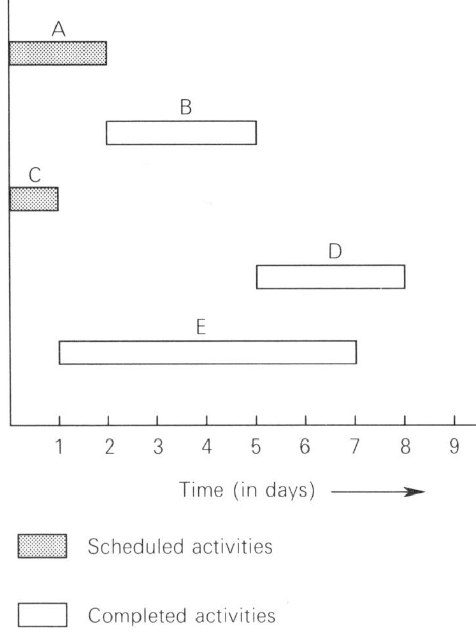

Fig 5.1 *A simple GANTT chart*

quickly reveal the **critical path** for the project. This is the series of activities in which any delay will cause an equivalent delay in the completion of the project as a whole – unless corrective action is taken. It is also possible to calculate the **float time** for each activity not on the critical path, i.e. that amount of delay which any activity can incur without any effect on the final completion of the project. The use of network diagrams has been greatly facilitated by the availability of powerful software on many types of personal or mainframe computers, built for the purpose of creating and updating a range of reports and diagrams for the network diagram user.

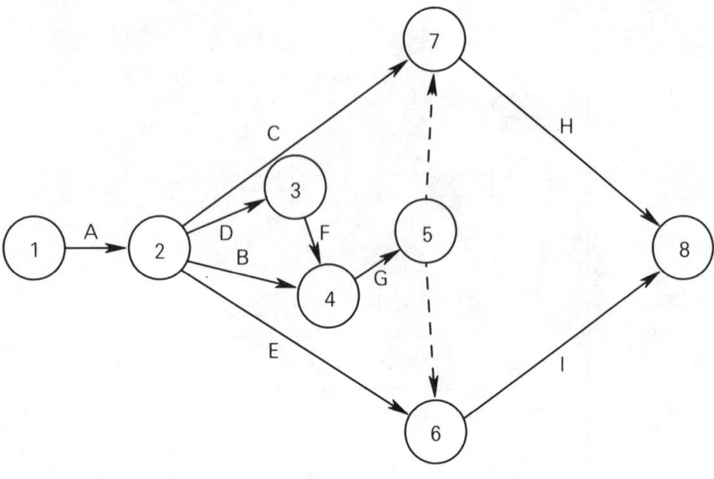

Fig 5.2 *A simple network diagram*

Activity

For your selected project, draw a network diagram of the tasks involved in the realisation of the project.

(ii) Limitations of network planning

In spite of the major advantages of network planning, it also has some limitations. First, the **current status** of the project cannot easily be seen on the diagram. Secondly, there is a need to include **dummy activities** to show activities that do not involve work or effort; two dummy activities are shown in Figure 5.2 linking event 5 to event 6 and event 5 to event 7 respectively. Thirdly, the preparation of a network diagram can be time consuming, especially when there are frequent **alterations**, even with the aid of computer software. Fourthly, a large network diagram is frequently too complex for use as a **planning document** in discussions with line managers.

(c) GASP Techniques

Network diagrams, although simple in theory, are therefore not widely used except by staff regularly involved in the planning of major projects. For systems designers, the chore of work necessary to keep the diagram updated and the lack of immediate visual relation to a time scale are the reasons most frequently quoted for not using network diagrams. However, to acquire the advantages of network diagrams while retaining the advantages of GANTT charts, a further technique of considerable value to the systems project manager has been developed. This technique has a number of names, including Job Progress Charting and *G*raphical Procedure for *A*nalytical and *S*ynthetical Evaluation and Review of Construction *P*rograms (GASP). For convenience, we will refer to the technique as GASP.

(i) Relationship between activities
Basically a GASP chart may be regarded as a GANTT chart which has been extended to show the **relationship between activities**. A simplified example of a computer implementation will show how a GASP chart is constructed and illustrate the advantages of the technique. Like all other planning techniques, the first task is to prepare a schedule of **activities** and estimated times for their **completion** (Figure 5.3). The next step is to identify the inter-

Fig 5.3 *Schedule of activities and estimated times*

SCHEDULE OF ACTIVITIES		
System: New Computer System		
reference	*activities description*	*estimated time (days)*
A	obtain agreement to proposed system	1
B	prepare and agree training programme	1
C	train user staff	10
D	write programs	6
E	test and debug programs	6
F	parallel run	3
G	system acceptance tests	1
H	order and await new stationery	7
Prepared by:	Date:	

relationships between the activities on the schedule. In Figure 5.3 no other activity can commence until activity A has been completed. Similarly, activity C will depend on the completion of B, activity E on D, activity F on H, E and C and activity G on F. A chart can now be prepared showing horizontal bars for each activity, the length of the bar being **proportional to** the **estimated time** for that activity (Figure 5.4). The relationships between the activities are then added to the chart (Figure 5.5), using solid vertical lines to indicate where the end of one activity represents the commencement of one or more subsequent events: for example, the line joining activity A to activities B, D and H in Figure 5.5.

Where there is **slack time** between the completion of one activity and the start of the next related activity (because this subsequent activity depends on another activity), the first activity is extended by dotted lines and linked to the subsequent activity by a vertical dotted line. This is shown with activities C and H in Figure 5.5, both of which have to be completed before the start of activity F, which itself cannot be started until activity E has been completed.

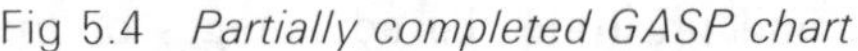
Fig 5.4 *Partially completed GASP chart*

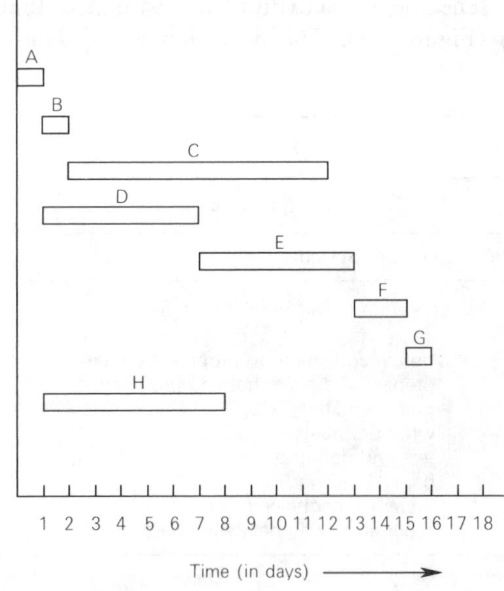

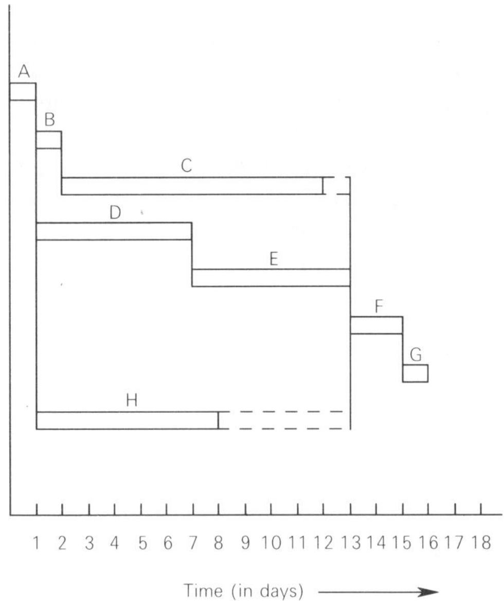

Fig 5.5 *Completed GASP chart*

(ii) The critical path

By adding the relationships to the chart, all activities for which a time float exists are thus immediately identified. The path along which there is **no time float** (A, D, E, F, G in Figure 5.5) is the **critical path**.

(iii) Value of GASP techniques

The GASP technique therefore retains all the advantages of the GANTT chart (especially its ability to show easily the current status of the project and the use of a time scale) and provides the major advantages of a network diagram in identifying the critical path and the relationships between activities. In addition, the learning period for the GASP technique is considerably less than that for a network diagram and the basic similarity to the well-established GANTT chart makes it more acceptable to line management.

The GASP technique is therefore a useful tool for the planning of a systems project. To aid resource scheduling, plastic strip charting media or magnetic strips on a magnetic board can be used to highlight the tasks of **individuals and manpower available**; colours can also be helpful to distinguish between 'waiting' activities (e.g. await delivery of equipment) and 'active' ones (e.g. writing a program). This can focus attention on those areas where the application of additional effort in the form of extra staff or material can result in overall time savings.

Activity

For your selected project, draw a GASP chart of the tasks involved. With your estimate of the time and resources needed for each task, what would be the total elapsed time of the project? If less human resources were available, what would be the impact on elapsed time? Would additional resources reduce the elapsed time?

The delays which frequently occur during the analysis, design and implementation of information systems can mostly be avoided by careful planning. The use of a simple technique such as GASP greatly facilitates this process. The implementation of systems on target plays a major part in the effective **use of resources** and in the acceptance of the operational system by the **users**.

5.4 Estimation Techniques

(a) Uncertainty

The inherent difficulty in planning is the **uncertainty** associated with each activity. In a good plan, the overall uncertainty of achieving the target on time should be less than the sum of all the uncertainties of the individual activities; in a poor plan, the level of uncertainty of the result will probably be so high that the plan will be of little value. Skilful planning allows for uncertainties, but avoids – as far as possible – the compound effect of stringing many individual high uncertainties together and makes additional resources available at points in the project where most uncertainty exists.

(b) Realistic planning

The problem is clearly reduced by experience in estimation. Although each project will have its own unique features, there is sufficient knowledge of systems development in general to enable realistic planning. The key points are:

* In formulating the project plan, allowance has to be made for activities **not within the project manager's control**, for example:

    senior management review and control
    staff training on non-project activities
    contract approval procedures
    outside contractors' own planning skills.

* High uncertainty activities should be kept **off the critical path** to the greatest extent possible.
* **Time estimates** should be checked with:

    experienced personnel outside the project
    the individuals responsible for carrying out the various activities.

* Estimating in a group should be avoided; a **joint estimate** is best made after individual estimates have been formulated.
* Each estimate should be made without consideration of the effect it might have on the **total project**, as there can otherwise be strong pressure to reduce estimates to give a more favourable project target date.
* A **contingency** of around 10% should be built into activities on the critical path.
* Making estimates is an **iterative process**: estimates need to be reviewed and revised as more information becomes available.

Self-check

Would you say that gaining the agreement of users on a system specification is within the control of the project manager? Is this activity likely to be on the critical path?

5.5 Monitoring and Control

(a) The project plan

The main tool for the monitoring and control process is the **project plan**. The latter should be updated according to events and improved estimates. The information for this updating depends on:

* Setting up the right channels for **feedback**. This includes weekly meetings of the project team, regular progress reports from contractors, etc.
* Defining **essential information flows** for progress reporting. Information on expenditure, revisions to the schedule for each activity, unforeseen events, etc. are key inputs for project monitoring.

(b) Progress reporting

An important responsibility of the project manager is to inform senior management of **progress**. This should focus on major milestones and, if needed, on exceptional situations (cost overruns, slippage of the final completion date, etc.). It is often practical to have a **steering group** set up for the duration of the project to monitor progress and help solve questions of policy. The membership would normally include the user department and the systems development department, plus other representatives as appropriate, such as auditors and quality control (see also Chapter 20).

(c) Consistency of approach

Frequently overlooked in project monitoring and control is the need to ensure consistency of approach among the different parties involved in the project. As the pressures build up during the design and implementation phases, a multiplication of small divergences in approach (for example, different documentation standards, different attributes for data elements, different methods for time accounting) can lead to considerable difficulties. It is the project manager's responsibility to make sure that such differences are **minimised**.

6 Step 4: Definition Phase

The objective of this phase is to obtain a systems definition, which will, if accepted, be the basis of **all subsequent work** on the system. The systems definition itself builds on the work done during the preceding phases, especially in the feasibility study. In fact, the systems definition may be regarded as a detailed rework of the recommended design scenario developed during the feasibility study which incorporates the results of the definitive systems analysis work carried out in the definition phase itself.

6.1 Activities of the Definition Phase

The eleven basic activities of the definition phase are:

* Specifying the **objectives** of the present system
* Studying the present system to determine the extent to which it **meets the objectives**
* Analysing requirements to develop **new objectives**
* Identifying **constraints** imposed by the users' environment
* Identifying responsibilities for **data capture**
* Examining **systems interfaces**
* Preparing detailed **user requirements**
* Preparing **design specifications**
* Planning for the **design and implementation phases**
* Updating the **cost-benefit analysis**
* Preparing a **report** for user and systems management.

6.2 Analyst/User Relationship

Like the feasibility study, this phase requires the analyst to work closely with the user – perhaps even more closely than during the feasibility study because of the necessity to work at finer levels of detail. It is during this phase, too, that a good working relationship must be built up between the analyst and user if the overall project is to succeed. The analyst will have to talk to many different levels of user and will have to sift and record a large volume of data. He or she should ensure that the underlying problem has been identified and that the proposed design scenario does not merely address the **symptoms** of the problem: a system that aims at alleviating the symptoms of a problem will invariably be much more complex, messy and difficult to implement than one which addresses the problem itself.

6.3 Systems Objectives

The key to this phase, then, is to ensure that the objectives of the activities being analysed have been **fully understood**. Once this is clear, the preferred design scenario can be safely expanded into a full systems definition.

(a) Overall objectives

Systems objectives can be defined at several levels and it is in fact desirable to do just that. First, there are the overall objectives of the organisation's total information system. The essential point about these objectives is that they contribute towards the organisation's own **objectives**. Examples of information systems objectives are:

* To maintain the company's **share of the market**
* To **increase net profits** over an extended period
* To increase the **return on capital employed** (ROCE)
* To maintain the **current level of customer service** during a period of expansion
* To maintain **current staff levels** in the face of an increasing workload
* To increase the company's **product range**
* To expand the **geographical area** in which the company operates.

(b) System and sub-system level objectives

Although these overall objectives are meaningful and important in determining systems strategy as discussed in Chapter 1, they do not help the analyst much in the determination of objectives at departmental level. The overall information system objectives should, therefore, be broken down into system and sub-system level objectives. In doing this, the following principles should be observed:

* All stated objectives must be **consistent with** and **support** the overall information system objective
* Wherever possible objectives should be **quantified** so that progress may be monitored
* The objectives should be **realistic** (i.e. achievable)
* Each sub-objective must be capable of being broken down into **sub-sub objectives**.

Figure 6.1 shows possible system and sub-system objectives for an order entry system.

The translation of the objectives of a system into sub-objectives expressed in more tangible terms **is an essential part of the analyst's task**. The analyst will initially identify the problem in general terms and then by systematic investigation progressively break it down into lower level objectives. This step by step process, proceeding gradually into greater detail is essential, as it enables the analyst to become familiar with the problem in a systematic manner and avoids the pitfall of being plunged straight into the detail with no framework for reference.

Activity

Make a list of suggested objectives and sub-objectives for a hypothetical system to computerise the inventory or stores records of a manufacturing organisation.

Fig 6.1 *Order entry system*

Objectives	*Sub-objectives*
* Reduce average delivery times	* By 20% for products A, B and C and 5% for products D and E
* Improve customer service	* Provide immediate response to 90% of customer enquiries * Reduce average order acceptance time by 15%
* Reduce stocks	* Reduce stocks by: 40% for products F and G 35% for products A and D 15% for products C and H

6.4 **Outputs of the System**

Having defined the objectives of the system, the best approach for the analyst to follow is then to identify all the outputs required from the system. These will include the **data** which is to be supplied to other systems as well as **screen displays** and **hard copy reports**. At this stage it is neither necessary nor desirable that these outputs be designed, merely that they be identified so that their data content may be defined. This requires all the **data elements** involved to be identified. A data element is the lowest level logical unit of information: for example, a name is a data element, so are the price of an article, a product code, date, etc. It is not normally meaningful to break these down any further.

Activity

Identify the major outputs likely to be required for a hypothetical computerised payroll system for a large organisation. Remember that the taxation authorities, accounts department, human resources (personnel) department, banks (for cash requirements and bank transfer payments) and the organisation's employees may all be considered as users of such a system.

6.5 **Data Capture**

After analysing the data elements to be present in the desired output from the system, it is necessary to examine the ways in which these are to be made available to the system. Where the organisation has a mature and well planned common data base and the proposed system either replaces an existing application or is closely linked to one or more existing applications, there is a good chance that procedures will already exist for the capture of many of the requisite data elements.

The fact that a particular data element is currently captured by a particular procedure does not mean that that is necessarily the way it **should be captured in the new system**. In many cases the procedure can be improved and sometimes it will be practical to move data capture back closer to the original source of the data (see also Chapter 7). Where the data elements are not already included in the data base, it is necessary to **define their source**. During this investigation certain relationships between data elements beyond those already known will emerge, and these should be recorded as they will be valuable in data base design.

6.6 System Definition

The analyst will by now have a comprehensive picture of the objectives of the proposed system and a detailed statement of the content of both the output and input to it, as well as a picture of how it relates to existing systems and data bases. This information will enable the analyst to expand the proposed system design scenario developed during the feasibility study into a fully fledged system definition. This should contain:

* A statement of the **objectives** of the system
* A statement of the **constraints** within which the system has been defined
* Data flow diagrams (DFDs) decomposed to a sufficient level of detail to define fully the **functional requirements** of the system (a description of the data flow diagramming technique will be found in Chapter 13).
* A data dictionary containing a narrative description of all the **processes** contained in the DFDs and definitions of the **data elements**
* Descriptions of the system **outputs**
* A statement of the **sources** of system **inputs**
* A definition of system **responsibilities** (including data input, updating, error control, etc.).

Note that the systems definition does not go far beyond the design scenario in defining how the system will be **implemented**. Rather, it specifies the content of the operational system and how it will be maintained. Note, too, that no consideration (beyond collating the essential information) is given to data base design. Similarly, the definition of responsibilities does not describe the procedure to be followed, merely where the responsibilities lie for input, updating, checking, etc. The way in which these functions will actually operate will be the subject of the succeeding design phase.

Once the system definition has been produced, the analyst is in a better position to estimate the **time** and **resources** needed to design and implement the system and to ratify the cost-benefit analysis.

6.7 **Project Control Planning**

If a formal planning technique (see Chapter 5) has not already been used during the feasibility study, this is the time at which it should be introduced. Although the number of activities will not be very large at this stage, the project will grow rapidly from this stage on and it is simply good management practice to ensure that the reporting and control procedures are in place at the outset. For most systems development purposes, one of the many PC based project control tools will be found very suitable for project planning and control. One of the reasons in developing a plan at this stage is to provide the eventual user with an idea of the **commitment** necessary and the **timescale** involved.

Activity

Obtain details of one of the PC based project planning packages on the market and make a list of the facilities it offers.

6.8 **Report and Recommendations**

The plan for the design phase, the revised cost-benefit analysis and the system definition are combined into a report for user and system management. Unless major problems have been encountered during the definition phase which have undermined the work of the feasibility study, this report will normally recommend that the project proceeds to the **design phase**, and it should clearly indicate the **resources** necessary for that phase.

Once user and systems management have accepted the report, the systems definition formally becomes the **specification for the design phase**.

7 Step 5: Design

7.1 Activities in the Design Step

In this step of the systems development process we proceed from the 'what' of the new system (discussed in Chapter 6) to the 'how': i.e. we move from the agreed definition of systems objectives and requirements to the detailed system design which is to be implemented. This means that the entire system has to be defined in terms of information flow, data, volumes, screen layouts, printed output designs, procedures (both computer operations and manual), program specifications, etc. In addition, a **revised estimate** of the **operational cost** of the system is calculated after the design has been completed and a **revised plan** for **implementation** produced.

The thirteen main activities which are undertaken in this phase (in approximate sequence) are:

* Definition of **output** requirements, volume, frequency, format and distribution
* Specification of **input** requirements, volume, frequency and format
* Estimation of **transaction volumes**
* Development of overall **systems logic**
* Determination of **controls** and **audit** procedures
* Finalisation of **information flow**, **data elements** and **data relationships**
* Specification of **data** requirements, i.e. development of the sub-schema
* Division of the total design into **programs**, **modules** and **procedures**
* Preparation of **program specifications**
* Development of **general test requirements** (type of data, source, control checks, etc.)
* **Revision** of **implementation plan**
* Revision of **cost-benefit analysis** (especially in the light of improved knowledge about operational costs)
* **Documentation** of the design.

Systems design is not easy. It takes skill and experience and despite many attempts to make it a precise 'engineering' type activity, it retains creative or 'craft' elements. To that extent, design cannot be 'taught' in the strict sense of the word, rather it is a learned process. Nevertheless, there are a number of canons or principles which are followed consciously or unconsciously, by designers of successful systems.

7.2 The Canons of Design

The thirteen canons of design are that:

* Data should be entered into a system **once and once only**
* Data should be captured **as close to source** as possible
* Computer systems should be fully integrated into **general work procedures**
* The design should be '**user friendly**'
* Each single element of data should be part of a **coherent data base** which limits redundancy and eliminates the problem of the same data derived from different sources
* The data base should be structured to facilitate the efficient **retrieval of data** in preplanned ways and also to support the retrieval of data in response to *ad hoc* enquiries
* Data should be **available** to everyone with 'a need to know'
* Systems should be designed for maximum **flexibility**
* Systems should be designed to facilitate **maintenance**
* Systems **performance** should be satisfactory for the users
* The ability to perform each transaction and access to all data should be controlled by **security measures**, and it must be possible to trace the **execution** of each transaction
* The system must incorporate **backup** and **recovery** procedures which enable the system and its data to be restored within acceptable time limits after human, hardware or software faults, however caused
* System **output** should be provided directly to the person requiring it in a format suited to his or her needs.

We will now consider each canon in some detail.

(a) Data should be entered into a system once and once only.

It is axiomatic that data (except key or identifying data) should be entered into a system only **once**. In properly integrated applications this principle should be extended to cover the full suite of systems.

(b) Data should be captured as close to source as possible

Closely related to point (**a**) is the concept of data capture as close as possible to its source. Ideally, data should be captured as a by-product of whatever process **creates** that data; this eliminates the data capture step *per se*, with its consequent delays and the possibility of introducing errors.

Activity

Make a list of the following everyday situations as potential data capture sources for computerised systems: car-parking ticket machines; dental records; close-down sales (price reductions); menus in restaurants; telephone ordering. What data could be captured at these sources and for what management purposes might it be used?

(c) Computer systems should be fully integrated into general work procedures

Well designed computer systems are fully integrated into the work procedures of their users. That is to say, they become an integral part of their users' normal work. The computer system is not 'an optional extra', but is part of the normal routine. As has been remarked above, this approach has additional attractions when applied to system inputs but is also extremely important in regard to systems **enquiries** and **output**. It follows that the designer must pay attention to such factors as the number, positioning and accessibility of terminals as well as the more technical aspects of design.

(d) The design is 'user friendly'

'User friendliness' has become something of a cliché in recent years. In practice, it means that the **man/machine interface** must be designed for ease of use by the particular user community concerned.

(i) Screen display
Nothing is more critical to the ultimate success of a computer system than the design of the man/machine interface. Whilst this has always been important, it has become almost a truism since a large percentage of systems users have had 'hands on' access via some form of terminal device. The most widespread and frequently encountered terminal is the ubiquitous 'screen' or Visual Display Unit (VDU) (Cathode Ray Tube or CRT in American usage). This unit usually includes a keyboard – normally one which follows the standard QWERTY typewriter layout but with some additional keys. Screen display may be single colour (monochrome), e.g. green on dark grey or may be multi-colour.

Self-check

Where do you see 'screens' in use in your daily life?

(ii) Nature of working use
Designing the interface between the user and the machine using such equipment is not easy. Consideration must be given first to the users' **working environment**. Here the nature of **use** becomes important. Where the user has to work at the terminal continuously, eg in many data capture applications, the positioning of the screen in the workplace needs to be carefully arranged in accordance with ergonomic principles (see Chapter 17).

(iii) User/machine dialogue
The second aspect of the man/machine interface design is the actual dialogue between the user and machine. Whole books have been written on this subject but the major principles are fairly simple.

* First, there should be some **consistency** to the layout of the various screens in the dialogue so the user is always looking in the same place for the same type of data (screens must not look so similar, however, that there is confusion as to which is which).

* Secondly, the user must be able to **move about** the system easily and without getting 'lost'. Practically, this means that the menus and transactions should be structured so that it is always clear how to return to a known place (the use of a function or **Pf** key to return to the next higher screen in the screen hierarchy or to the main menu is a useful feature).
* Thirdly, the design should minimise the amount of **keying** required, especially if the users are not used to keyboard operation. The use of menu driven systems, menu bars at the top or bottom of the screen, the display of tables of options or data from which selection may be made and the use of a 'mouse' (see Chapter 17) to reduce or even eliminate keying as such are all helpful in this regard.
* Fourthly, the users, especially part-time and infrequent users, should not be expected to memorise **complex codes**; again the selection of a choice from a list of options is generally a preferable approach.
* Fifthly, the user should always have access to **context sensitive help information**. Historically, this has been provided by documentation (user manuals) but with the advent of massive on-line storage capacity at relatively modest cost such help is increasingly provided on-line. Such help can be accessed from any point in a screen dialogue (usually by pressing one of the special or function keys), and will display one or more screens of explanation directly relevant to the screen or transaction being used.
* Sixthly, different **transaction paths** may need to be provided for regular and infrequent users. Where the user community includes a mix of frequent and infrequent users, consideration should be given to providing two different screen dialogues for the same transaction: a 'fast path' for the regular user who has keyboard skills and can be expected to have memorised some codes or 'short cuts' and a step-by-step approach for new or infrequent users.

(e) Each single element of data should be part of a coherent data base which limits redundancy and eliminates the problem of the same data derived from different sources

The subject of data management will be discussed in Chapter 18. From a design point of view it is much easier to design a modular, flexible and easily maintained application using a well structured data base than it is using an ill-thought-out collection of files. It follows, therefore, that unless the data base structure is a given for the designer, i.e. where he or she is using a pre-established (or at least pre-designed) corporate data base, then close attention needs to be given to **data base design** before the detailed design of the application *per se*.

Activity

Make a list of the data elements likely to be used in a stock control system for a retail store.

(f) The data base should be structured to facilitate the efficient retrieval of data in preplanned ways and also to support the retrieval of data in response to ad hoc enquiries.

Clearly, any data base structure designed must support the particular **application** in question, and do so in an efficient manner. Virtually all data bases, however, can provide other information or answer questions and queries which were either not considered (or at best not uppermost in the designer's mind) when structuring the data base. All too often data can be 'hidden' unintentionally at this stage, i.e. the designer structures the data base in such a way that potentially useful associations of data are difficult or even impossible to retrieve. Time spent in analysing **data relationships** and postulating **potential requirements** at this stage can be amply rewarded throughout the life of the system.

(g) Data should be available to everyone with 'a need to know'

Data is not the property of any single individual, department or system. Rather it is a **corporate asset**. It follows that it should be freely available to all members of that corporation whose work requires them to know, or would be facilitated by a knowledge of, that data. This is not to say that access to data should be completely unrestricted (the subject of control over access is discussed below), but it does reinforce the design philosophy of separation of applications from the underlying data and the requirement to make data available to multiple applications (see also Chapter 18).

(h) Systems should be designed for maximum flexibility

The systems designer should always remember the adage: 'If it can be changed, it will be changed'! With the best will in the world, users will solemnly declare that such and such will never be altered or that the absolute value of x is y. Such statements often fail to survive the first month of live operation of the new system! It is, therefore, imperative that the designer creates the most flexible possible design. Four major factors contribute to this end.

* First, the use of a **modular design** enables individual elements of the application (modules) to be redeveloped where necessary without a complete rework of the entire application.
* Secondly, the use of a data base approach which separates data storage from the processing of that data enables data changes (e.g. increasing the length of key data elements, such as part number) to be accommodated more easily than when data storage and applications are closely coupled.
* Thirdly, the use of a design approach which makes all constant and variable data (e.g. validation parameters, constants and formulae) **external** to the main programming sequence, greatly enhances the inherent flexibility of the system.
* Fourthly, no **constraint** should be built into the system unless it is unavoidable. It is amazing how many of the constraints built into systems are quite unnecessary. In one example known to the authors, a production control system for a factory with two assembly lines was designed with the constraint that the same product would not be produced on both lines at the same time. This constraint was quite arbitrary and did not add anything to the system in terms of functionality or control. Neither did it improve system performance. It merely enshrined the production manager's belief that this would be the case. Needless to say within days of the system going live it was decided that the same product would indeed be assembled simultaneously on both lines! Systems similarly should not be tied to organisational structures – these can, and frequently do, change!

(i) Systems should be designed to facilitate maintenance

Even with the most careful approach to systems design, systems maintenance is inevitable. It may be caused by legislative changes (e.g. changes in tax calculations for payroll systems), the need to eliminate 'bugs' or errors in the original system, or by changes (including minor additions) to the user requirements. Over the lifetime of a system the cost of these 3 categories of maintenance can equal, or exceed, the original cost of developing the system. Fortunately, the factors which make a system flexible are also those which facilitate system maintenance. There is thus a double bonus if the principles outlined in section (**h**) are adhered to – and a double penalty if they are ignored!

One further point about readily maintainable systems concerns **documentation**. Without good, clear and up-to-date documentation even the best designed systems can be very difficult to maintain: good documentation is, therefore, a prerequisite for easily maintainable systems.

Self-check

What are the key points for attaining maximum flexibility in system design?

(j) Systems performance should be satisfactory for the users

Although it should be obvious that a system's performance must be adequate, it is surprising how often new systems are installed with inadequate hardware, communications links and/or inefficient software. The result, too often, is sluggish system performance, manifest to the user in slow response times. Although, from an objective viewpoint, a 10-second response time at a VDU is much better than the 5 minutes or so that it probably took to answer the same enquiry using a conventional, paper based filing system, the 'wait' can and does seem lengthy to the user. Psychologically, there seems to be a break point at approximately 3 seconds; response times which are longer than this are often described subjectively as 'slow'. The designer should be aware of this when hardware and communications links are specified (testing the estimates by simulation whenever possible). Poor response times in the early days of system use can have a severely negative impact on the **acceptance of the entire system** by the user community.

(k) The ability to perform each transaction and access to all data must be controlled by security measures and it should be possible to trace the execution of each transaction

Although it has already been stated that data should be available to anyone with 'a need to know', this does not mean that there should be unconstrained access to data. Still less does it mean that anyone should be able to change or otherwise manipulate that data. It follows that **access** to a system and the **data accessed** by that system should be protected.

(i) Internal controls
The designer should make specific provision for the safe running of the system, to ensure that the organisation's interests are protected in the event of accidental or deliberate threats to the security of the data it uses and provides. Overall data processing security is of course the responsibility of the departmental manager aided by the entire staff. Nevertheless, good systems design takes into account all aspects of security and, where appropriate, builds in or recommends the adoption of additional measures.

(ii) External security
In addition to security measures required to meet the needs of a prudent management, certain controls may be imposed from outside the organisation. One example would be where an organisation's auditors required the adoption of specific controls. Of increasing importance is **privacy legislation**, which imposes limitations on the storage and dissemination of information held about individuals and provides such individuals with rights to know the data held about them. The system designer must be aware of all relevant legislative controls and discuss requirements with other external bodies which may have specific requirements for individual applications.

(iii) Security risk
It is important to note that **total security is never achievable**. This implies the acceptance of some risk. The degree of risk allowable for a given application can be decided only in the light of its

importance to the organisation as a whole. This residual risk can itself be the subject of insurance to lessen the financial effects if the risk materialises.

In general, such risk analysis is determined by the policy of the organisation and is not the immediate responsibility of the designer. The designer is, however, primarily responsible for providing the specific security measures for each application he or she designs. The designer is also responsible for developing **contingency plans** to be followed in the event of a breach of security.

(iv) Security measures

The different types of security measures to be considered may be classified under 3 main headings:

* Physical security (generic controls, see Chapter 20)
* Systems controls (specific controls)
* Audit and legislative controls (imposed controls)

'Systems controls' is the term used to cover all those controls which the designer builds into the system to provide **general operational control** (i.e. controls which are not imposed by outside sources or which are not provided to all applications within the organisation). The actual controls will, of course, depend on the sensitivity of the system , but there are a number of underlying principles to be observed during the design phase – for it is important that these controls be **embodied into the system** – not 'added on' at some later stage: designing in security measures reduces the risk that they can be circumvented in normal operation. Good control will result from adhering to four basic rules: exercise control as soon as possible, define the controls, provide adequate control and maintain error statistics.

* Exercising **control** as soon as possible is clearly a sound principle and helps avoid the problem which has come to be known by the acronym GIGO (Garbage In Garbage Out). The best way to ensure that data processing does not produce erroneous results is to ensure that the input is captured as close to its source as possible and subjected to the most rigorous **validity checking** possible before it is used in any calculation or processing.

* **Defining** controls is also of prime importance, especially where people become involved in authorising transactions or accepting data queried on validation by the system.
* The controls provided should be adequate. Although the usual design objective will be to secure zero errors, for many commercial purposes this will be neither attainable nor economically justifiable. Furthermore the concepts of **degree of error** and **timeliness of data** must be considered.

  Degree of error will distinguish between errors of say 5p and £1000 although conceptually both are a single 'mistake'.

  Timeliness of information refers to the fact that in many application areas virtually correct information now may be more valuable than totally correct data next week. For example, if a manufacturer of soap powder is conducting a special promotion or launching a new product, sales returns of 85% accuracy the morning after the sales have been made is likely to be much more eagerly welcomed than precise results 10 days after the event.

  Of course if it is possible to get both accuracy and timeliness at an **economic price**, then that is the best option (as, for example, when sales statistics can be captured at the point-of-sale, such as at a supermarket checkout, as a by-product of the routine processing rather than being collected manually).
* Any major system should have all errors **recorded** centrally and regularly **reviewed**. Such recorded facts can help determine what, if any, systems' amendments need to be made to reduce errors and are a valuable input into the post-implementation review (see Chapter 10).

(l) The system must incorporate backup and recovery procedures which enable the system and its data to be restored within acceptable time limits after human, hardware or software faults, however caused

No matter how carefully a system is designed, sooner or later some human, hardware or software fault will cause it to crash. Moreover, there is the ever present danger of external factors such as fire, flood, accident, acts of terrorism and other disasters. Murphy's law dictates that problems will occur at the most awkward part of the processing cycle and at the busiest time of the day! Fortunately, the most serious threat for most systems is well short of total destruction of the computer facility, the risk focusing on human, software and hardware faults – probably in that order.

(i) Backup and recovery procedures
It must always be possible to recover from these situations within **acceptable time limits**, which will vary from application to application. Thus for a process control application controlling, say, the flow of molten metal in a steel plant, hot backup (i.e. instantaneous switchover to a second computer) will probably be necessary, whereas for the majority of commercial batch systems, normal repair cycles will probably be adequate.

(ii) The transaction log
Like the security measures discussed in Section (**k**), it is essential that backup and recovery procedures (which again include generic installation and application specific elements) are designed into the system from the outset. A most important aspect of being able to recover from any interruption to processing is the transaction log or record of what has been done, by whom (the logged on user), and using what programs and data. Within specific applications the **audit trail** which enables the calculations performed on an item of data from its source to its destination to be traced serves this purpose as well as its primary one of providing a record for audit purposes.

(iii) Checkpoint procedures
Backup and recovery will also entail the use of checkpoint procedures whereby **status checks** of the data base or files being processed are taken at **predefined intervals** and subsequent changes retained so that not only can the data be recovered but also it will be unnecessary to return to the commencement of a long processing run but merely to the last checkpoint.

All these measures require to be properly documented and the operations staff to be properly instructed if they are to work effectively when needed.

Self-check

List the most important aspects of the security measures required for information systems.

(m) System output should be provided directly to the person requiring it in a format suited to his or her needs.

The design points associated with system output, whether by display on a VDU, on a hard copy (paper) report, or by some other means are simple, obvious – and, all too often, ignored.

* First, output should be provided directly to the person who is **going to use it**. There is no point in routeing output via supervisory staff if the impact is merely to introduce delay. As noted above, the essence of good computer system design is to integrate the system fully into the regular work procedures.
* Secondly, the output must be provided in a format suited to the **recipient's needs**. There are two aspects to this. Output should not include extraneous data. In general, reports should thus be constructed on the **exception principle** (i.e. they report only those items which are outside specified limits and need to be brought to the user's attention). Such exception reports should be backed by on-line enquiry or other means which provide access to the full data. It is also highly desirable for most systems to provide their users with a simple-to-use **report generator** which enables them to produce, quickly and easily, screen or hard copy reports containing the precise information to meet their requirements at that time. All these approaches help avoid that abomination known as the paper data base – the inches thick hard copy computer printout or listing through which the user must hunt to find the information he or she requires.

Activity

For any computer system with which you are familiar, make an assessment (on a scale of 0–10, with 10 the top) of the way it satisfies the 'Canons of Design'. Make a list of the ways in which the system could be improved.

8 Step 6: Buy/Build Analysis

8.1 The Need for Common Solutions

Many of the applications systems in use cover functions which are common to a large number of organisations, either within a specific industry or more generally across a range of industries. Thus, for example, all employers face the need to process payrolls and, within a given taxation jurisdiction, the procedures for calculation are usually much the same. In the same way, most organisations have basically similar approaches towards the maintenance of purchase, sales and general ledgers while many manufacturing companies in the assembly based industries (e.g. automotive and consumer durables (white goods)) face similar needs to schedule material to a production process or assembly line in response to orders (materials requirement planning or MRP for short).

In the early days of the computer age, each organisation set about developing its own unique set of computer programs to deal with these common requirements. It was not long, however, before it was realised that at least some of these business requirements were susceptible to the development of **common solutions** which could be applied across a range of companies or organisations which had, or were prepared to adopt, a basically similar philosophy to the function in question and were generally similar in terms of size, transaction volume, sophistication and organisation structure/management style. This realisation was the foundation of the **application package industry**.

8.2 Packaged Software

It is probably true to say that the application package industry has never fully lived up to the expectations of its greatest admirers. A major reason for this is the fact that many organisations have had to invest substantially to adapt 'off-the-shelf' packages to their own particular needs. Nevertheless, within clearly defined functional and technical boundaries an application package can clearly obviate the need to 'reinvent the wheel'. Moreover, the use of suitable packages can dramatically reduce application development lead times and release scarce human resources for the genuinely unique applications which exist within most organisations and which give them their 'competitive edge'. Packaged software also can, and does, reduce the risk factor associated with *ab initio* systems development.

Activity

Using one of the standard industry software reference books, make a note of the number of companies offering packages suitable for mainframe computers in the following application areas:

* General ledger
* Payroll
* Invoicing/accounts receivable/sales ledger
* Purchasing/accounts payable/bought ledger
* Inventory/stores control

8.3 Package Selection

One of the major reasons that packaged software has been less widely used than it theoretically deserves to be has been the absence of a widely recognised, simple to use, practical approach to the selection of packages. As a result, much of the packaged software which is in use has been 'sold' rather than 'bought'. Buyers have too often finished up with software which did not really meet their needs and were consequently dissatisfied, to the detriment of the packaged software market in general. Yet the business of selecting the most suitable package and determining whether or not an organisation should adopt that package or pursue a course of 'in-house' development is essentially straight-forward. The approach recommended comprises nine separate sub-tasks. These are:

* Preparation of a logical systems design **specification**
* Preparation of a 'Request for Quotation' (RFQ) for issue to **potential vendors**
* Compilation of a **potential vendor list**
* Development of **cost** and **timing** estimates for the 'build' or 'in-house' solution
* Conduct of the **initial vendor evaluation**

* Evaluation of the **functional fit**
* Determination of **technical suitability**
* Review of **user references**
* Evaluation of **commercial considerations**

This evaluation should be carried out by the project team responsible for the overall project (or a nominated sub-group of that team). It is particularly important that the team making the evaluation includes both **user** and **data processing** personnel.

(a) Preparation of a logical systems design specification

As has been remarked above, there has been a tendency for packaged software to be 'sold' rather than 'bought': vendors have often persuaded buyers that a package can meet their requirements **without a systematic analysis of those requirements**. Successful package selection cannot be made before a systematic review of user requirements. It follows that the buy/build analysis can take place only **after the definition phase** Step 4, Chapter 6) has been completed. The documentation produced during Step 4 does in fact form the template against which available packaged software is compared to ascertain the degree to which it meets the identified functional requirements. The data flow diagrams (DFDs) and supporting data dictionary which constitute the system definition are well suited to this purpose.

Self-check

What are the main objectives of a system's definition phase? (see Chapter 6).

(b) Preparation of a 'Request for Quotation' (RFQ) for potential vendors

The first major activity in the formal buy/build evaluation is the preparation of the RFQ. This document will be sent to all potential suppliers of suitable software packages. The objective of the RFQ is to obtain proposals in a form which facilitates their **comparison** and **evaluation**. A typical RFQ will contain four main sections: a summary of the general business environment; a detailed description of the system requirement (essentially the system definition prepared in Step 4); a description of the technical environment (the computers and software already in use); and a statement of the procedure and timetable to be followed in evaluating the vendor's proposals. A contents list for a typical RFQ is shown in Figure 8.1.

Fig 8.1 *Contents list for a typical request for quotation (RFQ)*

Background

Brief description of the organisation
Corporate objectives
Key operating data

The EDP Environment

EDP Strategy
Hardware in use
Software in use (systems software, DBMS, languages)
Communications environment
Methodology in use
EDP organisation chart

The User Environment

User department objectives
Current status of computerisation in department
User department organisation chart

Project Description

Description of policies/constraints affecting the system
General statement of the principles looked for in the proposed system
System definition
* Data Flow Diagrams (DFDs)
* Supporting narratives
* Key data element descriptions
* Key interface descriptions
Transaction volumes and trends
List of user locations and terminal requirements

Evaluation and Purchasing Procedures

Procedure
Timetable
Contact(s) for enquiries
Outline of evaluation criteria (but *not* weightings)

Glossary of Terms

Activity

For an organisation with which you are familiar, outline the information you would include in the 'EDP Environment' section of the RFQ to a packaged software vendor.

(i) Evaluation criteria

It is important that the selection criteria to be used in evaluating the proposals are identified and documented before the RFQ is finalised. There are two reasons for this. First, if the evaluation criteria are known, the RFQ can ask explicitly for information in a form to facilitate evaluation. Secondly, such identification eliminates the possibility that the selection criteria will be consciously (or even unconsciously) influenced by the initial impressions of the vendors' proposals, i.e. it avoids the risk of undermining the objectivity of the study.

(ii) Points weighting scheme

A practical way of evaluating packages is to adopt a points weighting scheme, the objective of which is to provide an overall, quantitative assessment of the packages to indicate which is 'the best buy'. Essentially a package needs to be evaluated under three main headings: **system functionality** (the degree to which the package meets the user requirements); **technical factors**; and **commercial considerations**. Systems functionality is, of course, assessed against the systems definition, while the main topics to be considered under each of the other headings are listed in Figure 8.2.

* In the first instance the group charged with making the evaluation should, in consultation with management, determine the relative importance of the three headings in the context of that particular organisation. It is convenient if the points awarded to each heading result in an overall total of 100. In a typical example, 60 points might be awarded to system functionality, 20 to technical factors and 20 to commercial considerations.
* The next step is to ascertain whether any of the topics listed represents a **go/no go decision point**, i.e. a criterion the absence of which will debar the package from further consideration. Although go/no go criteria should be kept to a minimum, it is

usually possible to identify a few criteria which fall into this category. If, for example, the organisation has standardised on (say) IBM hardware or the COBOL programming language, it may consider that any package which does not fit that technical environment should be disregarded, irrespective of its intrinsic merit as a solution to the business problem being addressed.

* Once the overall ratings and no go items have been decided, the next stage is to develop the complete evaluation criteria and to assign them weights. This requires the development of the full list of criteria. For system functionality this is most readily achieved by listing the process titles of the lowest level DFDs contained in the system definition. For technical factors and commercial considerations, an expanded version of Figure 8.2 tailored to the requirements of the organisation will normally be sufficient. The second step is to associate with each of the selection criteria a **weighting factor** which reflects its relative importance within each heading (i.e. system functionality, technical factors and commercial considerations). Again it is convenient if the weights within each heading add up to 100.

(iii) Scoring package

For evaluation purposes the most convenient way to score each package is on a scale of 1–10 (10 the top). This is readily understandable and provides sufficient flexibility to make distinctions between ‘good’, ‘very good’, ‘excellent’ and ‘perfect’. Moreover, it is easily and quickly applied when assessing the packages. It is then a simple mathematical exercise to convert the ‘scores’ to an overall rating both within each heading and for the three headings combined. (A simple spreadsheet on a PC is ideal for this purpose.)

Once this preliminary work has been undertaken there is a basis for a **quantitative assessment** of the functionality, technical and commercial considerations of a variety of packages and enables an objective analysis to be made of the available alternatives.

Self-check

What will be the main contents of an RFQ?

Fig 8.2 *Major evaluation topics*

Technical Factors

- Product Environment
  - Hardware
  - Operating system
  - Data Base Management System (DBMS)
  - Communications/networking software
  - Other systems software
  - Programming language
- Documentation Provided by the Vendor
  - User manuals
  - EDP operating manuals
  - System architecture description
  - Data architecture description
  - Program specifications
  - Data base layouts
  - Installation guide
- Technical Staff Employed by the Vendor
  - Number
  - Experience/special expertise
  - Turnover rate
  - Reliance on key individuals
- Performance of the Package
  - Response times
  - Batch run times
- Backup and Control
  - Restart and recovery
  - Access control
  - Audit trail
  - Adherence to privacy legislation
  - Transaction logging
- Customisation
  - Services provided by the Vendor
  - Possibility of modification/enhancement by the user
- Maintenance
  - Services provided by the Vendor
- User Friendliness
  - General and context specific help screens
  - Man/machine interface design
  - Frequent and occasional user transaction paths
- System Architecture
  - Menu or transaction driven
  - Hard coded or external parameters
  - Modular construction
  - Design methodology

Commercial Considerations

- Vendor Background
  - Financial viability
  - Length of time in business
  - Commitment to package/user's industry
  - Reliance on one or few key staff
  - Size
- Product History
  - Age
  - Number of installations
  - Development plans
  - Frequency of new releases
  - Availability of source code
- Commercial Terms
  - Is package copyrighted?
  - Purchase price
  - Licence fee
  - Maintenance fee
  - Training fees
  - Support service fees
  - Installation charges
  - Terms for upgrades/new releases
  - Limitations of purchase/licence agreement, e.g. single site, single CPU, etc.
  - Additional charges for multi-site/CPU installation
  - Discounts for subsequent purchases from same vendor
  - Frequency of maintenance fee reviews
- Installation
  - Distribution media/format
  - Vendor or user installation
  - Does package supplied incorporate all known 'fixes'?
- Fault Tracing/Fixes
  - Are fixes developed for one purchaser provided to all purchasers/licencees?
  - Reporting of faults
  - Responsibility for faults
  - Timeliness of fixes
- Warranty
  - Terms
  - Duration
- User Groups
  - Existence/membership of user group
  - Services provided
- Training and Support
  - User training
  - Systems/programming training
  - Operating staff training
  - Location/duration of courses
  - Duration of on-site support
  - Availability of additional on-site support
  - On-line diagnostics
  - 'Help' desk

(c) Compilation of a potential vendor list

While the RFQ is being prepared, a list of the companies to which it should be sent can be compiled. The aim should be to include all those vendors who could possibly meet the specified requirement whilst keeping the numbers involved (and therefore the evaluation exercise) within manageable bounds.

A number of trade directories are published which list software vendors and give brief details of the packages they offer - often classified by functional area (e.g. general ledger, payroll, personnel, stores control) and/or type of hardware for which they are designed. When consulting such directories to compile a potential vendor list, the analyst will often find that the information is insufficient to answer the question: 'Is this package a plausible solution for the requirement?' When faced with this dilemma, the advice must always be to **include** the package and its vendor on the list - packages eliminated at this stage cannot be evaluated later. Moreover, the list can also be expanded to include the providers of 'bespoke' (i.e. made to customer requirements) software. These provide an alternative to either packages or in-house development.

(d) Development of cost and timing estimates for the 'build' or 'in-house' solution

In parallel with the preparation and issue of the RFQ, work can proceed on refining the **cost** and **timing estimates** for the in-house development of the required system. These estimates will have been originally developed during the feasibility study and subsequently refined in each of the subsequent steps of the systems development process. For the purposes of the buy/build analysis they should be as accurate as possible, using the best available estimates of systems development effort and making sure that all significant elements are costed. Similarly, realistic estimates of **development lead times** are required and note should be taken of the impact that any in-house development will have on other potential projects (i.e. the opportunity cost of developing the system in-house).

(e) Conduct of the initial vendor evaluation

When the due date for the submission of vendor proposals is reached, all replies should be recorded on the master list of RFQ addressees and they should be subjected to a preliminary vetting. Typically, it will be found that the replies include some 'no bids' (i.e. the vendor does not wish to supply the package or considers that it is unsuitable for the requirement defined) and some cases where the package offered is clearly unsuitable. At the same time those proposals which do not satisfy one or more of the 'no go' criteria should be identified. For all packages identified in this process the master list of RFQ addressees should be suitably annotated and the relevant proposals excluded from the evaluation.

(f) Evaluation of the functional fit

(i) First evaluation

The purpose of this evaluation is to ascertain the degree to which each of the proposed packages meets the **user requirements** as specified in the definition stage. Typically, this evaluation will take place in two or three passes of increasing rigour. In the first pass, the evaluation team will work with the documentation supplied by the vendor and compare the functions and features of each package with the definition which serves as the template against which they are measured. A formal points weighting method of the type outlined in section **(b)** should be used during this process.

(ii) Second evaluation

Those packages which appear, on the basis of this first evaluation, to offer a good match to the stated requirements should then be subjected to a second evaluation in which the degree of **functional fit** is confirmed in detailed discussions with the vendors.

The team conducting these discussions needs to be well prepared. The objective is to confirm the degree of match to the requirement defined, not to listen to a well rehearsed sales pitch for the product in general or the virtues of particular features which are irrelevant to the users concerned!

(iii) Third evaluation

At the completion of this second pass the evaluation team should have a clear idea of the two, three or four packages best fitting the system definition. In a final pass this assessment must be tested by 'hands on' use of the package.

For major packages, some vendors will, at this stage, offer 'trial installation' for (say) 90 days with attractive purchase options at the end of this 'free trial' period. Such offers should be resisted. They are, in general, a sales technique whereas the objective of the approach described here is the **objective selection** of the most suitable package by the purchaser. It follows, therefore, that it is better to conduct such 'hands on' testing/verification (ideally using **real data** from the prospective purchaser) on the vendor's test installation or, best of all, on the system installed at an existing customer site. During the second and final passes of the evaluation the scores allocated in the first pass should be progressively refined.

The outcome of the evaluation should be a quantified assessment of the functional fit and a qualitative assessment of the 'user friendliness' of the system.

(g) Determination of technical suitability

Vital though functional fit is, it is not the sole determinant of the most suitable package. In all but green field situations (i.e. where a completely new or re-equipped computer centre is to be used to support the package), consideration must be given to how well the package will fit into the **existing hardware and software environment**.

(i) Existing DBMS and programming language

Some points are obvious: does the package run on the computer and operating system installed? (This is likely to have been a go/no go criterion.) Other points are more subtle but can have a significant impact on the overall viability of the package. To take one example, if an organisation has invested heavily in a specific data base management system (DBMS) and has a number of major applications using that DBMS, then the selection of a package based on an alternative DBMS will have a major impact on staff **training** and numbers of staff needed to **support** the package, and may make it difficult to **integrate results** from the package with those of the existing applications. Similar considerations apply to the programming language in which the package is written. Note that these considerations apply irrespective of the relative merits of the DBMSs and programming languages themselves.

(ii) Systems architecture

Another significant factor which must be considered at this stage is **systems architecture**. Is the package being evaluated modular in construction or does it consist of 'spaghetti code'? A package which is truly modular will be much easier to modify and to maintain and is, therefore, more likely to be a lasting success than one which is suitable now but cannot readily meet the changing requirements of its users.

(iii) Data structures

The technical evaluation should also address the question of data structures. Of particular concern is the ability of the packages to make use of the **data element definitions already in use** within the organisation. It can be a time consuming and expensive exercise to make such seemingly simple changes to a package as increasing the size of a single key field (e.g. customer number, or foreign currency total). This is especially true if the package under consideration is old or has a poor architecture.

There are, of course, trade offs to be considered at this point. Would it be possible for the organisation to alter its data structures to fit those built into the package? If this is practical, the costs of doing so must be taken into account in the cost-benefit analysis.

To take one example familiar to the authors, some airlines code all their spare parts with in-house numbers while others use the manufacturers' part numbers. The inventory and maintenance engineering packages available in this industry may adopt either approach but clearly the adoption of a package requiring an in-house numbering system for an airline previously used to manufacturers' part numbers has major implications in labelling parts and re-educating stores, inventory, purchasing and engineering staff – not to mention the potential for confusion during the changeover phase!

(iv) Package interface

Data structure compatibility (or a flexible way of dealing with variations) is also a major factor in being able to interface the package readily to other **existing applications**. Few applications are truly 'stand alone' and the effort in building bridges between existing applications and a package can be considerable.

(v) Documentation

Last, but no means least, the technical evaluation should consider the question of documentation. Whilst the functional evaluation should consider such aspects as user manuals, the availability and quality of on-line help, etc. the technical evaluation must address systems documentation including the documentation of the systems architecture, programs, data structures and operations procedures (including backup and recovery routines).

Like the functional evaluation the technical evaluation should utilise a predetermined points weighting evaluation method to achieve objective, quantified results.

(h) Review of user references

At the completion of the functional and technical evaluations the intending purchaser will have a good overall assessment of the packages under consideration and their relative merits. A worthwhile further check, however, is discussion with as many as possible **existing users** of the packages. These discussions (which should, of course, be independent of the vendor) will sometimes reveal unexpected flaws (e.g. glossy manuals superficially attractive but impractical in use) or, equally valuable, confirm the potential purchaser's own judgement. Such discussions can also be valuable in identifying the quality of the vendor's **support staff**.

(i) Evaluation of commercial considerations

The final stage in the buy/build evaluation process is to evaluate the commercial considerations. In part, this follows the same approach as for system functionality and technical factors. Such aspects as the degree (and quality) of vendor support can, and should, be quantified using the same points weighting scheme outlined above, as well as contractual factors such as limitations on use of the software, payment requirements, warranties, options for extension, etc.

(i) Costs and benefits

Factors such as cost can, however, be subject to additional analysis for the buy, the build and the bespoke alternatives. In particular the life-cycle costs and benefits associated with each of the packages and other alternatives under consideration should be subject to evaluation (again a PC based spreadsheet is ideal for the purpose). This evaluation should consider, *inter alia*, the initial costs of each alternative; the costs of modification to meet the system definition in full; annual maintenance costs; licence fees for any associated software (e.g. a DBMS); incremental hardware costs, running costs; etc.; as well as the money value of the benefits expected. All costs and benefits should be **time phased** over the anticipated life-cycle of the application and discounted cash flow (DCF) techniques applied (explained in Chapter 16) to give a clear financial comparison between the alternatives.

The evaluation team, with a quantified evaluation of system functionality, technical factors and the non-financial aspects of the commercial considerations will then usually have little doubt about which of the available packages represents the 'best buy'.

(ii) Whether to buy at all

The final question is whether the 'best buy' is a worthwhile buy when compared with the in-house and bespoke alternatives (both of which will, by definition have scored very high or perfect scores on the systems functionality and technical factors).

The cost-benefit analysis, with its consideration of the time phased costs and benefits, taken together with the analysis of systems functionality and technical factors will normally produce a situation where there is a clear cut winner (i.e. recommended alternative), or, at worst, a choice of two (rarely more) closely rated alternatives. Given closely ranked alternatives at this stage, conservative advice would be to choose the alternative with the shortest payback period – i.e. that alternative which at the earliest date shows a **surplus of cumulative benefits over cumulative costs**.

Activity

Do a build/buy analysis in an area not related to information systems (for example, in household maintenance work), and note how the principles of package analysis and selection are valid in different situations.

---

9 Step 7: Implementation Phase

The objective of this phase is to obtain an operational system, fully documented, which is accepted by the users as meeting the needs foreseen in the systems definition.

Many well-designed systems go wrong **during implementation**. Data bases become unreliable; programs go operational containing many errors; users find the new system too complicated. If this sort of situation occurs, the project risks failing completely, because the lack of confidence which prevails may well permanently bias the user against the system. Furthermore, other systems installed later will suffer from user doubts and the credibility of the EDP department will suffer.

Activity

Make a list of possible pitfalls during the implementation phase which may cause a project to:

* Take longer to develop than planned
* Exceed the development budget
* Fail to meet the users' requirements.

How can the systems analyst guard against each of these pitfalls?

9.1 **Control During the Implementation Phase**

The project leader must retain tight control during the implementation phase. The project plan set up during the project planning phase (Chapter 5) will be subject to much change during implementation. The points for special attention are:

* Make sure the objectives for each person involved in the implementation phase are clearly understood **by the individuals concerned**. Each individual should know precisely what is expected of him or her within the overall project objective.

  This is a sound management principle applicable to any type of project. It is, however, particularly important in the case of systems work in which there are many vaguely defined activities, such as checking data, data base design, monitoring user reaction, etc. Such activities may very easily stretch out in time without further contribution to the project being achieved. The project leader must therefore decide for each activity and for each member of the team what is the **maximum allowable** time for achieving the desired result.

* Ensure that all work is carried out in accordance with the **standards and working methods** which apply to this project. Chapter 20 identifies the main areas for attention.
* Once implementation has started, any change to the design must be subject to a **change control procedure**, such as that discussed in Chapter 11.

This approach is essential to maintain control over the many potential improvements that users and systems staff alike perceive when the design is being turned into a working system. Many of these proposed changes are likely to enhance the system eventually, but incorporation of such changes without careful study of their impact is a frequent cause of systems not meeting their objectives. Naturally, it will make good sense to incorporate some of the changes proposed (for example, to correct errors in the design), but only after a **formal review**. Any modifications made must be carefully **documented**. This is essential for subsequent testing and to give an exact record of what the system actually does.

Activity

Check whether the organisation for which you work or one with which you are familiar with has a formal change procedure. If it does, how does it differ from that suggested in the text? If a formal change procedure is not in use, how are changes requested and controlled?

9.2 System Construction and System Acceptance

There are two distinct parts to the implementation phase.

(a) System construction

This is the principal phase of implementation which brings into reality all the preceding creative work of definition and design. The activities will include the need to:

* Write and debug all computer **programs**
* Create **master files** and populate **data bases**
* Prepare **documentation** (including on-line documentation) for EDP and user departments
* Acquire all necessary **equipment** and **supplies**
* Train EDP and user **staff**
* **Test** and **prove** all parts of the system
* Supervise **phasing-in** of the different parts of the system (by module, by geographical area, etc.)
* **Tune** the system to improve performance.

(i) Training

The systems analyst's responsibility for training is very important. This includes training in input preparation, error correction, distribution of printed output and security procedures. To gain maximum user understanding, presentations and video films may be necessary. User and operating manuals should be distributed in good time.

(ii) Testing

The aim of testing is to achieve an error-free system, which fulfils the functions specified in the system definition, before it goes operational. This implies satisfactory completion of a thorough pre-defined testing programme. Guidelines for system testing will include the need to:

* Test each system **module** separately
* Test the system as an **integrated whole**, using both test and live data
* Have the **users** test the system, as soon as all known errors have been cleared
* Test all **procedural cycles** – month-end, year-end, year-beginning, etc.
* Simulate **peak-load** and other extreme conditions, including all possible combinations
* Have the **auditors** test the system
* Do at least one **parallel run** before going solo.

In addition to the above, the systems analyst should go 'on shift' with the users for the first few days (or even weeks), until the system is run in and users have attained confidence in it.

(b) Systems acceptance

(i) Declaration of commitment

No system should be declared operational without a formal **acceptance procedure**. This is particularly important for contractual reasons when the system has been bought from outside the organisation, as discussed in Step 6 (Buy/Build Analysis). But it is also a significant step for the users, as it is in effect a **final declaration of commitment** to the new system.

(ii) Phases in the procedure

The acceptance procedure has two distinct phases:

* **Provisional acceptance** – when all testing has been completed to the satisfaction of both the users and the systems department, the system may be released for live running. This point is designated as 'provisional acceptance', because operational conditions often reveal flaws not found in testing.
* **Final acceptance** – this point is reached when the system has been running error-free for a period of around 3 months and marks the transition to routine operational status.

Self-check

How can the performance of a system can be assessed in terms of compatibility with user requirements?

(iii) Benchmarks

One of the most difficult problems met in systems acceptance is performance. When drawing up the system definition, it is normally possible to give only general indications of performance – for example, response times, error rates, etc. Experience shows that unanticipated performance problems often arise after implementation and many judgements have to be made as to whether or not a given function of the system is acceptable. **Benchmarks** are useful in making such judgements.

The principle of a benchmark is the creation of a task which represents a **wider work environment**, in order to see how the system performs the chosen task. The usefulness of such evaluation depends on how well the representative tasks are chosen. Such tasks may be:

* retrieval of data using specified criteria
* file transfer
* validation of a test set of data.

The use of benchmarks requires considerable care and technical skill. The systems analyst will certainly not work alone, and will need to work with experienced computer specialists. Together they can use benchmarks very effectively to analyse performance of a new system and these benchmarks are useful reference points when the decision on system acceptance is taken.

10 Step 8: Post-implementation Review and Evaluation

10.1 Importance of Evaluation and Review

The work of a systems analyst on any given project does not cease when the system becomes operational and error-free. Yet many systems analysts move on to new projects without ever carrying out a **systematic review and evaluation** of their development work. This is unfortunate, as the purpose of such assessment is very important:

* First, the **achievements** of the operational system are compared to the **objectives originally set** and to the **system definition**.
* Secondly, the **efficiency** of the system is examined to see where improvements can be made.
* Thirdly, the evaluation process provides practical **feedback** which is essential for systems planning and for the systems analyst's own professional development.

Self-check

At what intervals do you think post-implementation review and evaluation should take place?

10.2 Points when Review and Evaluation Should Take Place

There are two distinct points at which review and evaluation should be undertaken.

(a) Post-implementation review

This review takes place after the system has been running operationally for several cycles. For example, in a system which is run once a month it is best to wait 5 or 6 months after start-up before carrying out the post-implementation review. This waiting period is necessary to make sure that the users and EDP staff are thoroughly familiar with the system. A weekly system should run for 2 months or so before review and a daily system several weeks.

The emphasis in this review will be on four key areas:

* user reactions
* systems performance
* errors and problems
* checking that the system is functioning as foreseen in the system definition.

The findings should be documented in a report for the users and systems management, giving specific **recommendations for action** according to priority and cost.

(b) Bi-annual review

After the initial post-implementation evaluation, the system should be reviewed after approximately 2 years, and at bi-annual intervals thereafter. As will be discussed in Chapter 11, most systems constantly undergo amendments because of the changing nature of user requirements, and very often so many modifications are made that an information system no longer fulfils its original purpose. To avoid having systems which, although apparently running efficiently, are in fact obsolete, good systems analysis will include periodic reviews of each operational system.

Five key points to review in a long-established information system are:

* Does the system meet the **needs** of user management?
* Are the benefits and costs of the system acceptable and do they show major **differences** from the estimates on which the system was originally justified?
* Is the system adequately **secure**? (Are there sufficient precautions to prevent incidents, including unauthorised use, and are there effective measures to recover from them, if they should occur?)
* Is the systems **documentation** up-to-date?
* What improvements are **desirable**, and at what cost?

Activity

For any system with which you are familiar, make an informal review covering the five key areas identified above. Is documentation available which enables you to trace the evolution of the system form the time when it was implemented?

10.3 Mapping the System's Future

Apart from any immediate actions that may be shown to be necessary, the results of the review will be an important input for the systems strategy and planning process described in Chapter 1. Sometimes expected benefits are not realised in practice, and the decision may have to be taken to phase out the system. More usually, the review shows that many changes in user requirements have arisen and that decisions are needed to determine to what extent the system can be adapted to the new situation. The bi-annual review is therefore an important focal point for assessing the **achievements** of an information system, and for mapping the way for its **future**.

11 Step 9: Maintenance and Enhancement

11.1 The Dynamic Information System

Most systems are **obsolescent the day they become operational.** That is not to say they are not valuable to the organisation, but that changes to the new system are invariably necessary right from the start. The systems analyst therefore rarely sees a system 'completed'. By their very nature, information systems are dynamic and subject to change.

Self-check

Why are changes to a system so often necessary after it has been implemented?

11.2 Reasons for System Obsolescence

Eight key reasons for such obsolescence.

* **Oversight** on the part of the systems analyst at the design stage
* Misunderstanding of the **requirements** of the user department
* Insufficient **testing** of systems before operational usage
* Desire to improve system **performance**
* Change in user department **procedures**
* **Company policy change**, e.g. pricing structures, credit policies
* Change in **legal requirements**, e.g. taxation laws
* Desire to take advantage of **technical developments**.

11.3 Need for System Maintenance

Changes are often made unnecessarily or without adequate analysis of their implications. Many, however, cannot be avoided. Inevitably systems maintenance forms part of the permanent workload of a systems department and an allowance should be made for future maintenance for every new system installed.

(a) Development *v.* system amendment

After a number of systems are operational, a significant proportion of the total workload of the EDP department is taken up with systems maintenance. This leads to the conclusion that there is a finite number of systems that can be installed and maintained with a given level of manpower.

This is confirmed by observation of mature computer installations, where it is not uncommon to find 60% of the systems department engaged in maintenance work. After some years' existence, the work of a systems department seems to slow down, as more and more effort is needed to keep the old systems going. Eventually, case by case, it is more sensible to redesign each system completely rather than continuing to amend it. At this point it becomes clear that only with the addition of more staff can the old systems be rewritten while truly new systems are being created. Once this policy decision has been reached (that development should not be increasingly neglected in favour of amending old systems) the consequences are clear. An expansion in staff (or increase in expenditure for external development support) must occur. This process often results in a step function change in the pattern of resource utilisation.

(b) Cost implications

The cost implications can be wider than the direct cost of staff. Not only is extra space needed for the personnel, but also more resources for testing, and so on. Systems maintenance is therefore an important factor in the tendency of EDP budgets to rise over time. Anything that can be done to control it will benefit the whole organisation.

(c) Essential and inessential maintenance

Whereas every effort (through careful agreement on user needs at the system definition phase, for example) should be made to minimise subsequent changes to the system, some types of maintenance of course bring significant benefits. Examples are:

improved performance, greater ease of use, better 'help' facilities, etc. The important point for systems management is to differentiate between **essential** and **not-so-important** maintenance, and to control the whole process in such a way that resources which could be better utilised elsewhere are not constantly consumed.

11.4 Types of System Modification

Three types of system modification may be distinguished:

* Corrective maintentance
* Ongoing maintentance
* System maintentance

(a) Corrective maintenance

This is the work needed to put right what was wrongly implemented in comparison to the original system definition. Corrective maintenance is frequently urgent, and typically occurs **early in the operational life** of the system. Key actions are:

* to prevent the problem arising at the **operational stage** by thorough checking of the design and the pre-operational system against the system definition
* to ensure that the problems identified really are **errors**, and not changes made as 'new user needs' during implementation
* when a corrective modification is made, to repeat all tests necessary to ensure that the rest of the system **has not been affected**
* to maintain a **detailed record of changes**, and update the system documentation accordingly
* to inform all those who need to know about the change (users and systems department personnel).

(b) Ongoing maintenance

An information system must reflect the **changes in its environment**. For practical reasons, it is impossible to make changes on a continuous basis, but periodic adjustment to meet evolving user needs is an essential part of the systems development function. The problem is to enable the process to take place in an **orderly way**, and to ensure that the changes in the information system are genuinely in line with the interests of the **organisation**. To achieve this, it is important to:

* establish a formal procedure for handling requests for modifications; this can be used for all types of modification; a suitable procedure is described in Section **11.5** below.
* implement agreed modifications according to a plan, which groups together related amendments: for large systems, groups of amendments can be introduced in the form of periodic 'releases' of the system; this approach greatly helps the procedures for testing, new documentation, etc.

(c) System enhancement

'System enhancement' is a form of systems development which falls short of becoming a project. It is a matter of judgement for the systems developer whether or not a specific enhancement belongs to ongoing maintenance or should form a new project.

The initiative for systems enhancement usually comes from the systems department. The systems analyst will see areas for improvement, and can identify opportunities for making non-urgent but beneficial changes. These opportunities may be prompted by such events as:

* changes in basic software (for example, the data base management systems used by the organisation)
* developments in other systems, which open possibilities for more up-to-date input, geographical extension, etc.
* new requirements in the area of security
* awareness that performance or ease of use of the system could be improved by relatively small changes.

The emphasis in deciding whether or not to make a modification should be placed strongly on **cost-benefit assessment**. In addition, the overall view of systems evolution should be maintained. Systems can always be improved, but too many changes – even if justifiable individually – irritate the user. Stability has a high value in operational information systems and changes of the enhancement kind should be made only on the basis of clear benefit to the organisation.

Activity

Estimate the percentage of human development resources in your organisation (or one with which you are familiar) which are devoted to:

* Corrective maintenance
* Ongoing maintenance
* System enhancement
* New projects.

Are the calculated percentages stable? If not, which ones are increasing?

11.5 Modification procedure

It is important to have a formal procedure for **controlling changes**. Many users are not in a position to understand the implications of changes (even modifying a simple screen layout consumes time of the systems analyst, programmer, operations department and computer resources). Often this desire for change is made out of enthusiasm and there are occasions when it may indeed be best to pay the cost of making some changes in order to retain the goodwill of the users. But of course even in this situation one must retain control.

(a) Three key points of control procedures

The control procedure should be based on the following points:

* Any request for modification must be put **in writing** and signed by a responsible person in the user department
* The request should be evaluated by the systems analyst in terms of **cost** for doing the job and of **effects** of the change on other systems, performance, etc.
* The cost figure should be presented to the user department, whose agreement must be obtained that the modification is worthwhile. If the modification shows **direct savings**, there is generally no problem. If the benefits are more vague, then insistence on a signed agreement to proceed may cause the user department to review their request. Putting a signature to a request for expenditure has an amazing psychological effect

– people think much more carefully about the justification for a sum, if they know they can be identified later as the originator of the expense!

(b) Modification documentation

These three key points can be conveniently moulded into one simple procedure by having a special document, which includes the following information:

* The **name** of the person requesting the modification
* A **description** of the modification required
* The **reason** and **justification** (including estimated benefits) for the modification
* The estimated **cost**
* A statement of the **implications** of the modification – for example, increased running costs, effect on people's tasks, etc.

A suitable form for this purpose is shown in Figure 11.1. Such a simple procedure can have a significant beneficial effect in minimising the systems maintenance load, while ensuring that errors are put right and that the system adapts to evolving user needs.

(c) Introduction of change

After agreement on the need for modifications has been reached, it is essential to maintain close control on the way these changes are physically introduced. Such control is needed not only to ensure that the changes are correctly made, but also to satisfy the formal **audit** requirements of the organisation. Thorough testing and comprehensive updating of documentation are essential elements in this process. There are powerful software aids available to help the analyst in this work, notably in change control, releasing new versions, etc. Furthermore, some tools available facilitate 'reverse engineering', i.e. the ability to work backwards from the implemented system's code, data base formats, etc. to a physical and to a logical design. Such tools enable the analyst to delay the need completely to redevelop older systems and to take at least some advantage of technological advances since the original system was developed.

Fig 11.1 *System modification request*

SYSTEM MODIFICATION REQUEST		Reference number
		Title
		Sheet number
Supplement each section as necessary with additional notes and/or diagrams		Author
		Date
Name position and dept. of requestor		
Description of the modification required		
Reason for the modification		
Date by which the modification is required		
Reason for the required date		
Estimated cost of the modification (one time costs)		
Implications of modification (include effect on running costs)		
Authorisation	Requestor: ______ Date: ______	Systems Dept: ______ Date: ______

Activity

Using the format in Figure 11.1, prepare a system modification request for a desirable improvement to any system with which you are familiar.

Part II

Techniques

12 Fact Gathering and Reporting

12.1 The Analyst's Personal Skill

(a) Human relations skills required

Many analysts believe that well over half the skills they bring to any project are concerned with human relations rather than with technical matters. This human relations content does itself have a number of aspects, among the most important of which may be considered:

* **Choosing** a team to conduct a project
* **Leading** a team
* **Communicating** ideas
* Giving **technical instructions**
* Obtaining **information**

(b) Need for training in human relations skills

This last category of 'obtaining information' itself covers a number of techniques, but easily the most important of these is **interviewing** – it is, after all, the principal way in which the analyst obtains the detailed information needed about the present system, and especially the requirements for the new system.

Notwithstanding its importance, this part of an analyst's training rarely receives the attention it deserves. In cases where analysts are specifically recruited, and due consideration is paid to the personal skills required in the job, the results may not be too serious, but in cases where analysts are recruited only for their technical knowledge of computers (as is often the case with ex-programmers) the results may be little short of disastrous. Indeed it is the authors' opinion that much of the gap that persists between the technical capability of computers and the realisation of that potential is due to the neglect of the human relations and communications skills of analysts in general.

How may this part of the analyst's training be undertaken? There are all too few courses which address human relations and communications skills in the context of systems analysis – it being supposed, presumably, that these skills are either naturally possessed by all staff selected for such work or, alternatively, that they are of insufficient importance to justify a place in the normal analyst's training syllabus.

It is, to a certain extent, true that some individuals have more natural aptitude in these subjects than their peers, but it is emphatically not right to conclude that these skills cannot be improved by suitable training.

In Chapter 12 we address some of the most important human relations and communications skills which should be part of the skills portfolio of every analyst.

12.2 **Interviewing**

There are a number of guidelines which, if observed carefully, will enable interviews to be conducted satisfactorily, in terms both of eliciting the information required and of helping to build the **rapport between analyst and user** which is an essential ingredient of successful systems development. These guidelines are mainly simple common sense, but all too often they are not followed. Sixteen key guidelines can be distinguished, and we shall look at each in some detail.

- **Make an appointment**. Whenever a lengthy interview is planned (say more than 15 minutes), or when a new contact is being made, it is advisable to make an **appointment**. This serves two major purposes.

  First, it ensures that the interviewee is available and thus minimises the possible **waste of time**.

  Secondly, if advance notice is given of the topic(s) to be discussed during the interview, it enables the interviewee to collect the necessary **information**.
- **Be prepared**. The interviewer must take great care to be prepared; he or she must be perfectly clear as to what is **wanted** from the interview, and whether this is **facts** or **opinions**. It is recommended that a short checklist be drawn up to ensure that no points are missed. This will also have the effect of minimising the disturbance to the interviewee caused by having to go back and ask questions **forgotten the first time round**.

- **State the reason for the interview**. Whether or not the interviewee has previously been acquainted with the purpose of the meeting, it is as well to prevent any possible misunderstanding by stating briefly at the outset the purpose of the meeting. Some such sentence as: 'I would like to obtain some detail of the order taking process' will usually be sufficient.
- **Observe good manners**. This heading also covers some of the other guidelines, notably those concerning the making of appointments and avoiding interrupting the speaker, which many would regard as particular examples of normal manners. It is included as a separate heading, however, to remind the interviewer to observe good manners throughout the interview. Particular examples of ill manners frequently occurring in business circles which may cause offence are:

  * Smoking without asking permission
  * Failure of the interviewer to introduce him or herself
  * Failure to be punctual or stick to time limits

- **Use the interviewee's language**. Most departments within any organisation have their own specialised jargon. Failure to understand this language may mean that the analyst may not obtain all the information required – or, worse still, may misinterpret it. In any case, it may well leave the interviewee with the impression that the systems department does not understand his problems. It is, therefore, extremely desirable that the analyst, as part of his preparation, makes sure that he understands the **departmental jargon**.
- **Don't interrupt**. The analyst must guide the interview to a considerable extent. It is the analyst, after all, who requires the information. He or she must not, however, interrupt the interviewee if this can possibly be avoided. It is far better to wait until a convenient moment occurs to turn the interview back to a more pertinent line of enquiry than to interrupt, as this may well **inhibit the interviewee from expressing himself or herself freely** later on.
- **Avoid Yes/No questions**. The object of an interview is normally to find out facts or opinions from the interviewee; this being so, it is more effective to avoid questions which may be answered 'yes' or 'no' unless necessary to clarify a particular point. At first sight 'yes/no' questions may appear the easiest and quickest way of obtaining facts, but in practice they will

invariably mean that **important qualifying information** is **omitted**. The interviewee will also not feel that he or she has been properly consulted or the opinion offered listened to, if he or she has merely answered 'yes' and 'no'. It is much better in nearly all cases to use relatively **open-ended questions** which invite the interviewee to expand his or her ideas about the subject as well as provide the information directly sought. The interview may take rather longer but the interviewer will obtain a much better picture of the overall situation and is likely to leave a satisfied interviewee, since most people like to talk about their work in this way.

- **Don't express your own opinions**. When conducting an interview an analyst will often be asked to state his or her opinion about persons, departments or systems. It is dangerous to express such opinions and the temptation to do so must be resisted. An extension to this guideline, which is perhaps even more important, is that the analyst must not **contradict** or **argue** with the interviewee. Except for rare occasions his or her duty is to obtain facts and opinions: this purpose will not be served by arguing!
- **Compliment when possible**. Most people are encouraged by being paid an occasional compliment, especially when it shows that the analyst is genuinely interested in the person to whom he or she is talking. Even such general remarks as: 'That's a fine plant you have on your windowsill, Mr Brown' can be very effective in encouraging people to relax and express themselves freely.
- **Distinguish between fact and opinion**. Many people express their own (or their department's) opinions as proven facts. The analyst must take special care to check which of the items of information falls into each category.
- **Distinguish between need and desire**. This is particularly important when producing the systems definition. The general remarks in **(10)** above also apply to the necessity to distinguish between need and desire.
- **Don't be asked to leave**. In many ways the success of an interview may be judged by the final impression left on the interviewee. If the analyst has failed to observe the signs that the interview has gone on long enough (or has exceeded the time limit that was previously set), the final impression will be adverse. Observe, therefore, signs of restlessness, particularly

glancing at a watch or clock or collecting papers together, and be prepared to make an appointment to resume the interview later if the subject has not been covered in full.

- **Watch the interviewee's body language**. People do not only communicate with their voices. Every look and every gesture, indeed the very way people sit or stand, helps to add meaning to or modify the message being conveyed by the words being spoken and the tone of voice being used. The analyst should be aware of this extra 'language' (which is well described in a number of books) and responsive to the information it contains.
- **Check information received**. With the best will in the world people often make mistakes when quoting facts or alternatively may give only partial or obsolete information. It is, therefore, vital that the analyst should cross-check facts whenever possible.
- **Take notes**. Few people have the power of total recall over a conversation even a few minutes after it has taken place. For this reason it is always advisable to take notes and jot down facts during an interview.

  Some precautions do, however, have to be exercised.

  * First, the **permission** of the interviewee should be sought; some general introduction like 'If you don't mind, I'd like to note the main points of our discussion to help refresh my memory later' will usually suffice.
  * Secondly, do not take **verbatim** or even copious notes; these will only serve to distract the interviewer and will almost certainly inhibit the interviewee. It is better by far to make a few key notes in 'bullet point' form (probably using a pad on a clipboard for this purpose) as an *aide memoire*, and to write the notes up in full as soon as possible after the interview (or to use a dictating machine for this purpose – although, of course, permission to use such a machine must be sought at the start of the interview).
  * Thirdly, be prepared to **stop taking notes** (and to be seen to be doing so) if the interviewee starts to divulge personal or confidential information.
  * Fourthly, **summarise** the notes for the interviewee at the end of the meeting (this is also a useful check that the analyst has captured the main points accurately).

- **Confirm results of the discussion.** After the notes have been written up in full, it is good practice to send a copy to the interviewee so that any facts may be confirmed and to serve as a record of the meeting for both parties.

Case Study 1: The Bad Interview

A = Systems analyst
B = Accounts Manager being interviewed

A Good morning, I'm from the Information Systems Department. We sent you a memo telling you I would be coming to see you.

B Yes, I did agree with Mr Poppit, manager of the Information Systems Department, that I would be free for a discussion with one of his staff.

A Well I'm the one doing the job. You see we want to computerise a lot more of the work of your department. You have an awful lot of staff and we feel that we could do a lot of their work by computer.

B What did you say? Take away some of my staff? My staff are badly overworked as it is.

A No, you don't understand. Let me explain. We are going to set up a data base of all customer accounts and keep them on disk. Of course, we'll do an updating run before we use the data base to input to the invoicing run and monthly reports. Here, let me show you this data base layout. (Shows complex diagram and immediately launches in to a detailed description of the structure of the data base using technical jargon. After some minutes, **B** starts looking at his watch – a gesture that becomes increasingly frequent and obvious as the meeting goes on.)

B This is all very well, but you know my department is probably the most important one in the company. We control all financial matters very carefully, and we . . . . .

A (Interrupting) Oh, don't worry about that! The computer is much more accurate than humans. (Lights cigarette.) In fact, that's going to be a problem after the new system has been installed. Unfortunately, we will still have to rely to some extent on human beings. I mean your people will still have to provide the input data to the system but they'll have to be a lot faster than they are at present.

B I'd like you to know that my department won the group award last year for courtesy and efficiency. Furthermore, we always . . . .

A (Interrupting) Yes, but we're talking here about the new upgraded computer with 48 MIPS, which will certainly be a lot faster than any of your staff. Just you wait and see.

B No, I will not wait and see. (Looks at his watch again.) I am going to speak to Mr Poppit personally about this matter and we'll see then if . . . . .

A (Interrupting) You can if you like, but I'm afraid it's too late. I've already put in my recommendations and this represents such a big technical advance that I'm pretty sure they'll be accepted.

B You've already put in your recommendations! Why did you come to see me then, may I ask? I shall see the Managing Director himself about this. Now I'm sorry but I have to go to a meeting, so if you will excuse me I'll . . .

A (Interrupting) Well, I just have some more questions to put to you. We need more data about some of your activities. When do you require the customer accounts statements, every calendar month or each accounting cycle?

B I think we can discuss this some other time. I'm in a hurry now.

A Well just one last question. How many customers are there who . . .

B (Interrupting) Good-day, Mr . . . What did you say your name was? My secretary will show you the way out!

Case Study 2: The Good Interview

A = Systems analyst
B = Accounts manager being interviewed

A Good morning, Mr Smith. My name is Dolittle from the Information Systems department.

B Good morning, Mr Dolittle.

A It's very kind of you to give me half an hour like this. We realise you are very busy and I'll try not to take up too much of your time.

B Well yes, I must admit that I am rather busy these days. What can I do for you?

A As you know, we in the Information Systems department have been trying to see how we can improve the support we give managers like yourself. We have already done some preliminary work and, in fact, you kindly let us talk to some of your staff last month. We have tried to concentrate on your area to start with because your department is a key part of the company, which affects most other company activities. So, naturally, we want to take advantage of your experience and ideas.

B Well, I'll certainly try and assist all I can.

A Thank you. One of the problems with which we are very much concerned at the moment is the enormous amount of paperwork which is being thrust on departments such as yours. You have probably felt this problem increasing over the years.

B I certainly have! It's getting quite out of hand. I spend half my time just filling in forms and writing reports. It doesn't leave me enough time to be doing all the things I should be doing.

A Exactly. This is what is worrying us. Managers like you want to concentrate on activities like analysing the results of your department's work, decision making and staff training and supervision.

And your staff should be able to control the customer accounts rather than getting buried in the daily paper-work.

B Quite. I must admit that most of my staff are doing nothing more than routine clerical tasks, though they are all good people and capable of doing much more valuable work if they had the time.

A Well, we've been trying to get on top of the problem and we have some proposals on which we would very much appreciate your advice. We think one way in which we could help alleviate your problem would be to put more of the routine paperwork onto the computer. This should help you and your staff to have enough time for decision making and control of the business.

B I am certainly interested in what you are trying to do and will do my best to give you whatever information you need. I am glad that at long last somebody is trying to do what I have been saying should be done for the last ten years.

A If we may, we'll contact you again in the next week or so and ask your permission to talk to some more of your staff. You've been most helpful. I'll be confirming the details we discussed in a memo. Thank you very much for giving me so much of your time this morning.

B It was a pleasure. Good-day, Mr Dolittle.

A Good-day, Mr Smith.

Activity

With a colleague set up a number of role playing exercises in which you alternatively play interviewer and interviewee. Suggested scenarios are:

Interviewee	*Interviewer*
Cooperative, helpful user interviewed as part of series of meetings	Systems analyst seeking data
Nervous user, uncertain of facts, initial meeting	Systems analyst seeking data
Uncooperative, anti-computer user, latest in series of difficult meetings	Systems analyst seeking data
Systems analyst	Difficult user demanding many modifications to an operational system
Clerical assistant, responsible for maintaining integrity of data in newly operational system which is working unreliably	Head of department, in which the clerical assistant works

After each exercise, conduct a full debrief on the ways in which the interview could have been more productive, less antagonistic, etc.

12.3 **Other Fact-finding Techniques**

Although interviewing is the most important fact-finding technique, it is not the only one, and consideration must be given to the other **sources of information** available to the analyst.

Self-check

Where would you, as a systems analyst, look when trying to collect information before setting up a new system in an organisation?

Useful sources for such information will include **company documentation** within the data processing and user departments (and sometimes other departments as well), examination of **trade** or **national statistics**, use of random sampling techniques, observation and questionnaires. We shall consider each of these in some detail.

(a) Company documentation

Searches of company documentation will, of course, reveal a multitude of sources of information ranging from minutes of board meetings (which may, for example, reveal areas of future expansion and thus influence the computer capacity and number of terminals required for a new system) to the detailed documentation of an existing computer system. The documents searched in the analysis and design phases of a project will, of course, vary from system to system and organisation to organisation. There are, however, a few general points which should be remembered in all cases.

* First, check to ensure that the information is still **current**. It is of no value to base system design on obsolescent information.
* Secondly, **cross-check** information wherever possible. There is a tendency to assume that written information is more reliable than verbal information. This is not necessarily true: the mere fact that the information has been committed to paper does not guarantee its accuracy.

* Thirdly, ensure that the information is **relevant**. It is easy to be misled into making the basic mistake of accepting statistics which are almost what is wanted as being exactly what is wanted. If, for example, in designing a computer system the analyst requires to know the **number** of weekly paid employees who are paid by direct bank transfer, it is not sufficient to be told the **percentage** of all employees who are paid in this way. The information will not be correct for the purpose for which it is intended.

(b) Examination of trade or national statistics

All the points listed in (**a**) are equally important when seeking facts from trade or national statistics, but special care must be taken in assessing the relevance of the information to the needs of the study being performed.

(c) Random sampling techniques

These techniques are an extremely valuable aid during the fact-finding phase of a project, but great care must be taken if the results are to be properly applicable to the whole population of the study. Basically the technique consists of selecting a **proportion** (the sample) of the total (the population) and, based on the assumption that the sample is representative of the population, drawing inferences about the whole. For example, if a sample of 10% of the invoices received in a week had an average value of, say, £50 and a total value of £10,000, it could be inferred that the average value of all invoices was £50 and their total value was £100,000.

In the use of this technique there is, however, a major pitfall. If the sample is insufficiently large or not representative of the population as whole, no valid conclusions can be drawn from the analysis of the sample. In the above example the invoices from some major suppliers might be received only monthly, thus distorting the picture obtained from a sample drawn from a single week (whether or not that sample included the monthly invoices).

This pitfall, and the way in which samples may be selected so that there can be a high degree of confidence in the statistical validity of the results obtained, is explained in any textbook on statistical techniques and the analyst is strongly advised to study one of these or to consult a statistician before using the technique.

Activity

Obtain a textbook on business statistics and review the chapters on sampling techniques.

(d) Observation

One of the ways in which an experienced analyst collects information is by observation. This is not a specific technique which can be taught but is rather a **subjective assessment** of those factors likely to prove of importance. Observation may take the form of simply 'keeping one's eyes open', or the formal observation of an activity over a period of time (which may be either **continuous** or at **specified** or **random intervals**).

The key to successful observation is to take a purely passive and patient role, not interfering in any way with the process itself, which must be allowed to take place as nearly as possible as it normally would. (The analyst should be aware that the mere act of observing may alter the behaviour of the individuals concerned: the so-called 'Hawthorne' effect.) The use of observation as a fact-finding technique will come readily to the analyst trained in O&M and work study techniques.

(e) The use of questionnaires

Facts obtained from answers to questionnaires are less likely to be accurate than those obtained from answers to questions posed at a direct interview. This is because the interviewer is in a position to explain his or her questions more clearly, and to interpret the replies. The interviewer is also able to make a subjective assessment of the probable **validity** of the information. These aids are denied to the analyst working with information supplied in answer to a questionnaire who does not even know whether the person who completed the questionnaire completed it accurately or merely guessed at the answers.

There is also a further reason why questionnaires often result in highly suspect information. Unless designed very carefully the questions asked may prove **ambiguous** or **misleading**. For example, a questionnaire on staff turnover included the question: 'What was the percentage staff turnover in the data processing department in 1989?' No further instructions were given, so answers could have been calculated on the staff level at the beginning or the end of the year, or on an average figure. Moreover, respondents may, or may not, have included part-time staff, staff on maternity or other long-term leave, sandwich students on attachment to the department or contractors.

(i) Pilot survey

There are, of course, many instances (for example, where the size of the survey to be undertaken is too great for individual interviews) where the use of a questionnaire is the only possible method. In these cases great care must be taken in **framing the questions** and, if possible, expert advice obtained. It is also good advice to conduct a small, pilot survey using a preliminary version of the questionnaire so that practical problems not apparent to the authors may be **identified** and **eliminated** before the full scale survey is undertaken.

(ii) Personnel involved

The use of semi-trained personnel to present the questionnaire and assist the recipient to complete it will remove many of the anomalies in the information obtained. Furthermore, the use of a well worded covering letter (or better still a briefing meeting) explaining the **need** for the survey and requesting the assistance of the person to be questioned will also serve to improve the accuracy of the replies.

Activity

Develop a questionnaire to obtain personnel data for inclusion in a human resources data base. Get a number of friends to complete the questionnaire and compare the results to identify any ambiguities: e.g. does the question 'Next of kin' invite the response of a name or a relationship (wife, parent, etc.)? Revise the questionnaire and re-test.

12.4 Recording Facts

Mention has already been made of the value of taking notes during an interview. This is also true of any other fact-finding technique.

Facts should be recorded **as soon as possible**. Once the facts have been recorded they should be **checked** and any necessary **corrections** made. All documents produced must state clearly what they contain, the source of the data, the author and the date.

12.5 Writing Reports

It will have become apparent from the description of the approach to systems analysis in Part I that at many stages of the development cycle the analyst will be required to write formal reports. This is true even when one of the Computer Aided Systems Engineering (CASE) tools described in Chapter 2 is used. It follows, therefore, that the analyst must develop the skill of writing accurate, readable reports. Yet although it is such a basic skill, a depressingly large number of business reports are overlong, difficult to read, and even when the reader has ploughed his or her way through them the message remains unclear!

(a) Guidelines for a good report

The guidelines for a good report are, however, surprisingly simple and obvious and, given a little attention, can make both report writing and report reading much less of a chore.

(i) Content and audience

The first step is to decide what you want to say and **to whom** it is addressed. Obvious, perhaps, but nevertheless a point worth stressing. A few minutes setting out in bullet point form the message(s) the author wants the reader to comprehend and the action or response which is required will do much to focus the subsequent work. Similarly, jotting down a list of the likely readers will help the author determine the **language** and degree of **detail** required.

(ii) Framework and structure

The second step is to set out a **framework** or **structure** for the report. Many organisations have standard report layouts and where these exist they should, of course, be followed. Similarly, many reports of the types described in this book will of necessity follow a set format. Where, however, the analyst has no prescribed format to follow, the outline given below will generally be found satisfactory.

- Cover page
- Table of Contents
- Introduction
- Management Summary
- Recommendations
- Main Text
- Glossary of Terms
- Appendices

1 **Cover page**: The cover page should provide sufficient information for the report to be fully identified. It should contain:

- A descriptive title
- Reference number
- Date of issue
- Author's name
- List of recipients
- Status: draft, interim or final report, etc.

2 **Table of contents**: For all but the briefest reports, a table of contents is essential. In addition to providing an index to the document it also gives a short overview of the scope of the report.

For long reports, the table of contents should be sufficiently detailed to enable the reader to go immediately to a section of the report only a few pages long when looking for specific information – not being faced with the task of wading through twenty or thirty pages of text to find what he or she wants. It follows that the report must be constructed in such a way that **headings** are used every few paragraphs or, at worst, every few pages. (Headings will be discussed below.)

For reports like those that are produced at stages in the systems development life-cycle, and where the content will follow a predetermined pattern it is helpful to establish a **report folder** early in the relevant phase of the project. The report folder (a lever arch file is ideal) can then be sub-divided into sections corresponding to the table of contents and material can be added to the folder as it is created. This approach substantially eases the task of **report writing** at the end of the phase.

3 **Introduction**: The purpose of the introduction is to introduce the report, not to present its findings. It should state clearly but concisely what the report is **about** and **why** it has been written. It is also useful if the introduction explains in a sentence or two the **content of each main section** of the report.

4 **Management Summary**: The objective of the management summary is to provide a quickly read **overview** of the work reported. It is, in essence, a short précis of the report, setting out in a few pages the main arguments and salient factors.

Management summaries should rarely exceed three or four typed pages even for the most complex reports and if they exceed six pages they should be completely rethought. In general the management summary does not contain detailed cross-references, footnotes or other distractions and the use of graphics should be limited to a very few which make points which are essential to the main theme of the report. The management summary is normally best written after the main body of the report.

5 **Recommendations**: Where a report makes specific recommendations, it is advisable to summarise them in one place, cross-referring them to those sections of the report where the case for them is argued. Those responsible for accepting or rejecting the recommendations can then see, at a glance, what is being proposed in total. This section of the report should tabulate for each recommendation:

- **What** is being recommended
- **Who** is expected to action the recommendation
- **When** the recommendation should take effect
- What the **financial implications** of the recommendation are (usually a single expenditure figure, a single benefit figure and a time scale)
- **Cross-references** to the arguments in the report leading to the recommendation

Like the management summary, the recommendations section is usually prepared after the main body of the report has been written.

6 **Main text of the report**: Before writing the main body of the text it is necessary to go back to the list of bullet points (i.e. one- or two-sentence descriptions) of the main message(s) to be conveyed by the report and the list of expected readers.

- The list of messages should be rearranged so as to provide a **logical flow or sequence of ideas**. Where there is no logical flow or sequence, other criteria such as **perceived urgency** or **time scale** may be used to impose some structure onto the material (the analyst should also, in this situation, carefully consider whether all the messages actually belong in the same report).
- The next stage is to determine the **relative importance** of the various messages since this should, in general, determine the space devoted to each one. Then with the list of readers firmly in mind, the analyst should construct a **space budget** (number of pages of text and graphics) for each message.

Only when this background work is complete should the analyst put pen to paper (or fingers to keyboard).

The actual writing of the text brings up the whole question of **style**. Whilst style is essentially subjective, there are a number of points which are generally considered good practice when writing business reports:

- Write in the **third person**.
- Use clear, concise English (generally simple, fairly short sentences) avoiding **jargon** and excessive use of **colloquial** expressions.
- Divide the text into **paragraphs**.
- Use **headings** for each paragraph or group of paragraphs.
- Relegate detailed tables, background material, etc. to **Appendices** – do not overburden the main text.
- Avoid **ambiguity** – e.g. in a report to be circulated to both American and British readers, write dates as 12 November 1990 rather than 12/11/90, which could mean 12 November or 11 December, depending on the nationality of the reader.

  Similarly, do not introduce abbreviations unless you are positive that they will be understood by all likely readers. It is good practice to spell all abbreviations out in full the first time they are used. For example, 'Electronic Data Interchange (EDI), is used . . . .'.
- Use **graphics, charts and tables** to illustrate key points (a picture is worth a thousand words) but make sure that the graphic really does support the point being made and is

properly **titled** and is **referred** to in the text. Where appropriate, reference should be made to the **source** of the data.

- **Substantiate all facts quoted** and clearly state where **opinions** or **deductions** have been introduced, e.g. 'In the opinion of the Project Team, therefore, ...', or, 'From the foregoing it may be deduced that . . . .'.
- **Cross-reference** the text to other parts of the report and other documents precisely, but only if it is not possible to structure the report in such a way as to avoid cross references or duplicating text.
- Use a **numbering system** which helps the reader find his or her way around the document but, not so complex that it becomes intrusive. Generally, the numbering of individual paragraphs is unnecessary. For most purposes the following guidelines will prove satisfactory.

  Use **arabic numerals** (1, . . .) for each section of the report (e.g. Introduction, Management Summary etc.) each sub-section and each sub-sub-section, separating the numbers by decimal points. These numbers will therefore be in the sequence 1 . . .; 1.1 . . .; 1.1.1 . . .; etc.

  Within sub-sub-sections, individual paragraphs or groups of paragraphs may be identified by unnumbered, descriptive headings, distinguished, if possible, by **emboldening** or the use of a distinctive **typeface** or different **size of type**.

  Finally, **lists** within paragraphs may be identified by bullet points (•) or asterisks (*) or, where they are subsequently referred to, by lower case letters or roman numerals ((a) . . .; (i) . . . .). Where letters or roman numerals are used, make sure that they are not repeated within the same level of the report hierarchy – i.e. they should run sequentially within each sub-sub-section.

  The use of increasing levels of **indentation** of the text to reinforce the hierarchical structure is of material assistance to the reader as is the use of **page numbers** throughout the report.

7 **Glossary of terms**: In this section of the report, all technical terms and abbreviations should be **listed** and **explained**.

8 **Appendices**: The Appendices should contain any detailed and background material necessary for a full understanding of the report but which is not essential in following the main argument of the text – i.e. they **support** the main text but are not part of it.

(iii) Importance of report presentation
The use of word processing technology supported by electrostatic copying machines, many of which can collate documents, has greatly simplified the production of business reports. Although most such documents do not require the full facilities of Desk Top Publishing (DTP) packages, there is no doubt that a well presented report makes an immediate, favourable impression. The use of a clear, uncluttered layout, different typefaces and sizes, emboldening of text and the use of attractive graphics all help in this process.

There is a risk, however, that presentation can become an end in itself and the analyst should always ask what **added value** the latest bell or whistle brings to the process of communication.

Activity

Obtain a report (e.g. annual report of a company, scientific report, committee report, etc.) and review it critically with regard to its presentation, clarity of expression, etc. In what ways do you think the report could be improved?

12.6 Making Presentations

Like writing reports, making presentations is part of the analyst's 'stock in trade'. Presentations may be to large or small audiences, formal or relatively informal, and may be carefully prepared and rehearsed well in advance or short notice ad hoc events. In all cases, the quality of the presentation (and thus its ability to **convey its message** to the audience) is greatly enhanced by preparation and by observing a few simple guidelines.

(a) Content and length

The two critical activities in planning a presentation are deciding **what** you want to say and finding out **how long** you have to say it.

* When deciding what you want to say, it is again good advice to **limit the number of messages** you want to communicate. The human mind does not absorb material continuously. The analyst should note the points that he or she wishes to make in bullet point form and then prioritise them on the basis; 'If I

could leave only one message with this audience, what would it be?'. Then repeat the question with the remaining messages.

* When the potential messages have been prioritised, it is necessary to decide **how many** should be included. This is a function of the time available. In most cases only two-thirds of the total available time should be taken up with formal presentation, leaving plenty of time for questions and discussion. How many messages can be conveyed in two-thirds of the total time is a matter of judgement and will obviously vary with their complexity and the extent to which the audience is familiar with the subject matter. As a rule of thumb, any message will take at least 5 minutes of presentation and many, if not most, will take 10 minutes to develop properly. Thus if 1 hour is allowed for a presentation (40 minutes' presentation, 20 minutes' questions and discussion), from four to eight messages can be communicated. The authors' preference would be to err towards the lower figure; many more presentations are unsuccessful because too much is crammed in than fail because the material is spread too thinly.

(b) Structure

After the messages to be conveyed have been decided, the **structure** of the presentation should be planned. The standard advice:

* **Stand up**
* Tell them what you're **going to tell them**
* **Tell them**
* Tell them what you've **told them**
* **Sit down**

remains sound. No audience is attentive continuously, so some element of repetition is not only permissible but desirable – unlike a report, the audience cannot turn back to a previous page and many even senior personnel are inhibited from asking a question that might reveal that they have not been paying attention all the way through!

(i) Formal visual aids

Within this basic structure, the analyst must decide how he or she wants to **convey the messages**. Most often this will involve the use of some form of visual aid, typically overhead projectuals (transparencies), 35mm slides or flip charts. When using visual aids, remember that each one will account for a minimum of 2 minutes' and more usually 3 to 5 minutes' presentation time.

Many otherwise good presentations are spoiled by poor visual aids, the most common problems being irrelevance, poor legibility and verbosity.

* Little can be said about irrelevance. All visual aids must be **appropriate**. Using graphics because they are attractive, available or interesting rather than relevant will confuse the audience and distract the presenter from the main theme. When designing visual aids, the question: 'How does this support the message(s) that I'm trying to convey?' must always be uppermost in the analyst's mind.
* All visual aids must be clearly **legible** to each member of the audience. Overheads produced quickly by photocopying a page of a report rarely satisfy this criterion and, moreover, often introduce distractions or irrelevances in the form of extraneous text or data. Handwritten visuals which are prepared using multi-coloured felt tip pens and transparencies are often a better alternative for a presentation given at short notice.

  Another cause of poor legibility is the attempt to cram too much onto a visual aid, a comment which leads directly to the next point on verbosity.
* Not only is **verbosity** a prime cause of illegibility it is also a problem in its own right. As a rule of thumb a 35mm slide or overhead should contain no more than 12–14 words. If the number of words is 20 or more, then consideration should be given to dividing the text between two or more visual aids.

  In addition to avoiding verbosity and the closely related fault of 'busyness' where too many lines, figures or too complex diagrams are included on the visual aid, good visual aids are aesthetically pleasing. The help of layout artists or public relations (PR) personnel should be sought if available. Generally, only a limited range of colours and typefaces should be used (lower case is often easier to read than UPPER CASE). The use of a common style or theme (e.g. a standard border with the company logo or project name on it) can help give cohesion to a presentation and, for long presentations, the use of marker or **index** visuals which indicate where the presentation has reached compared with the agenda, can be helpful to both audience and presenter.

(i) Opinion is divided on the best **medium** *for visual aids*
For big presentations, the quality and colour attainable using 35mm slides is hard to beat, but this medium does require the room in which the presentation is being given to be at least partially darkened, thereby restricting the interaction between presenter and audience.

For most purposes overhead projectuals are suitable. These may be handwritten, produced by electrostatic copying or commercially produced and may include colour. They also have the advantage that they can be used in near normal lighting conditions and can act as the 'script' for the presenter as they can be read even when not being projected.

Other visual aids (e.g. video tapes and projector guns for large scale display of computer terminal screens on-line) may also be appropriate where circumstances require and preparation time and budget permit.

(ii) Informal visual aids
In addition to the formal visual aids, it usually desirable to have some medium available for drawing **impromptu sketches**, etc. in response to questions or to list points arising during discussion. Flipchart boards, blank transparencies (or transparency rolls) for use on an overhead projector, white boards or chalk boards can all be used for this purpose, although the first two are to be preferred since they provide a **hardcopy record** of the sketches or lists.

(iii) Multi-media/screen presentations
Sometimes multi-media or multi-screen presentations may be considered. Although these can have considerable impact if done properly, they can also be extremely 'bitty' and difficult to follow as the audience keeps having to change its focus of attention. Such extravaganzas are rarely worth the effort and expense for the sort of presentations most analysts will be called upon to perform. Where they are required, the analyst should seek the assistance of PR or other suitably experienced personnel in preparing, and possibly giving, the presentation.

(c) Venue

Having agreed the messages to be delivered, structured the presentation and prepared the visual aids, consideration can be given to the room in which the presentation will be given. Often the actual venue will be beyond the control of the analyst, but there are often things which can be done to make the presentation more likely to succeed.

The simplest of these is the **arrangement of the room**. For audiences up to thirty or so in size, a 'U'-shaped arrangement is usually preferable to a room arranged 'schoolroom' fashion. With a U-shaped seating arrangement, it should be easy for the presenter to move forward into the open end of the U to 'command' the audience.

Secondly, the screen and projector should be placed so that all members of the audience have a clear view and the presenter can use a pointer to draw attention to items on the visual aids without blocking the view.

(d) The presenter(s)

Before the presentation itself two other points must be considered: should the presentation be a solo performance, and should hand-outs be made available?

* Sometimes the answer to the first of these questions is immediately obvious. Where only one person has been involved in the work being presented, or where the presentation is short (say 15 minutes or less), the use of more than one presenter would be artificial. With longer presentations, a change of presenter can often be a way of keeping an audience attentive, offering a change of voice, pace of delivery, etc.

  Where it is decided to use multiple presenters, care must be taken about where the **natural breaks** occur in the presentation. Typically these will be at the end of the introduction (tell them what you are going to tell them), at the end of each message and immediately before the summary (tell them what you've told them).

  To avoid fragmentation do not use too many presenters. This means that the temptation to give everybody who has been involved in the work something to say should be avoided: more than three presenters would be an exception. All presenters should be chosen on the basis of their capability to give the presentation, irrespective of seniority or status. No presenter should speak for less than 10 minutes (shorter 'slots' tend to give the impression of a row of 'Jack-in-the-box' toys!). It is recommended that the same presenter should give both the introduction and the summary.

(e) The dress rehearsal

The final stage in preparation for a presentation is the 'dry run' or dress rehearsal. Note that no mention has been made of writing a 'script'. Few analysts can actually deliver a presentation well using a verbatim script: it is much better to use a series of headings and the visual aids as the guidelines for the presentation.

* By all means write the introduction out in full and learn it verbatim and always write out quotes and references and read them from a written text, but for the bulk of the presentation use the words that come naturally from the headings (the authors' technique is to write these in large print on single sheets of paper and interleave them with hard copies of the visual aids and any quotations or references and then join them all together with a treasury tag. In this way they are easily read and manipulated but do not lose their intended sequence if accidentally dropped.
* A naturally delivered (i.e. not fully scripted) presentation will sound much more convincing than almost all scripted presentations and will, moreover, avoid the twin traps of reading head down from a written text oblivious to the audience and the risk of being completely 'thrown' by an unsolicited question or interruption.

(f) Using handouts

The final pre-presentation consideration is whether handouts should be given to the audience and, if so, **when**. Handouts (usually just copies of the visual aids but possibly supplemented by more detailed figures when the visual aids have been greatly simplified in the name of clarity) are normally a good idea and well received by the audience which does not, therefore, have to take notes and can concentrate fully on the presentation.

* Distributing handouts at the beginning of the presentation enables the audience to make margin notes on the appropriate copy but the presenter runs the risk that the audience will read the notes, not listen to the (much expanded) script.
* Conversely, distributing handouts at the end of the presentation runs the risk that some members of the audience may feel obliged to take copious notes (distracting their attention from the content), while there may be questions (particularly if the visual aids are less than perfectly legible) which would have been avoided by the availability of hardcopy.
* On balance, the authors prefer distributing handouts after the presentation (and stating their availability at the beginning), but in reality the decision is finely balanced.

Self-check

You are to make a presentation on a new system development plan to the board of directors. What will be your key points in preparing for the presentation?

(g) Delivering the presentation

No discussion of presentations would be complete without a few remarks on the actual techniques of **delivery**. The following list of do's and don'ts is not exhaustive and may even be broken (with discretion) by the experienced presenter projecting his or her own particular personality or style. It will, nevertheless, serve as a guideline for all presenters:

* Do **stand up**.
* Do speak **clearly** in your natural voice and **slowly** and loudly enough to be heard in all parts of the room.
* Do use **short sentences** (but not so short that they sound clipped and unnatural).
* Do **alter the pitch** of your voice – emphasise what needs to be emphasised.
* Do use a **pointer** to draw attention to points on your visual aids – but don't wave your pointer like a palm tree in a hurricane!

* Do make sure you don't block the audience's **view of your visual aids**.
* Do **watch your audience**: the response will tell you if you can be heard.
* Do watch your audience's **body language**: are the listeners warming to your message (leaning forward, nodding in agreement) or withdrawing (sitting back and crossing their arms across their chests)? Body language is contagious and the experienced presenter will try and isolate those withdrawing and build on the support of those sympathetic to his or her script by the use such language as: 'I can see many of you have experienced what I've just been talking about' or, 'I can see you don't all agree but ....'.
* Do stay **within the time allocated**. A good way to do this is to note during the final dry run the intermediate times in the abbreviated script so that you have milestones during the presentation. The authors, along with many others, place a watch on the table next to the script, propped so it can be easily read without the obvious distraction of having to look at the wrist.
* Do **edit on your feet** if you run out of time. If you suddenly realise you are going to overrun by more than, say, 5 minutes, do go through the remainder of your presentation in bullet point form then deliver your planned summary using such language as: 'I'm sorry I'm running out of time and I don't wish to detain you longer than planned, but if I could briefly introduce the other topics I had hoped to cover today'.
* Do **move around** – but not too much! Standing stock still for 20 minutes is totally unnatural and as unnerving for the audience as perpetual movement. Move deliberately, don't fidget and above all move naturally.
* Do **use your hands**. Hands are a stage prop for the presenter: do use them to amplify your points but don't wave them aimlessly or continuously.
* Don't put your hands in your pockets and jangle the keys or loose change (such items are best taken **out of pockets** before the presentation).
* Don't stand face down to your script and **ignore your audience**.
* Do get friends and colleagues to watch your presentations and tell you about **mannerisms** of either **speech** or **action** which may be irritating to your audience.

* Don't crack jokes or tell anecdotes unless they are **apposite**, **suitable** for the audience, and you can tell them **well**. This does not mean that the presentation must be deadly serious. A little levity or light relief is often highly desirable, especially during a long presentation on a complex subject. Neither jokes (especially risqué or ethnic ones) nor anecdotes (especially long or complex ones) have a high success factor. Better by far the (carefully rehearsed) 'spontaneous' one liner or 'impromptu response to the audience (one of the authors frequently responds 'Gesundheit' or 'Bless you' to a sneeze by a member of the audience). The key is to be yourself – but yourself under careful (and premeditated) control.
* Do decide how you want to **handle questions**. These may be taken as they occur during, or held over until the end of, the presentation. Once you have decided (questions taken during the presentation seem more natural for a small to medium sized audience but are more likely to distract the relatively inexperienced presenter and make it harder to stay within the planned time), tell the audience at the **beginning** of the presentation. If a question arises during the presentation which is addressed later on, reply using such language as: 'I'll be covering that point later on so I'd prefer to leave the answer to then but if I don't cover your question in full, please raise it again'.
* Don't be **nervous**! Take a deep breath and relax.

Activity

Plan and prepare a 10-minute presentation on a topic of your own choice (a hobby or subject you know well is recommended). After you have prepared the presentation, rehearse it in front of a full-length mirror taking care to time your delivery. Refine the presentation and repeat the rehearsal. When you are confident you have a well prepared presentation, present it to a group of friends or colleagues. Invite constructive critique and repeat the exercise as necessary.

Note:
This activity is best conducted in groups with each member taking turns to make a presentation with the remainder making up the 'audience'.

12.7 Walkthroughs

Walkthroughs (also called walkthrus) are an approach to peer group reviews in which staff of similar levels within the organisation review each other's work in a formalised manner.

(a) Value of the approach

Properly conducted walkthroughs are a valuable way of promoting group participation in both analysis and design, and provide a measure of **quality assurance** by ensuring that all aspects of the work concerned are critically reviewed by people who are closely involved with the relevant technology and, usually, the subject matter, without being directly responsible for it or subject to the cost or deadline pressures experienced by the line manager in charge of the work.

(b) A 'professional' culture

The key to successful walkthroughs is the development of a culture in which all concerned can express their opinions fully and frankly without any form of **personal censure** being implied. That is to say that the debate is conducted at a purely professional level without fear of recrimination or other comeback. To achieve this aim takes time, but it can be fostered if walkthroughs become a regular feature of the systems development process and all staff take their turn both as presenters and reviewers.

(c) Format

The format of a walkthrough is basically that of a small, formal meeting at which one member makes a presentation (i.e. he or she 'walks through' some aspects of the analysis or design), in such a manner that a group of his or her peers (the reviewers) have a full opportunity to understand, evaluate, question, comment upon and ultimately accept or reject the work concerned. The walkthrough is run by a chairman and a secretary records the meeting.

(d) Conducting a successful walkthrough

The ten key points in conducting successful walkthroughs are:

* Restricting the size of the group to a level at which all attendees can be expected to **participate actively**: in practice, this means a group of six to eight.
* Ensuring that all attendees are sufficiently well versed in the general project under consideration to be able to make a **useful contribution**.
* Limiting the participation to staff who are sufficiently homogeneous in status and organisational grouping to avoid **defensive or aggressive attitudes**.
* Circulating the data flow diagram (DFD) or other document to be 'walked through' sufficiently well in advance of the walkthrough to allow all attendees to have **studied it**.
* Limiting the walkthrough to a reasonable time – avoiding the twin pitfalls of open ended discussion about the entire project and curtailing discussion about the subject matter. 2 to 2½ hours should be sufficient for the most complex material – especially if participants are **properly prepared**.
* Allowing the presenter to explain **why** things have been done in a particular way, as well as **how**.
* Conducting walkthroughs **before** the presenter has become **totally committed** to a particular method of achieving his or her objective.
* Discouraging **passive attendance**.
* Controlling the meeting through **effective chairmanship**. The chairman should ensure that all questions and comments are **objective** and **relevant** to the topic under discussion. The chairman must also ensure that no remarks of a **personal nature** are allowed.
* **Recording** the points raised. The secretary should record all points which lead to significant **clarification** and all points which lead to the **modification** of the document being walked through (excepting minor typographical or grammatical points).

(e) Outcome of the walkthrough

There are three possible outcomes of a formal walkthrough.

* The meeting may decide to accept the document concerned 'as is'.
* It may accept the document subject to the inclusion of specified changes.
* It may require some rework of the document and its submission to a future walkthrough.

The chairman should establish the findings of the meeting, ensure that they are properly documented and, where the agreement is for rework and another walkthrough, establish the date of the next meeting.

After the walkthrough, the secretary should **circulate** the record of the meeting and a copy of this record together with a copy of the document walked through should become part of the **project log**.

Activity

Conduct a walkthrough with a small group of friends or colleagues, with one of the participants presenting and arguing in favour of the content of a magazine article.

---

13 Charting Techniques

In Chapter 12, various ways in which an analyst may obtain information were described and it is natural to follow this with a discussion on some of the ways in which the information obtained can be **documented**.

13.1 **Value of Charting Techniques**

Charting techniques are, however, more than just ways of recording information: properly used, they can prove valuable design aids and, in some cases, are effectively the key element of a total methodology.

13.2 **Charting Techniques Available**

Some of the most useful charting techniques are now described; they are:

* Data flow diagrams
* Bubble charts
* Flowcharting
* HIPO charts
* Procedure charts
* X charts

13.3 **Data Flow Diagrams (DFDs)**

(a) Function of DFDs

DFDs are diagrams which show the **logical interrelationships** between processes and the way in which data moves to **support** those processes.

* DFDs may be logical, in which case they depict **what needs to take place** in an overall process or procedure in order to achieve a given aim.
* DFDs may be physical, in which case they describe how a process or procedure is **carried out**.

DFDs can, therefore, be used to depict both 'what is' and 'what should be'. They make no distinction between computer based or manual processes within a system.

A further key feature of DFDs is that they may be 'decomposed' or 'exploded' to provide ever increasing **levels of detail**, whilst retaining full consistency with all higher levels of DFDs for the same system and other DFDs at the same level of decomposition. It is this attribute of DFDs which makes them the core technique of a variety of structured methodologies or approaches to systems analysis and design.

(b) Diagramming conventions

A number of diagramming conventions exist for DFDs and the symbols associated with three of these are shown in Figure 13.1. Each of the notations shares three common elements – processes, data stores and data flows – and two of the notations also provide a symbol for external entities.

* In DFDs, **processes** are used for the activities which **transform data**. That is to say, processes represent things that happen to data (e.g. calculating, selecting, matching, etc). Processes are described by using an 'action' verb followed by a description of the data being processed (e.g. 'prepare purchase order').
* **External entities** represent the **point of origin** of **inputs** into or the **destination** of **outputs** from the system being diagrammed. As such, they may be persons, organisational units (either within or external to the organisation whose system is being diagrammed), or other systems.
* **Data stores** represent data **at rest**. That is to say, data which is subject to either short- or long-term storage. In physical terms, storage may be in computer or any other format (e.g. hard copy in a four-draw filing cabinet or data semi-permanently displayed on a wall chart for reference purposes).
* **Data flows** represent data **in motion** (i.e. the flow of data between processes, data stores and external entities).

(c) Logical processes and flows

When preparing DFDs the emphasis is primarily on what is **logically taking place**. Physical considerations are taken into account only where necessary. It is this focus on the logical processes and data flows which makes the DFD a powerful

Fig 13.1 *Symbols used in Data Flow Diagramming*

SYMBOL NAME	DESCRIPTION	USING FLOWCHARTING SYMBOLS	USING de MARCO NOTATION	USING GANE & SARSON NOTATION
PROCESS	An activity which transforms data			
DATA FLOW	Data in movement (arrow shows direction)			
DATA STORE	Data at rest			
EXTERNAL ENTITY (Interface)	The origin of input within the system being depicted or the destination of output produced by the system being depicted		NOT USED	

analytical tool. By focusing on the logical, the question as to **why** such and such a process is taking place is readily highlighted, and thus analysis is facilitated. (In practice, it is often convenient to draw DFDs of existing systems in physical terms first, and then to distil the logical processes and flows from the physical DFD.)

(d) Drawing a DFD

The steps to be followed for drawing a DFD are given in Figure 13.2. An example of a completed DFD is shown in Figure 13.3.

(e) Conventions and validation rules

A number of conventions and validation rules exist for use with DFDs. The most important of these are given in Figure 13.4.

Fig 13.2 *Steps to be followed in preparing a DFD*

Step 1 Identify the **aspect** or the **extent** of the system to be diagrammed

Step 2 List and draw the **processes** included in the system or partial system being diagrammed, making sure that all process names begin with an **action verb**

Note: If the system or partial system being diagrammed includes more than eight processes, consideration should be given to dividing the diagram into two or more parts or combining some of the processes for decomposition on subsequent DFD.

Similarly, if the DFD contains less than four processes at this stage, consideration should be given to combining the DFD with another or sub-dividing the processes into sub-processes. The aim should be to include 6 + or −2 processes on each DFD in order to achieve the desired level of detail at each level of decomposition

Step 3 List and draw the **outputs** (data flows) produced by each process and connect them to the appropriate symbol for their destination (which may be one or more external entities, another process on the same DFD, a process on another DFD or a data store

Step 4 List and draw the **inputs** (data flows) used by each process and connect them to their point of origin (the options are the same as for output destinations)

Step 5 Label and name each **data flow**, **external entity**, **data store** and **process** on the DFD

Step 6 Restructure the DFD to give the clearest possible **graphical representation**

Step 7 Ensure that the DFD respects the **conventions** listed in Figure 13.4

Step 8 Prepare a 'fair copy' of the DFD by hand drawing or using computer graphics, making sure that it is properly **identified**

Fig 13.3 *A completed data flow diagram*

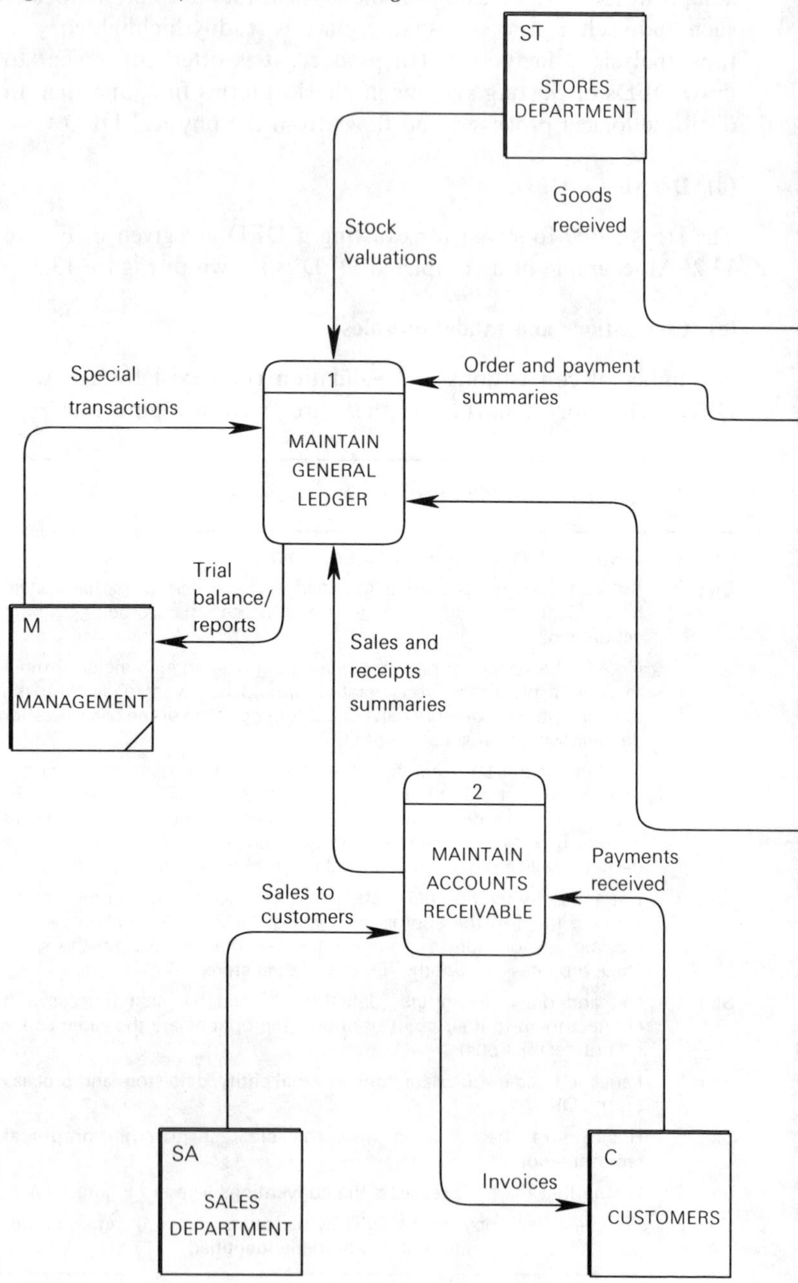

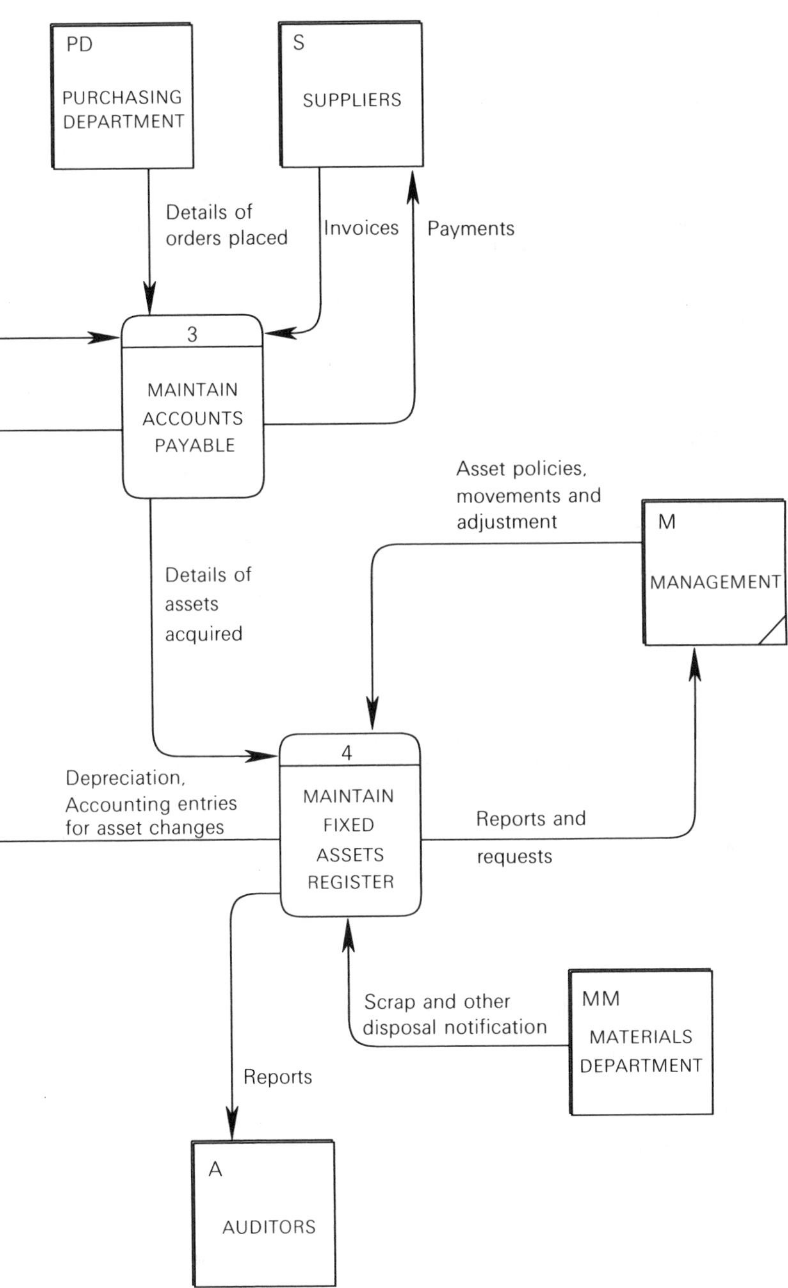
PD
PURCHASING DEPARTMENT
S
SUPPLIERS
Details of orders placed
Invoices
Payments
3
MAINTAIN ACCOUNTS PAYABLE
Asset policies, movements and adjustment
M
MANAGEMENT
Details of assets acquired
4
MAINTAIN FIXED ASSETS REGISTER
Depreciation, Accounting entries for asset changes
Reports and requests
Scrap and other disposal notification
MM
MATERIALS DEPARTMENT
Reports
A
AUDITORS

Fig 13.4 *Conventions and validation rules for use with DFDs*

1 All symbols on a DFD are connected by **data flows**

2 Data flows are permitted only between certain **combinations of symbols**, as shown on the following table:

To: \ From:	EXTERNAL ENTITY	PROCESS	DATA STORE
EXTERNAL ENTITY	No	Yes	No
PROCESS	Yes	Yes	Yes
DATA STORE	No	Yes	No

Note:
In practice this means all data flows are activated by or for processes.

3 Each process within the system, or partial system, which is the subject of a DFD, must have at least one data flow **entering it** and one data flow **leaving it**

Note
On explosion charts, processes which serve as 'interfaces' or connections to other DFDs are not subject to this rule (e.g. processes 1, 2 and 3 (all outside the boundary) in Figure 13.5).

4 Each process within the system, or partial system, which is the subject of a DFD, will normally have at least **three data flows** into and out of it (a process with only one data flow in and one data flow out is unlikely to be transforming data in any logical way)

5 Each data store within the system, or partial system, which is the subject of a DFD, will normally have at least **one data flow into** and **one data flow out** of it: that is to say, data stores cannot spontaneously create data (immaculate conception) nor be a permanent unused repository (a data sink)

Note:
There are **exceptions** to this general rule. The most important are:

(a) Where a data store serves as an 'interface' or connector to other DFDs exploded from the same high level DFD; in this case the data store may be created or used on another DFD
(b) Where the data store is used as an archive
(c) Where the data store represents a public data source external to the organisation whose system is being diagrammed (e.g. the use of Teletext or Oracle for timetable or exchange rate data)

6 For processes and data stores, it must be possible to generate the **outputs** from the **inputs**

7 Any explosion DFD must be logically consistent with the **next higher level DFD**

8 Processes in explosion DFDs have a reference number which starts with the reference number of the process from which they are decomposed, with a suffix to provide a **unique identity** on the new DFD

9 All symbols and data flows must be clearly and unambiguously **labelled**

10 Where symbols are repeated on the same DFD, this fact should be indicated; the convention used in the DFDs in this book draws a diagonal line across the lower right corner of external entities and adds a triangle to the left hand side of data stores

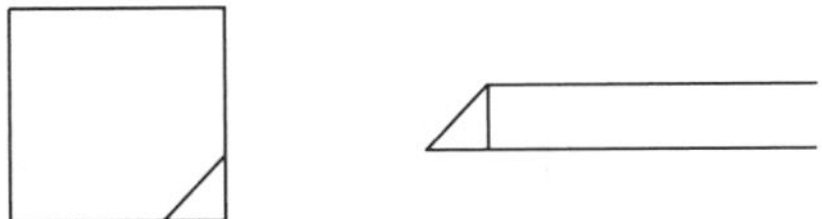

11 All DFDs must be identified in accordance with the principles of **good** documentation; in particular each must have: a title, reference number, the author's name and data

---

* It has already been noted that DFDs may be 'exploded' or 'decomposed'. This is achieved by taking any one of the processes from an existing DFD and creating a whole DFD **for that process alone**, showing the various sub-processes which exist within the process itself. When creating an 'explosion' in this way, it is important to ensure that all the data flows into or out of the process shown in the higher level diagram are included in the lower level diagram.
* These data flows may **themselves be decomposed** (i.e. a single data flow on a high level chart may be shown as multiple data flows on the exploded diagram). For example, 'Customer correspondence' might appear as a data flow on a high level diagram but be decomposed into 'Enquiries', 'Orders' and 'Complaints' on the next level of diagram.
* The important thing is that all the data flows are carried onto the lower level diagram. Additional data flows may also be included where they have not been considered important enough to show on the higher level diagram. **Exceptions**, for example, are typically on detailed diagrams shown only where they account for a **significant proportion of the workload**, being excluded from high level diagrams where, by definition, they are exceptions. The DFD in Figure 13.5, is the explosion of process 5 from the DFD shown in Figure 13.3.
* The processes in a DFD can be exploded to any required level of detail. As can be seen from Figure 13.6, exploding a DFD

Fig 13.5 *Maintain fixed assets register*

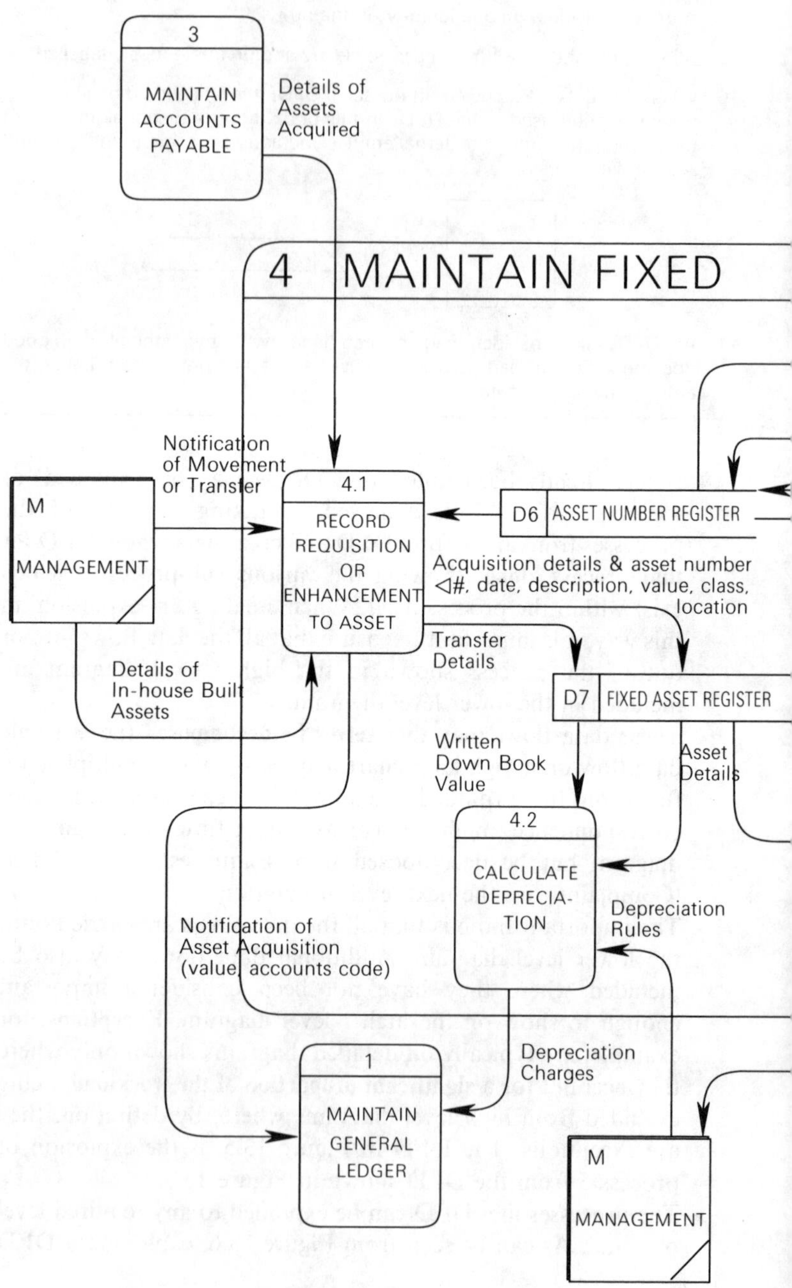

Note: This figure is an 'explosion' of a process from Figure 13.3

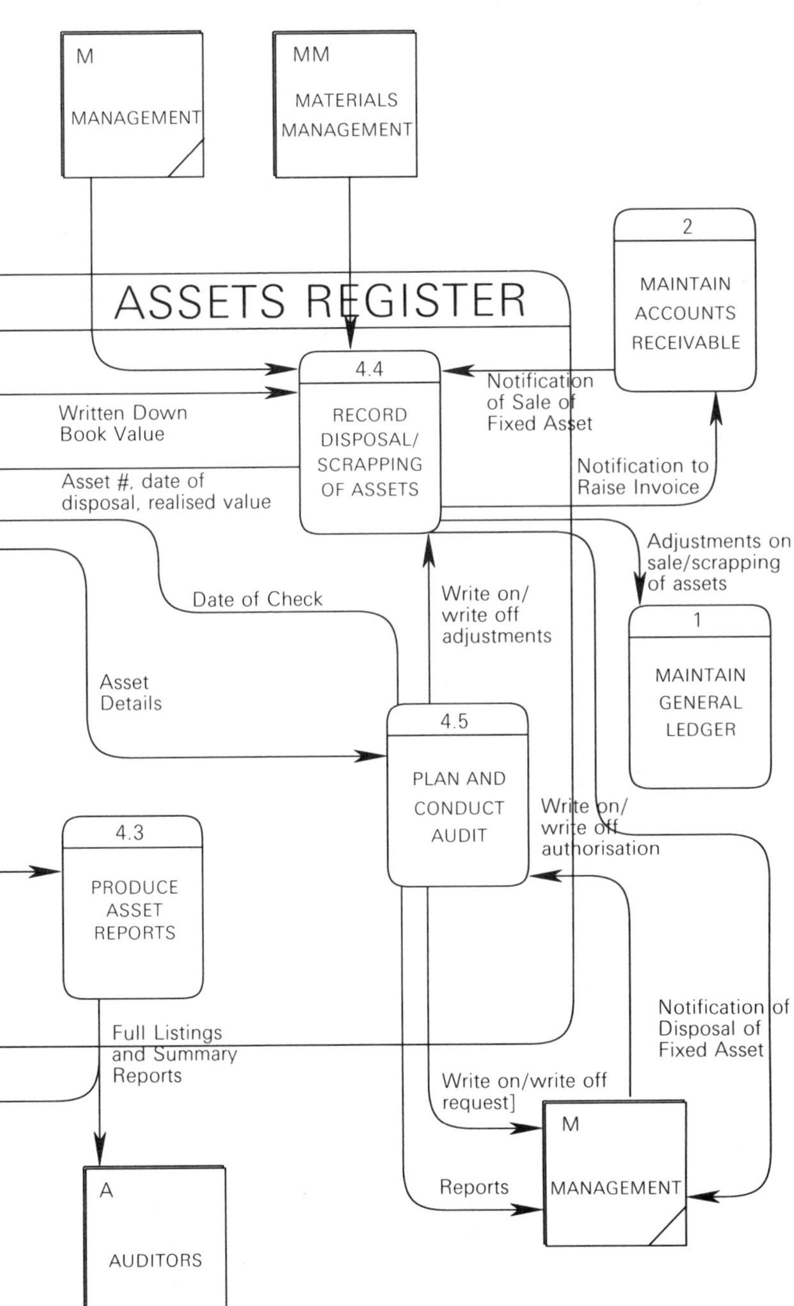
M
MANAGEMENT
MM
MATERIALS MANAGEMENT
2
MAINTAIN ACCOUNTS RECEIVABLE
ASSETS REGISTER
4.4
RECORD DISPOSAL/ SCRAPPING OF ASSETS
Notification of Sale of Fixed Asset
Written Down Book Value
Asset #, date of disposal, realised value
Notification to Raise Invoice
Adjustments on sale/scrapping of assets
Date of Check
Write on/ write off adjustments
1
MAINTAIN GENERAL LEDGER
Asset Details
4.5
PLAN AND CONDUCT AUDIT
Write on/ write off authorisation
4.3
PRODUCE ASSET REPORTS
Notification of Disposal of Fixed Asset
Full Listings and Summary Reports
Write on/write off request]
M
MANAGEMENT
A
AUDITORS
Reports

Fig 13.6 *The decomposition or 'explosion' of DFDs*

HIERARCHICAL LEVEL	0 (ZERO)	1 (First Level of Explosion)	2 (Second Level of Explosion)	3 (Third Level of Explosion)
DEFINITION	Major business or operational areas Each process relates to the logical requirements of the organisation, not the existing organisation of the requirements	Sets of operations which are sub-sets of the level 0 processes and which transform data logically or physically according to a set of rules or process logic	Processes which are sub-sets of higher level processes	Processes which are sub-sets of higher level processes equate to a clerical task, computer program or transaction
LEVEL OF DETAIL INCLUDED	Major business functions and principal interactions only	Main line business operations and data flows at important document level, e.g. invoices	Significant exception and error processing routines included	All exeception and error conditions included
TYPICAL EXAMPLE (PROCESS NAME)	MANAGE CORPORATE MATERIALS	PURCHASE RAW MATERIALS	PLACE ORDER	EXTRACT SUPPLIER DATA FROM DATA STORE
TYPICAL ACTION VERBS	MANAGE ADMINISTER CONTROL ESTABLISH	SPECIFY DETERMINE ARRANGE MONITOR APPLY RECORD	PRODUCE PLACE SELECT ISSUE OBTAIN VALIDATE	ROUTE CALCULATE CONFIRM COMPARE EXTRACT SORT
NUMBER OF PROCESSES ON DFD AT THIS LEVEL	6 + or − 2	6 + or − 2	6 + or − 2	6 + or − 2
NUMBER OF PROCESSES IN SYSTEM	6 + or − 2	16 TO 64	64 TO 512	256 TO 4096

can rapidly take the analyst to a very fine level of detail. Nevertheless, the overall integrity of the analysis is preserved and it is easy to see where each piece of detail fits into the overall picture.

* DFDs may be hand drawn, but there are also a number of PC based software graphics packages available to assist the analyst in drawing DFDs. The DFDs in this chapter were originally drawn using one such package, DFDdraw, which is a registered trademark of McDonnell Douglas Corporation. Where the graphics tools also include a data dictionary (see Chapter 18) and some facilities for logic or error checking on the diagrams created (e.g. ensuring that the conventions mentioned in Section **13.2** above have been observed and/or checking that the data elements contained in the output from a process are all included in the input to that process), the package becomes one type of Computer Aided Systems Engineering (CASE) tool (see also Chapter 2).

Activity

Draw a DFD of the process of booking a holiday, taking the viewpoint of a systems analyst working for a travel agent. Remember that the customer will be seeking information about a variety of holidays and the travel agent is likely to consult a number of different datastores. Write a process description for each process included in your DFD.

13.4 **Bubble Charts**

Bubble charting is a graphical technique used to help the analyst describe the **relationships between the items of data** within the system which is being studied (for a discussion on the nature of data see Chapter 18).

(a) Symbols on bubble charts

Bubble charts take their name from the ellipse or bubble shaped symbols which are used to represent **items of data**. The other main symbol used in a bubble chart is a line which is used to **link** bubbles. The link is marked with arrow heads and other symbols to explain the nature of the link. The bubbles thus represent items of data whilst the lines represent the associations between the items of data.

(b) Associations on bubble charts

* The associations represented are the **logical connections between items of data**. For example, employee name and employee address are clearly connected data items. In this case, the association will typically be one-to-one, i.e. each employee will have a single address. (For the few employees who have more than one home, most personnel systems record only the normal residence and ignore the second or holiday address.)
* On a bubble chart the one-to-one association is shown by **joining** the bubbles representing the two data items (employee name and employee address) with a line and superimposing on the line a single arrow head which shows the **direction** of the relationship.
* Although each employee may be expected to have an address and it can therefore be presumed that the association just diagrammed will exist, there will be many cases where a relationship is optional. A typical example is the employee–spouse association. In western cultures each employee may or may not have a single spouse (i.e. there may be a one-to-one relationship, or there may be a one-to-none relationship). This situation is often represented by including the letter O (for optional) on the arrow to form a 'collar'.
* **Not all relationships are one-to-one**. Each employee may, for example, have any number of children from zero to, say, twelve. This situation is represented by placing a double headed arrow on the link and is known as a one-to-many relationship (where 'many' is understood to mean from zero to infinity).

The basic symbols used in bubble charting, one-to-one, one-to-one (optional) and one-to-many relationships are shown in Figure 13.7.

(c) Reverse relationships

If there is a relationship between an employee and his or her address, there is also a relationship (known as a reverse relationship) between address and employee. This relationship can, at least theoretically, be one-to-one, one-to-one (optional), or one-to-many. The same is true of the relationships with spouse and dependents. The nine relationships theoretically possible between two items of data are shown in Figure 13.8. In practice, reverse relationships are normally included in bubble charts only where

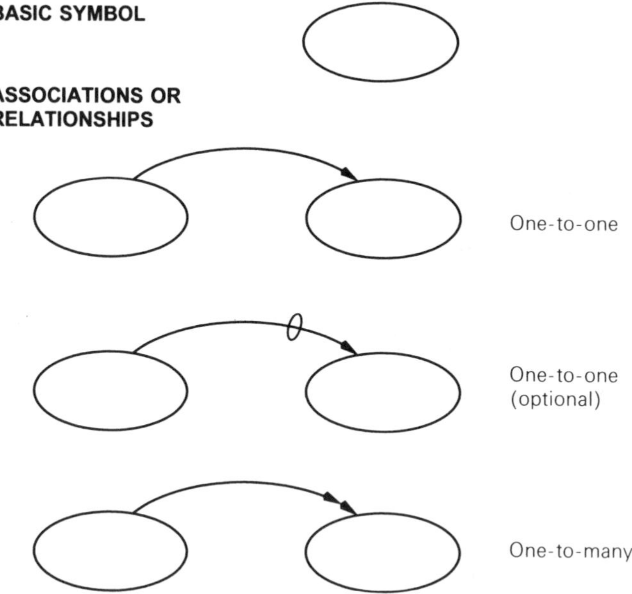

Fig 13.7 *Bubble chart notation*

they are considered meaningful, although the analyst is well advised to include them if there is any doubt in the matter.

(d) Data organisation

Bubble charts are a useful technique for recording the way users 'see' data. Using the bubble charting technique the analyst (or indeed the user) can quickly build up a graphical representation of how the data appears to be organised. A number of other techniques have been developed which are basically similar to bubble charting including the **entity modelling** technique. This uses boxes (with either square or rounded edges) in place of the ellipse and a symbol popularly known as a 'crowsfoot' in place of the arrowheads used with bubble charts. This notation is shown in Figure 13.9.

(e) 'User view' of data

An example of a 'user view' (in this case of personnel data as seen by a personnel manager) is shown in Figure 13.10. Note that only

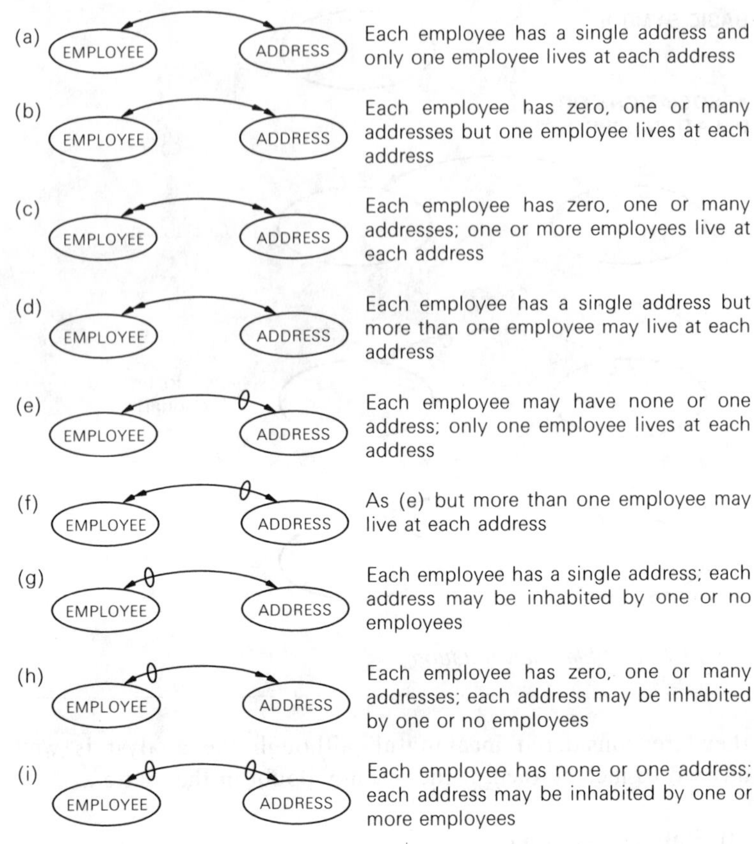

Fig 13.8 *The nine relationships theoretically possible between two items of data*

some of the reverse relationships are included. This user view indicates that the personnel manager is concerned with such questions as: 'Which employees have a B.Eng in Chemical engineering'?, 'Which employees are paid over $35000'?, and 'Which employees work in Department X'?, as well as the obvious employee based questions, e.g. 'What is Joe Soap's address?'

A 'user view' of the type shown Figure 13.10 can be prepared in consultation with the user whose view is being documented. One practical approach is to make a list grouping the key data items by

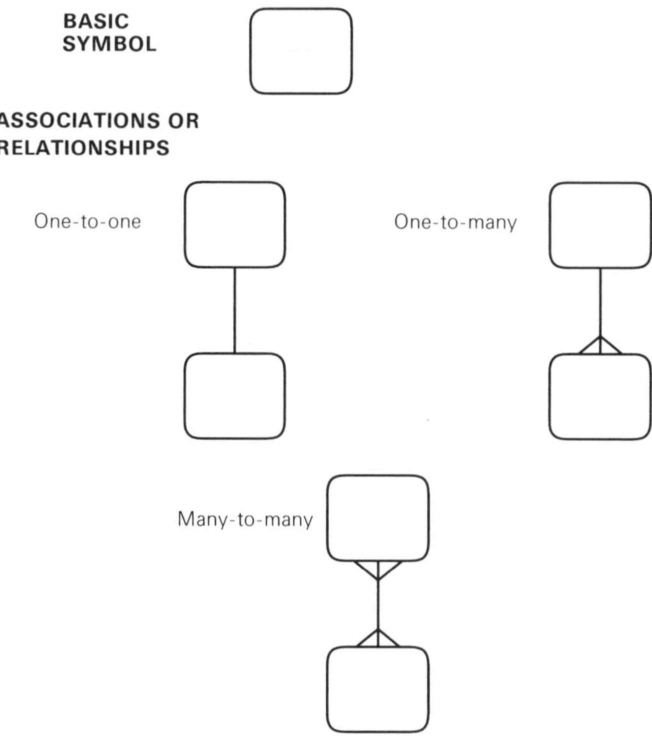

Fig 13.9 *Entity model notation*

reference to the main documents, forms, files and reports referred to by the user in the normal course of his or her work. The associations which exist between these items, and the associations which should exist between these items, are then added in discussion with the user.

Of course, the personnel manager is not the only member of the organisation who will be interested in personnel data. The service manager may, for example, be interested in knowing which employees have both specific qualifications and a knowledge of a particular foreign language. This user view is shown in Figure 13.11. Similarly, the payroll manager will be interested in the relationship between employee and salary and, if wages are related to age as they are for junior staff in many organisations he or she

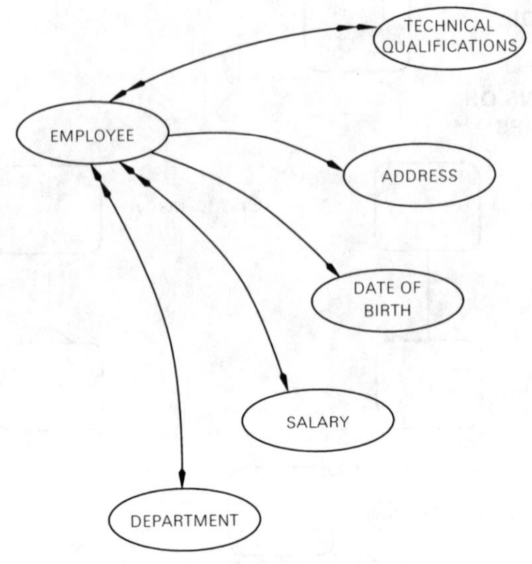

Fig 13.10 *User view of data: a personnel manager's view of personnel data*

Fig 13.11 *User view of data: a service manager's view of personnel data*

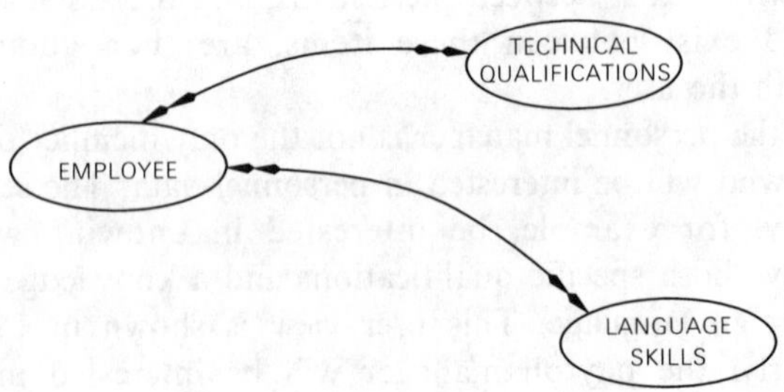

will also be interested in the relationship between date of birth and employee so that rises can be awarded at the correct time. This user view is shown in Figure 13.12.

Where different user views contain at least some of the same data items, they may be combined to produce a data model which is, therefore, a **synthesis** of the views of the various users. At this stage it is necessary to eliminate the many-to-many relationships found in the majority of user views. A many-to-many relationship actually means that the value of the data at any time cannot be found by using either of the data items as the key. Rather both data items must be used together. Figure 13.13 shows the two stages of synthesis for the three user views shown in Figures 13.10, 13.11, and 13.12. In the first stage, the three user views are simply combined, a process usually most easily accomplished by superimposing the simpler user views onto the most comprehensive. In the second stage, the many-to-many relationships are eliminated by the construction of an extra data item between the two data items and giving it a name formed by joining the names of the two data items. This extra data item is called a **concatenated key**. Data models constructed in this way are used as the basis for logical data base design.

Fig 13.12 *User view of data: a payroll manager's view of personnel data*

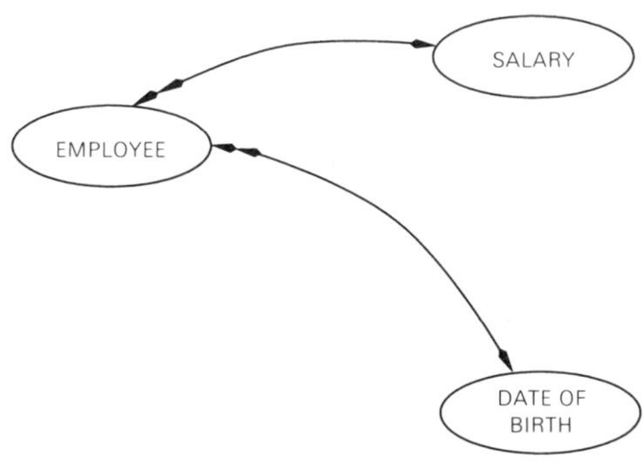

Fig 13.13 *Synthesising user views*

a *Stage 1 – combining user views*

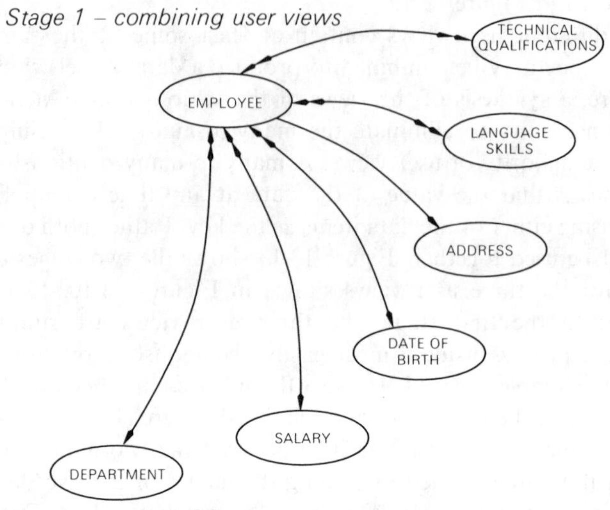

b *Stage 2 – eliminating many-to-many relationships*

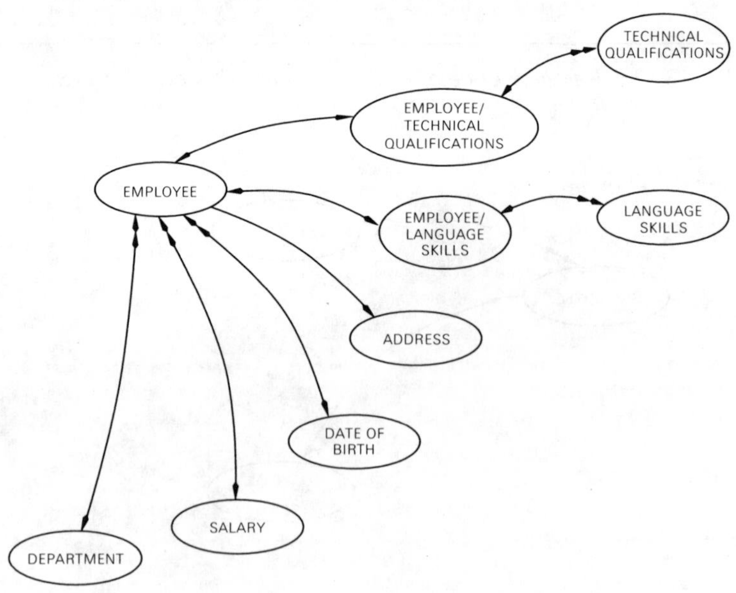

Activity

Make a list of the attributes of the entity 'employee' likely to be maintained within a large organisation. Check your list, if possible, against the information actually maintained by an organisation with which you are familiar.

Note:
The information requested on job application forms will help indicate the details maintained.

13.5 **Flowcharting**

(a) Uses of flowcharting

Flowcharting is the diagrammatic representation of information usually expressed in **time sequence**. Until the advent of the structured approach, it was perhaps the most important technique for the analyst and systems designer. With the advent of more rigorous techniques which facilitate the analysis process and eliminate the risk of creating huge monolithic systems and programs (the latter often unflatteringly but accurately called 'spaghetti code'), the use of flowcharting has diminished sharply. Although it can no longer be recommended for analytical purposes it remains, nevertheless, a useful notation and serves as a 'lingua franca' among systems personnel. Among the uses for which flowcharts are suitable are: computer hardware configuration charts and computer run diagrams (i.e. the sequence in which modules or programs should be run in large scale batch applications).

(b) Flowcharting symbols and conventions

Although a wide variety of symbols have been proposed and used in flowcharting, only a few are actually essential when using the technique. The symbols in Figure 13.14 (which are a sub-set of those contained in the International Standards Organisation (ISO) standard 1028), will be found suitable for virtually all purposes. In addition to the basic symbols a number of conventions govern the use of flowcharts. These are summarised in Figure 13.15.

Fig 13.14 *Flowcharting symbols (the symbols are a sub-set of the full ISO standard)*

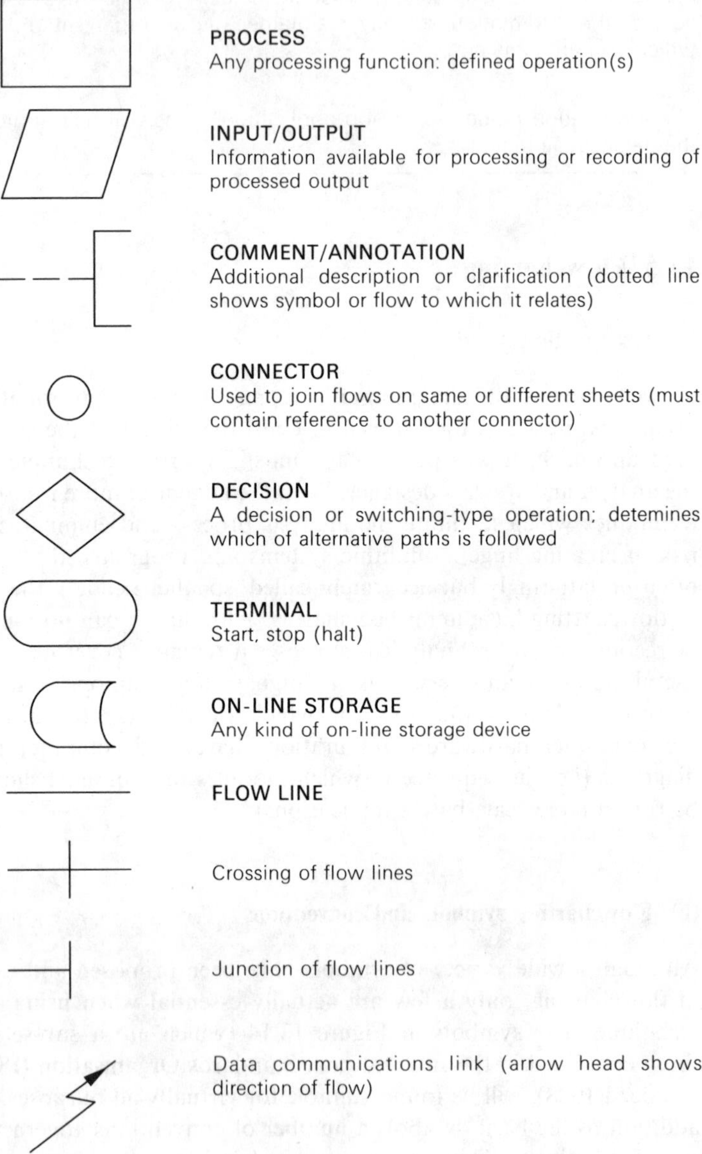
PROCESS
Any processing function: defined operation(s)
INPUT/OUTPUT
Information available for processing or recording of processed output
COMMENT/ANNOTATION
Additional description or clarification (dotted line shows symbol or flow to which it relates)
CONNECTOR
Used to join flows on same or different sheets (must contain reference to another connector)
DECISION
A decision or switching-type operation; detemines which of alternative paths is followed
TERMINAL
Start, stop (halt)
ON-LINE STORAGE
Any kind of on-line storage device
FLOW LINE
Crossing of flow lines
Junction of flow lines
Data communications link (arrow head shows direction of flow)

1 The general **direction of flow** in any flowchart is:
 * From top to bottom
 * From left to right

2 Arrowheads will be used whenever the flow of information **or sequence of events** is not as indicated in 1 above **and** whenever necessary to improve the clarity of the flowchart

3 Flowlines crossing shall imply **no logical connection** between those lines

4 Two or more flowlines may join without any explanatory note, two or more flowlines may diverge only at a symbol which is annotated to show **under what conditions** divergence occurs

5 Flowchart symbols may be drawn any size, but the ratio between dimensions should be maintained within reasonable limits in order to facilitate **recognition**

6 Any flowchart should be **identified** with a title, date and the name of the author

7 **Annotation and cross-references** should be made when the meaning is not apparent from the symbol(s) used

Fig 13.15 *Conventions for the use of flow charting in data processing*

(c) Activity, purpose and information

The first step in drawing any flowchart is to be quite clear about what **area of activity** is to be shown and for what **purpose** the flowchart is being drawn. These objectives having been clearly identified, the second stage is to obtain the **information** to be included. Depending on the complexity of the activities to be charted, it may be necessary to produce a simple narrative description as an interim stage.

(d) Drawing the flowchart

Once the information has been obtained, the way is clear for the actual charting to begin. When drawing a flowchart, the following points should always be considered:

1 Do not hesitate to specify detailed procedures outside the body of the main flowchart by the use of the **predefined process symbol**. This has the effect of simplifying the main flowchart and thus allowing the main points to be assimilated more readily.
2 Make full use of the **comment or annotation symbol** to ensure that the flowchart is comprehensible.

3 If preparing the chart manually, be as **neat and tidy** as possible. A little more care exercised in the preparation of a chart can eliminate the need to redraw and thus lead to an overall saving in time and effort.

4 When the chart is complete, it must always :

* be fully **identified**
* be **dated**
* have the **author's name** on it
* be **checked** to ensure that no uncompleted flow remains.

Self-check

What was the original use of flowcharting? For what is the technique still useful today?

13.6 HIPO Charts

A useful charting technique which probably deserves greater usage than it actually enjoys is the Hierarchy plus Input Process Output (HIPO) technique. In fact there is a series of different HIPO charts which, taken together, can be a valuable documentation and design aid. Developed to help the technical aspects of computer systems design, the higher level of HIPO charts can also be profitably used when considering the overall system.

(a) Objective of HIPO charts

The objective of HIPO charts is to provide a structure to facilitate the understanding of the **functions of the system**. A complete set of HIPO charts (called a 'package') is constructed on top-down design principles, so that each level of chart in the package is a sub-set of the level above.

(b) Levels of chart in HIPO package

There are three levels of chart in the typical HIPO package: the Visual Table Of Contents (VTOC), overview diagrams, and detail diagrams.

(i) Visual table of contents

* This chart – the first in a HIPO package – provides a schematic representation of the **system** and the **hierarchical relationships** between the elements of the system. As each element represented on the chart will normally be the subject of a separate chart within the package, the visual table of contents also serves, as its name implies, as an **index** to the complete HIPO package and/or other documentation used to describe the system. As will be seen from the example in Figure 13.16 for software, the VTOC becomes effectively a representation of the structure (conveniently represented in topdown form).
* The starting point for the preparation of the VTOC is usually a **narrative of user requirements**. From this, the overall heading is extracted and used as an identifier for the top box in the hierarchy. This function is then sub-divided into its constituent elements and the first horizontal line of the table is completed. These functions or elements (each represented by a box in the table) are in turn sub-divided, working line by line, until the necessary level of detail is achieved (normally no more than four or perhaps five levels of detail can be accommodated on a single chart). For analytical purposes it should be noted that there is usually a number of ways in which the basic function may be sub-divided and the systems analyst or designer should experiment with a number of approaches before finalising the VTOC (which will exert considerable influence on the final design).
* The boxes or elements in a VTOC are numbered by means of a simple convention. The top box is numbered 1. Boxes at the next level are numbered 2, 3, 4, . . . *n* sequentially from left to right across the table and all boxes in subsequent levels are numbered with the number of the heading box plus suffices; the number of digits in the suffix denoting the level in the hierarchy (see also Figure 13.16).
* A VTOC may refer not only to other HIPO charts but also to other charts or documentation, e.g. decision tables.

(ii) Overview diagrams

* Overview diagrams make use of the fact that business systems can be represented by a simple model containing **input, process and output elements**. An overview diagram lists the elements in a stylised manner (Figure 13.17).

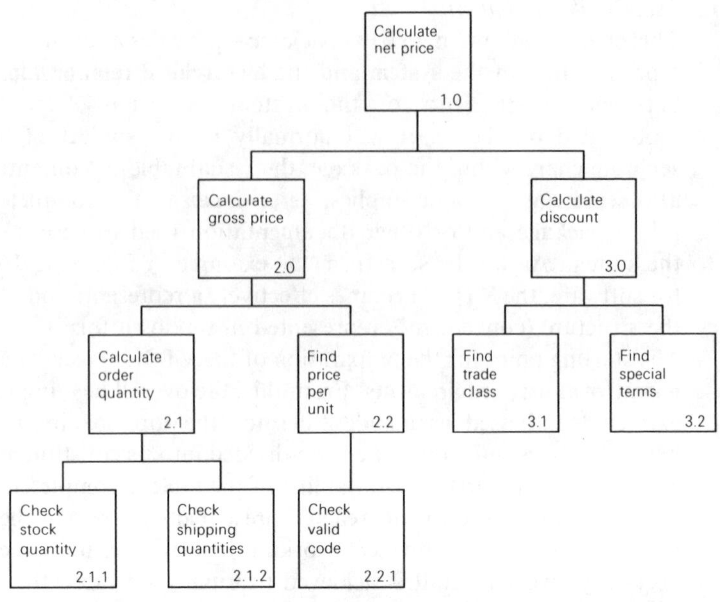

Fig 13.16 *A visual table of contents for a simplified pricing procedure*

---

* To prepare an overview diagram, an outline of the basic chart is used and all known output for the process being represented is entered in the appropriate box. Following this stage, the processing necessary to produce the outputs and the requisite inputs should be identified and entered into the appropriate boxes. The analyst should then review the list of processes to make sure each is expressed in a concise statement beginning with the action identified (e.g. calculate, search, determine, compare, encode, etc.). It is now possible to connect the appropriate inputs and outputs to each process, although this step may be reserved for the detail diagrams, with the overview diagram showing only basic associations.

(iii) Detail diagrams

* Detail diagrams follow the same basic pattern as overview diagrams but carry the definition of each step to a finer level of detail. When preparing detail diagrams, care should be taken to ensure that the scope of each diagram remains a sub-set of

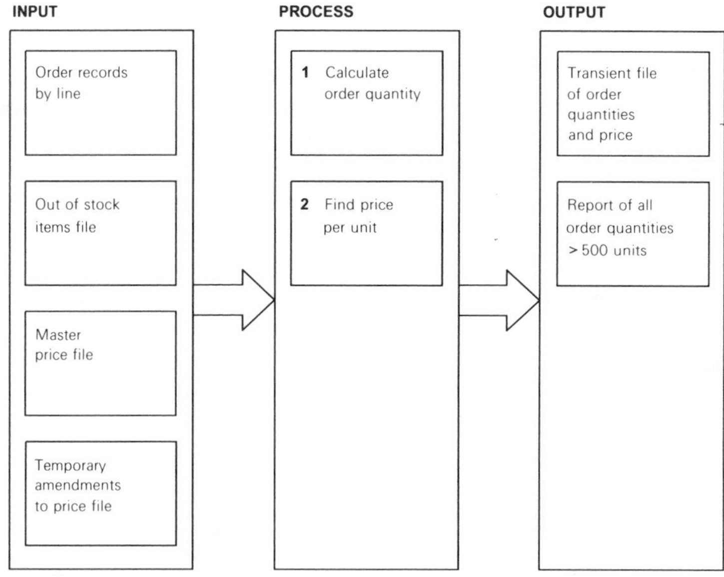

Fig 13.17 *An overview diagram of an element of a simple pricing procedure (calculate gross price element 2.0 of Fig 13.16)*

the next higher level diagram within the same hierarchy. This point stresses that HIPO charting is a way of enforcing **top down design principles**.

* Where additional detail or description is needed on any level of HIPO chart, this may be added as a **narrative description** at the bottom of the chart.

Self-check

How does the basic structure of a HIPO package of charts make it such a valuable documentation and design aid?

13.7 Procedure Charts

(a) Value of procedure charts

Unlike some of the other techniques described in this volume, procedure charting is not rigidly defined. The term 'procedure charting' covers a variety of basically similar approaches for **analysing work graphically**. Such charts, which may be prepared at various levels of detail, can be particularly valuable in identifying non-productive job steps and designing the non-computer aspects of a total system, and have long been part of the stock-in-trade of Organisation and Methods (O&M) and Work Study practitioners. Since there are many variants of the basic concept, the analyst is advised to utilise that which is most familiar within the environment in which he is working, or if there is no such *de facto* standard, that technique most appropriate to the situation he or she is attempting to chart.

(b) ASME symbols

One of the simplest and yet most effective of the conventions for procedure charts is the use of five symbols based on those originally promulgated by the American Society of Mechanical Engineers (ASME). These five symbols, which are illustrated in Figure 13.18, enable nearly all procedures to be represented easily.

(c) Levels of detail required

Before a procedure chart is constructed, it is first necessary to decide what **level of detail** is required to represent the procedure. Where the analyst is supported by O&M or Work Study practitioners, he or she will generally be concerned only with the broader aspects of clerical and other non-computer functions, but with the increasing emphasis on on-line systems fully integrated into the working environment, this is less often the case and the analyst must be prepared to analyse and document these aspects of the system as well as the purely computer aspects.

(d) Construction procedure charts

Procedure charts can be constructed using either **horizontal** (landscape) or **vertical** (portrait) format. They record the events in the

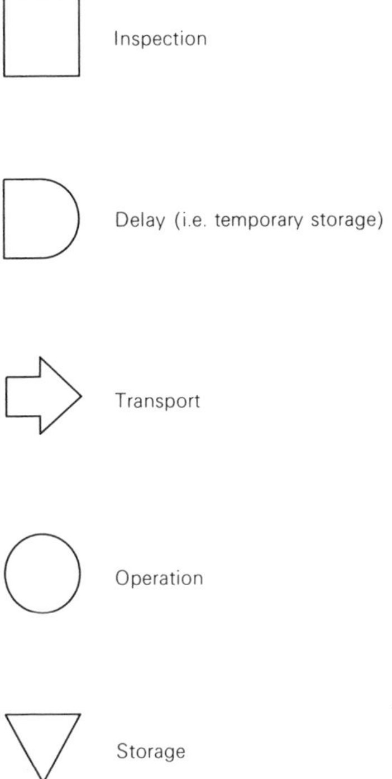

Fig 13.18 *Procedure charting symbols (based on those recommended by ASME)*

---

procedure (as represented by the five symbols) in a **sequential** manner. Typically the chart will do this by following the sequence of events for each document in the procedure, but the activities of individuals may also be recorded in this way. A simple procedure chart showing the preparation and clerical activities for a source document which is created at a branch and then sent to head office, where it is used for data capture, is shown in Figure 13.19. A simple extension of this type of chart is to introduce vertical columns to represent the various individuals or organisational units involved in the in the procedure. In Figure 13.20 Figure 13.19 has been redrawn with this modification incorporated. Charts of this type are often called **Procedure Flow Charts**.

Fig 13.19 *Part of a flow process chart showing the preparation of a typical source document*

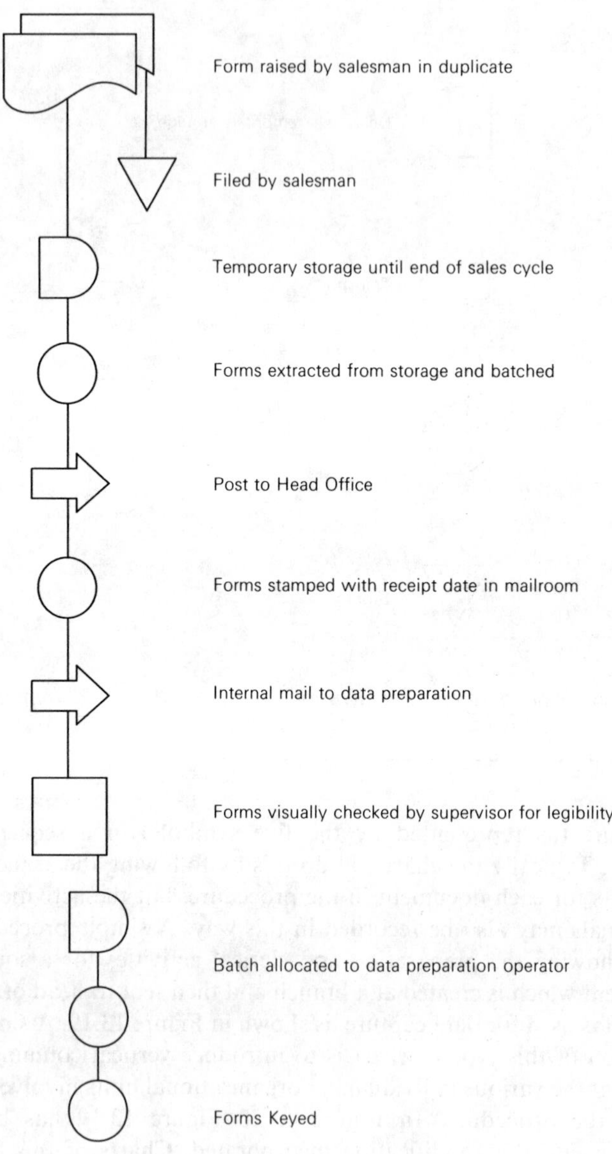
Form raised by salesman in duplicate
Filed by salesman
Temporary storage until end of sales cycle
Forms extracted from storage and batched
Post to Head Office
Forms stamped with receipt date in mailroom
Internal mail to data preparation
Forms visually checked by supervisor for legibility
Batch allocated to data preparation operator
Forms Keyed

Fig 13.20 *Part of a flow process chart showing the preparation of a typical source document: note that transport is implied without the need for a separate symbol*

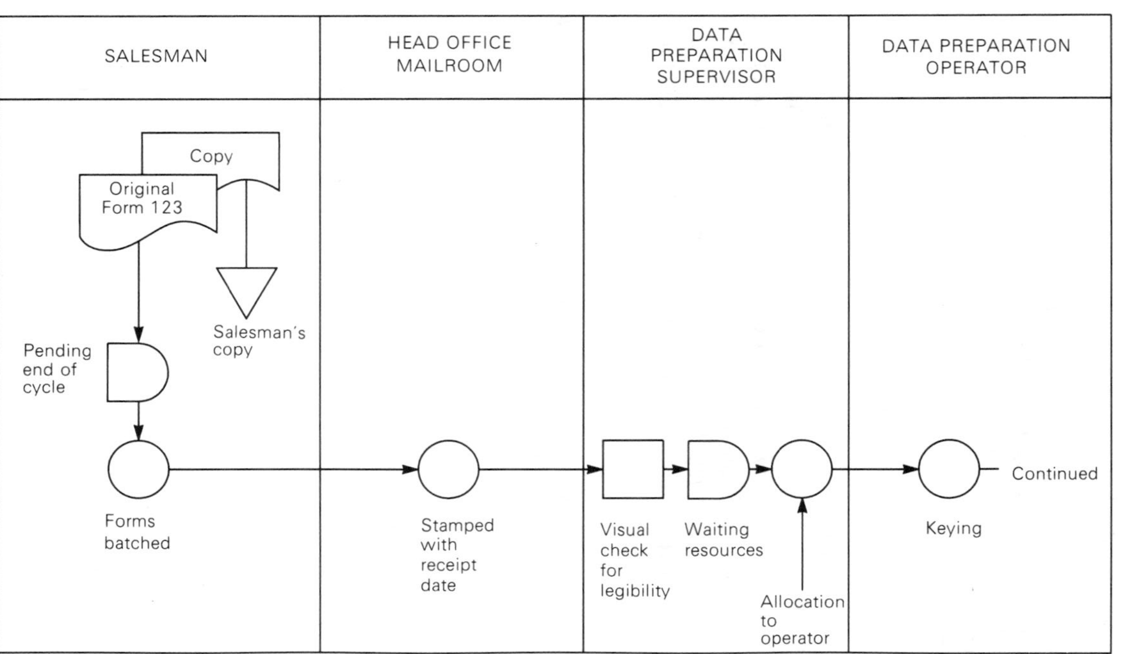

Activity

Draw a procedure chart (using ASME symbols) of the process of applying for a job.

Note:
In addition to the personnel department, applications are likely to be reviewed by the departments in which the applicant might be employed; references may be requested and taken up and qualifications may be checked.

13.8 X Charts

The final type of chart described in this chapter is the X chart. X charts are used to reveal the **overlap** or **distribution** of **activities** or **information between various sources**. In data processing for example, an X chart might be used to portray graphically the degree of overlap between a number of files or data bases (as illustrated in Figure 13.21). The same technique might also be used

Fig 13.21 *X chart showing overlap of information on typical conventional files*

Data element \ *File*	*Master payroll file*	*Personnel file*	*Labour costing file*
Name	X	X	
Works number	X	X	X
Department	X	X	X
Standard pay rate	X		X
Job class	X	X	
Marital status	X	X	
Tax code	X		
Date of birth		X	

to portray the amount of source data that is being captured more than once, or to show the overlap in activities between clerical personnel.

Self-check

What key role can X Charts play in comparing two information systems?

---

14 Decision Trees and Tables

14.1 Role of Decision Trees and Tables in Systems Analysis

One of the most challenging tasks for the systems analyst is to understand, and to record unambiguously, the **ways in which users perform their work**. The major techniques for doing this have been described in Chapters 12 and 13. When the user's work involves multiple options and decision-making, it can be particularly difficult to analyse and describe the user's methods in a way which allows an information system to be designed to support the process. In Chapter 14, two related techniques are described which are useful for the analysis and design of those areas where users operate in an environment where multiple choices exist in their normal work.

Frequently, the techniques of decision trees and tables highlight **deficiencies** in the user's existing methods, and in those information systems used to support them. It is the rigour of the techniques which makes them so useful to the analyst.

14.2 Decision Trees

(a) The concept of the decision tree

The concept of the decision tree is basically simple. When alternative actions are possible, the options are broken down systematically showing **all possible outcomes** as the decision making process progresses. This results in a tree-like structure, as shown in Figure 14.1, which illustrates a series of related marketing decisions. For each option the probability of the result can be estimated enabling a quantitative analysis of the "best" decision at each point to be made; this is, however, normally beyond the scope of the analyst's responsibilities and the technique is described here as a means of systematically understanding the information needs of the user.

(b) Role of information systems

The role of information systems in such decision making processes is important, since the alternatives can be evaluated more precisely with better information. In order to define the information that could most help the decision maker, the analyst should take the four following steps:

* Identify the range of decisions which have **common input, processing or output**. For example, sales management, marketing and pricing decisions depend largely on the same basic data.
* Relate each group of decisions to a **specific user group**. Each organisational unit which uses the common data or procedures to make its decisions should be identified and analysed, including the hierarchical steps involved in each decision (approval by superiors). Different information may be required at the various levels in the hierarchy.
* Identify **decision making inputs and outputs**. At this stage the precise inputs and outputs for each decision are specified for each organisational unit.
* Identify **decision rules**. Here the analyst needs to understand the ways in which the users **make their decisions**, so that an information system can be designed which will, as far as possible, prepare the options for the user. It is at this point that the analyst uses the graphical approach of decision trees to build up and analyse the structure of the user's decision making process, in the form shown in Figure 14.1. At the completion of this phase the analyst is in a position to prepare **decision tables**.

Activity

Draw a decision tree on the process of deciding which of two job offers to take. Factors needing evaluation may include:

* Initial salary
* Promotion prospects
* Company stability
* Training opportunities
* Ease/cost of travelling to/from work
* Value of job experience

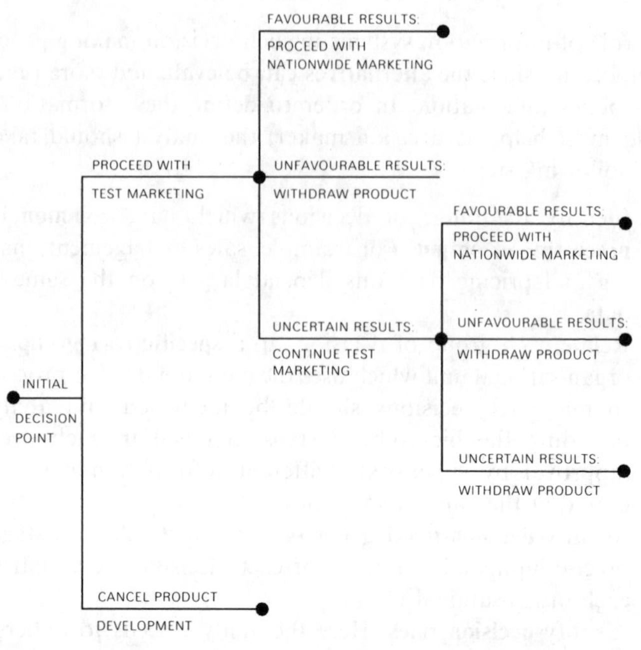

Fig 14.1 *Decision tree analysis: marketing example*

14.3 Decision Tables

(a) What decision tables express

Decision tables are an effective way of expressing the **relationship** between **data, actions and people**. Suppose that a systems analyst working in the production information field establishes the following facts:

1 The production planning manager wishes to receive a report about any deviations of more than 10% from plan in factory unit A.

2 The sales manager wishes to receive a report about any falling behind of plan by more than 5% for product P.

3 The standard cost section head must receive a copy of all production performance reports for product W in factory unit A.

Each of these statements is clear in itself. Yet in reading one after the other the relationships which obviously exist are difficult to grasp. A decision table showing the facts and their relationship is, however, very simple to create (see Figure 14.2).

(b) Form of the decision table

The general form that a decision table takes can be seen in the above example, and is illustrated in Figure 14.3. The three steps for creating a decision table are therefore:

* Identify the **general conditions** and list them in the upper left-hand part of the table.
* Identify the **general actions** and list them in the lower left-hand part of the table.

Fig 14.2 *Simplified decision table*

Deviation from plan > 10%	Y	–	–
Factory unit A?	Y	–	Y
Product P?	–	Y	–
Deviation from plan < –5%?	–	Y	–
Product W?	–	–	Y
Send report to Production Planning Manager	X	–	–
Send report to Sales Manager	–	X	–
Send report to Standard Cost Sectional Head	–	–	X

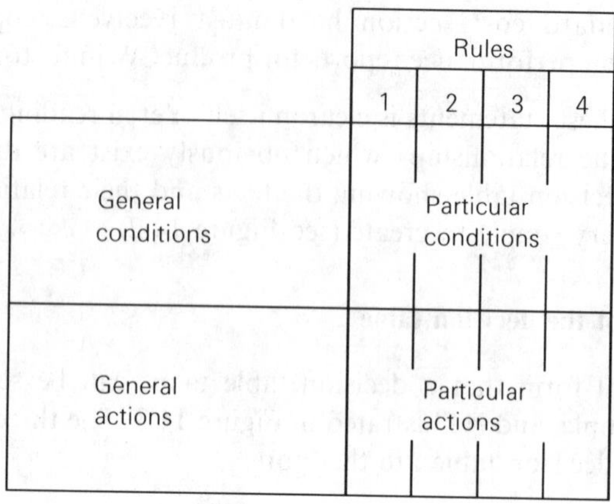

Fig 14.3 *General structure of a decision table*

* Examine each required combination of general conditions, marking them with a '**Y**' (yes) or '**N**' (no) as applicable, or a '–' (dash) if not applicable; for each set of conditions the corresponding actions are indicated by an '**X**'.

A suitable proforma for use in constructing decision tables is shown in Figure 14.4.

(c) Power of the decision table

The approach outlined so far can be made more rigorous. For example, in rule (1) in the above example the first two conditions:

* Deviation from plan equal or greater than 10%?
* Factory unit A?

were sufficient to cover the case of the production planning manager. However, the addition of the condition:

* Product W?

would also satisfy (if the answers were positive) the requirements of the standard cost section head. Hence the decision table becomes more comprehensive if combinations of **general actions** are shown which satisfy combinations of **general conditions**. The example shown earlier can thus be extended to that shown in Figure 14.5.

DECISION TABLE		
	Reference number	
	Title	
	Sheet number	
	Author	
	Date	

	Rules												
	1	2	3	4	5	6	7	8	9	10	11	12	13

Fig 14.4 *Decision table form*

This begins to indicate the power of a decision table. It can be used for more than just representing a set of logical relationships (highly valuable though this is) – it can be used as a check on the **consistency, accuracy and completeness** of the analysis.

* For example, if we find certain combinations of general actions always occurring together, we have identified **redundancy** in the table. These associated general actions could therefore be combined, as logically they are one unit of action. We may also find on our first draft of the decision table that certain general actions **never seem to be needed**. This is therefore a good pointer to re-analysis of the rules to see why a general action was earlier identified but later not used.

	1	2	3	4	5	6	7
Deviation from plan > 10%	Y	Y	Y	N	Y	Y	N
Factory unit A?	Y	Y	N	Y	Y	Y	Y
Product P?	N	Y	Y	Y	N	Y	Y
Deviation from plan < –5%?	–	Y	Y	Y	–	Y	Y
Product W?	N	N	–	N	Y	Y	Y
Send report to Production Planning Manager	X	X			X	X	
Send report to Sales Manager		X	X	X		X	X
Send report to Standard Cost Sectional Head					X	X	X

Fig 14.5 *Sample decision table*

* In this way the decision table can be a general aid to the systems analyst in the analysis of the logical relationships in a system – always the most difficult part. Note, too, that these relationships can be at any level – for example, overall system logic, analysis of user procedures and decision making, program relationships, data relationships, input-output relationships, etc.
* It should be pointed out that a decision table contains less information than an equivalent flowchart. The basic concept of a decision table is simply the **expression of relationships**, and no significance is normally given to the sequence of conditions, actions and rules. Graphical techniques generally express a procedure better than decision tables.

Self-check

What, for the system analyst, are the relative advantages and disadvantages of decision tables compared to techniques based on graphical representation?

(d) Decision tables *v*. graphical representation

A comparison between decision tables and forms of graphical represention, such as flowcharting, is shown in the following table.

Decision tables	*Flowcharting and other forms of graphical representation*
• Good at showing logical relationships; do not show procedural sequences	• Good at showing procedural flows, less clear for logical relationships
• Easy to introduce changes in logic	• Clumsy when introducing changes in logic
• Can be used to verify logical consistency and completeness	• No check provided for for logical consistency and completeness
• Shows logical relationships in a way easily understandable by non-systems personnel	• Not easily understood by by non-systems personnel

1 It is therefore convenient to use graphical methods, such as flowcharts, for the **procedural** parts of analysis and design, and decision tables to express the **logical** relationships.

2 Most of the benefits of using decision tables can be obtained by using them in their simplest form. However, the provision of means to convert decision tables into **machine code** is a useful aid in reducing the overall workload of systems development and programming.

A practical problem which sometimes arises in the use of decision tables is that of **size**. A simple way to deal with this problem is to split a decision table by making one or more of the conditions generate an action to go to another decision table, as illustrated in Figure 14.6. In this way, a structure of **interrelated decision tables** can be built (see Figure 14.7).

Decision tables are a useful tool for the systems analyst, from the initial survey of overall requirements, through the system definition stage, to the actual programs produced during the implementation phase.

Activity

Draw a decision table recording the rules which determine whether or not a job applicant should be offered a job. The criteria might include:

* Satisfactory references
* Meeting specified academic criteria
* Interview results (possibly with multiple interviewers)
* Whether the candidate is 'affordable' (i.e. current salary compared to the pay offered for the job in question)
* Whether the applicant meets the organisation's policy with regard to age for grade, etc.
* Whether the applicant contributes towards the organisation's policy/quotas/legal obligations with regard to the employment of women/the disabled/other minorities, etc.

Fig 14.6 *Sub-dividing decision tables*

	1	2	3
Customer category A?	Y	N	Y
Cash < £100?	Y	–	–
Cash > £1000?	–	–	Y
Inform Sales Manger	X	–	–
Create new file			X
Inform Credit Manager			X
Go to decision table 'B'		X	X

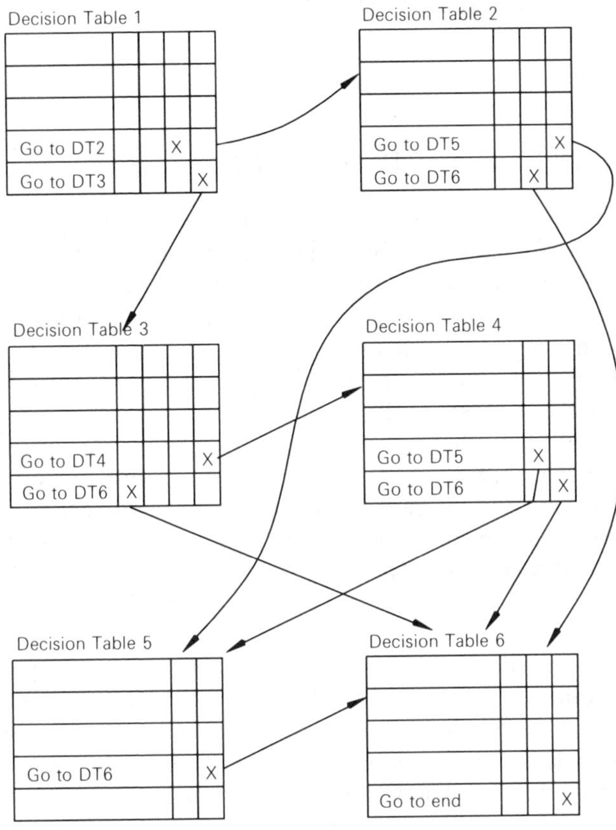

Fig 14.7 *Linking decision tables*

15 Data Analysis

15.1 Objectives of Data Analysis

Data analysis is a generic term for the formalised process of studying the **data used within an organisation** (or a part of it) and the **relationships** between the various **data types**. This formalised process is not only the basis of the data driven approaches but is also an integral part of the process driven approaches to systems development (see Chapter 2 for a discussion of the various approaches to systems development).

As with the other techniques practised by systems analysts, the underlying objective of the data analysis process is meeting user requirements. In the case of data analysis, the immediate objective is the development of **data bases** which are responsive to the identified **user needs**. The way in which the techniques described in this chapter contribute to this objective are indicated in Figure 15.1.

In many, if not most, medium to large sized data processing installations, data analysis will be primarily the responsibility of specialist data administration staff (see Chapter 18), but it is nevertheless incumbent upon the systems analyst to have an adequate working knowledge of the techniques involved.

15.2 Technical Data Analysis

Two of the most important techniques in the data analysis field are those of **entity modelling** and **normalisation**.

(a) Entity modelling

'Entity modelling' is the process of producing a **graphical model** of the data used within an organisation and the relationships between that data. Entity models are drawn for two major reasons:

* To provide an **overview of the entities** (an entity is something about which the organisation keeps information) used within

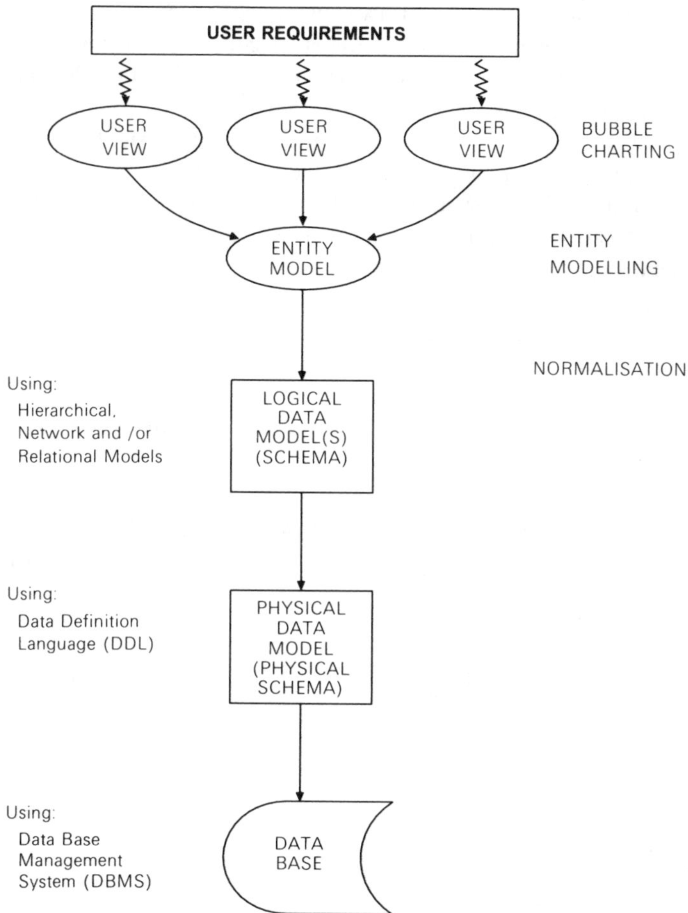

Fig 15.1 *Schematic of the use of data analysis techniques in the development of data bases*

the organisation. In this role the entity model summarises either the result of a comprehensive study of the data requirements of the organisation or, more narrowly, the data requirements of a single application area.

* To provide a **logical model** upon which a logical data base design may be based.

Entity models may be drawn using either of the notations introduced in Section 13.4, and the rules contained in that section are applied throughout this discussion. When using bubble charts to produce entity models, it is, of course, mandatory that each bubble should represent an **entity** rather than an **attribute** (i.e. one of the items of data which is maintained for that entity). Thus, for most organisations, 'customer' will be an entity while 'customer name', 'customer address', 'customer contact name', etc. will be **attributes** of that entity.

Self-check

When and how does one use bubble charting? (See Section 13.4)?

Part of a typical entity model is shown in Figure 15.2. This may be contrasted with the bubble charts shown in Figures 13.10–13.13,

---

Fig 15.2 *Part of a typical entity model (before elimination of many-to-many relationships*

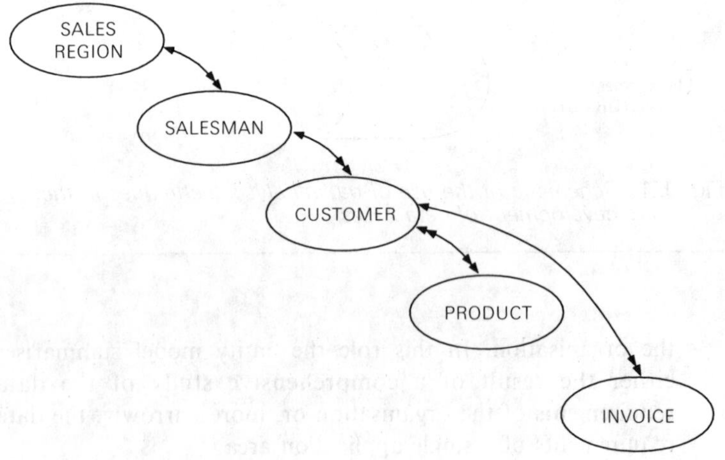

which show the relationships between the entity 'employee' and its attributes.

(b) Normalisation

* 'Normalisation' is a technique which **clusters or groups data fields** to be stored in a data base into records in a way which reduces storage requirements and minimises repetitive updating. Five normal forms are recognised, although, in practice, the fourth and fifth forms are less frequently applied. The characteristics of the five normal forms are shown in Figure 15.3.
* Normalisation is applicable in the design of hierarchical, network or relational data bases (see Chapter 18).
* To transform data into one of the higher normal forms (i.e., normalise the data) a series of steps is followed. These steps are summarised in flowchart form in Figure 15.4, while an example of normalisation which transforms unnormalised data into third normal form is shown in Figure 15.5.

Fig 15.3 *Levels of normalisation*

Level	*Description*
First Normal Form (1NF)	A record in which there are no repeat groups
Second Normal Form (2NF)	No non-key field depends on part of the key (applies only where the key is concatenated, i.e has multiple fields joined together)
Third Normal Form (3NF)	No non-key field depends on another non-key field (third normal form is often described as the situation in which each non-key field depends on: 'the key, the whole key and nothing but the key')
Fourth Normal Form (4NF)	The key does not contain independent facts about the entity which is the subject of the record
Fifth Normal Form (5NF)	Normally as Forth Normal Form: Fifth Normal Form differs when there is a symmetric constraint in the record

Activity

Using an example from your own organisation or educational institution, convert a data sample into third normal form (TNF). Among the examples you might choose are:

* Orders
* Parts
* Personnel data.

Fig 15.4 *Steps in the normalisation process*

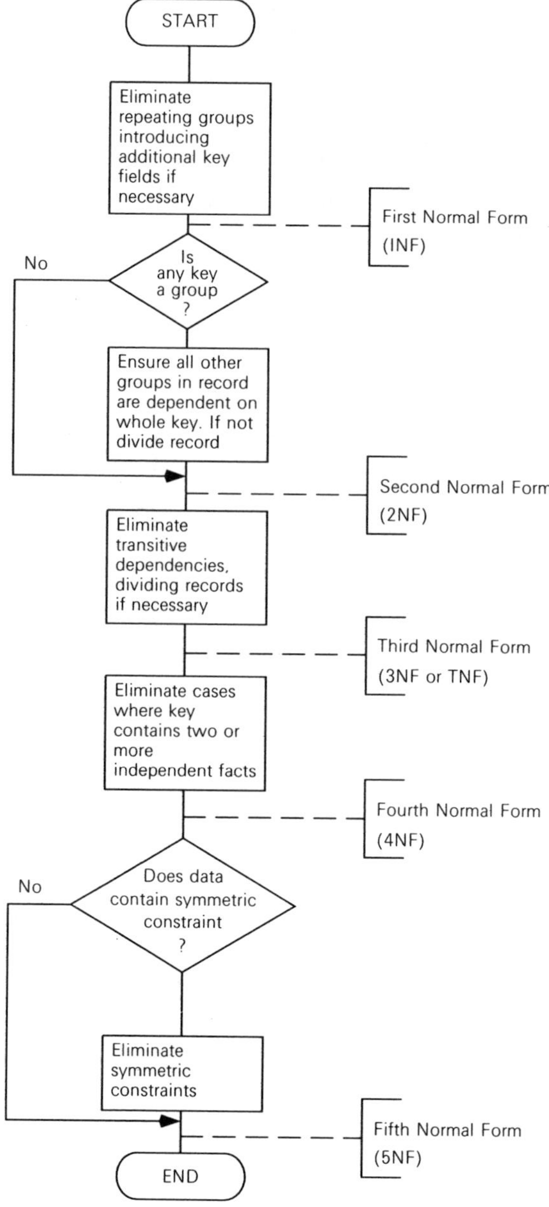

Fig 15.5 *Normalisation of data*

1 The unnormalised logical model shown is for a vendor's invoicing application. The group 'invoice line data' includes: date of sale, product reference, line number, description, size, quantity, unit price and value (i.e. quantity multiplied by price).
2 The first stage is to eliminate repeating groups. This produces two sets from the logical model called here 'invoice' and 'line item'. Note that each 'line item' must be identified by the concatenated key invoice number and line number.

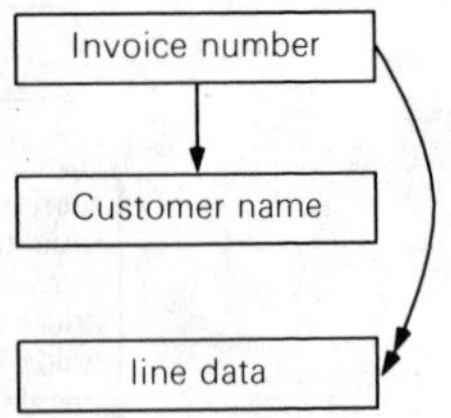

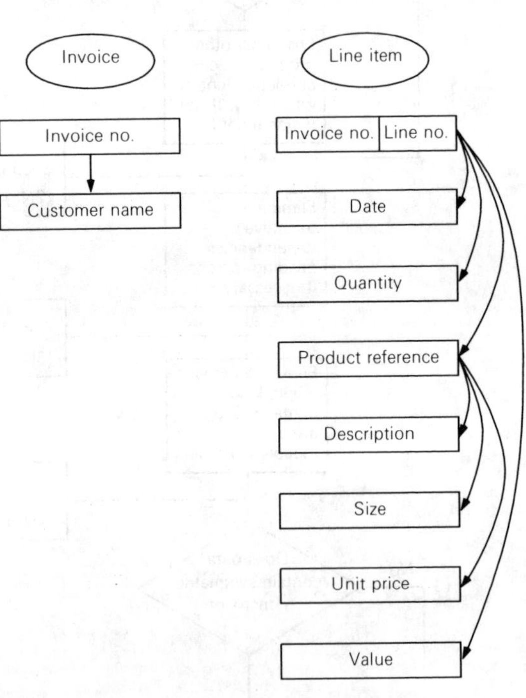

Notes: (1) It is necessary to add 'invoice no.' to 'line item'.
(2) The group 'line data' has been expanded into its constituent elements for clarity.

THE MODEL IS NOW IN FIRST NORMAL FORM

3 The second stage of transformation is to remove elements not dependent on the whole of a concatenated key. This step removes 'date' (dependent only on 'invoice no.' not on 'invoice no.' and 'line no.').

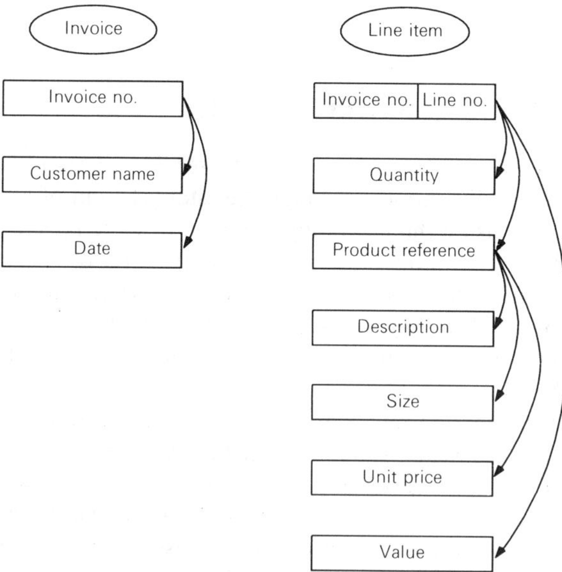

THE MODEL IS NOW IN SECOND NORMAL FORM

4 The third stage of transformation is to remove elements dependent on data items other than the primary key (i.e. eliminate transitive dependencies). This leaves three sets, called here 'invoice', 'line item' and 'product'.

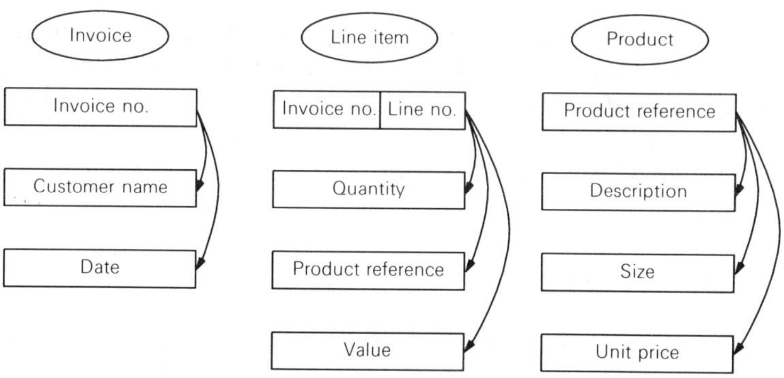

THE MODEL IS NOW IN THIRD NORMAL FORM

Note: It is probable that in most cases unit price would be dependent on description and/or size rather than solely on product reference as shown here. This illustrates the necessity of user input to data analysis specifying the real relationships of the data involved.

16 Cost-benefit Analysis

16.1 The Cost-benefit Evaluation

Despite the increasing tendency to see information systems as a way of making money through the establishment of a 'competitive edge' (i.e. using the technology to achieve some benefit in product, or, more commonly, service compared to other, competitive organisations), rather than as a way of saving money (through improved efficiency or staff reductions), systems development should always be subject to a rigorous evaluation of both costs and benefits.

This evaluation must consider not only the absolute levels of cost incurred and benefits, but also the **timing** of the cash flows into and out of the organisation if a true picture of the financial situation is to be obtained. The cost-benefit evaluation therefore consists of three parts: an assessment of **cost**, an assessment of **benefits** and a time phased analysis of the **cash flows** arising from the costs and benefits.

16.2 Costs

The costs associated with the development and use of an information system may be conveniently considered as either **one time costs** or **running costs**. 'One time costs' refer to all costs associated with developing and implementing the system while running costs include all those associated with the on going operation of the system.

(a) One time costs

The main elements of one time cost are: systems personnel costs, user personnel costs, equipment costs, and other costs.

(i) Systems personnel costs

* These include the salary and overhead costs associated with the systems development staff, together with some proportion of

the costs associated with the management of the information systems activity. (In the absence of a well defined corporate policy on internal costing, the objective should be to construct an **internal cost** for each of the main types of development staff, analysts, programmers, etc. which will fully recover all the budgeted costs, including corporate overhead, when applied to the work actually done by the systems development staff.)

* The calculation of these costs demands not only the calculation of a **rate** but also the estimation of the **time** involved in developing and implementing the system. Estimation of systems development effort is notoriously difficult but the fact that software houses can and do enter into fixed price contracts for such work proves that it can be done!
* In practice, the only realistic way of estimation is to develop a plan of work in sufficient detail that each of the individual tasks may be assigned to a particular grade or type of **system development resource** and a reasonably accurate estimate of the **time required to perform it** made.
* It follows that planning is itself a fairly lengthy exercise which must be performed by someone with extensive experience of the type of work involved. The use of one of the many PC based packages for project planning is strongly recommended for this purpose (see also Chapter 6).

(ii) User personnel costs (which may be calculated on the same basis as systems development personnel costs)

* These should include all the time which the user community is expected to spend on **providing information** to the systems development team, as well as the time of any user staff allocated full or part time to the development project. Systems implementation frequently makes heavy demands on users' time, often including overtime payments for more junior staff, and these costs must also be estimated.
* It is frequently argued that staff costs (and especially user staff costs) should not be included in development costs on the grounds that the staff are employed anyhow and no additional cost accrues when they are working on systems development. Whilst there is some validity in this point, the authors would argue that management has a duty to know the full costs of activities and that therefore all costs must be identified. Since,

however, most organisations treat recurring and internal costs such as salaries differently than out of pocket expenditures ('blue' dollars as opposed to 'green' or real dollars), then the different types of cost should be **clearly identified**.

(iii) Equipment costs

* These should include an allowance for **computer time** used during development and the **capital cost** of any equipment, of whatever nature, purchased exclusively for the new system (e.g. dedicated mini computers, communications links, terminals, etc.).
* Where the new system requires the expansion of existing facilities (e.g. the upgrading of a CPU or the installation of additional general purpose peripherals which will subsequently be used for all systems), the new system should not, in general, bear the capital cost involved but the **running cost** calculated (see below) must take into account the higher overall investment in computing facilities.

(iv) Other costs

This heading covers all such additional costs which may be associated with the development and implementation of the new system. These costs may include: **travel and expense costs** for both systems and user staff to attend specific training courses or conduct a buy/build analysis, **training fees** associated with the new system, costs such as building work, transportation, insurance and decorating associated with the **installation of equipment** specifically for the new system.

Self-check

What are the main categories of one time cost that will be incurred when developing an information system?

(b) Running costs

Running costs for a system will typically consist of staff costs, equipment and communication charges and other costs.

(i) Staff costs

* These should be limited to the **user staff** operating the new system, (e.g., data input staff) together with any computer staff specifically employed to operate the systems (e.g. a network controller employed to manage a communications network dedicated to a single application).
* The only other staff charge which should be included in operating costs is some provision for **systems maintenance**. This charge should be restricted to that part of the total system maintenance cost associated with keeping the application running (i.e. it should not include provision for those systems enhancements so often labelled as 'maintenance'). (Enhancements should be subject to cost-benefit analysis in their own right.)

(ii) Equipment and communication charges

* Equipment charges will typically be of two types: the complete rental, lease and maintenance charges associated with **dedicated** equipment and a charge (usually based on time or some measure of usage) for the use of **centralised** computing facilities. This charge will normally include operator costs, power, light, heating, etc. – in fact all the costs involved in providing the computing service.
* It is because this charge includes a wide range of cost elements that care must be taken to ensure that items are not accounted for **twice**. For example, is pre-printed stationery treated as a direct cost and passed on to the user, or are all stationery charges related to the system treated as overhead and recovered through the computer usage charge? Similarly, communications charges may be treated as direct computer department costs (and recovered through the computer usage charge) or as corporate overhead.

(iii) Other charges

Other charges associated with the operation of a system may include direct stationery costs, consumable materials (paper, printer ribbons, etc.) associated with dedicated equipment, and in some cases such items as postage or other delivery charges.

Self-check

What will be the main categories of running cost for an operational system?

(c) Costs over time

It is important to consider how costs **vary over time**. Clearly, development costs precede running costs (although the boundaries may become blurred – especially in the case of systems developed using a prototyping approach) and running costs tend to be fairly constant over the life of the system, at least until equipment maintenance costs rise as the equipment approaches the end of its useful life. Development costs, however, are by no means constant during the development period, tending to rise progressively to peak shortly before the new system is due to go 'live'. A typical pattern of cost distribution for the phases of a system's life is shown in Figure 16.1.

(d) The system life-cycle

It should be noted that the individual phases of the system life-cycle are not of equal length. The operation or running phase may confidently be expected to exceed the development phase by a large multiple and within the development period there will be a significant variance in duration between, say, the relatively short feasibility study and the implementation phase. When time is introduced, the typical distribution of costs over the life of the system from the commencement of development is as shown in Figure 16.2.

16.3 Benefits

The benefits to be obtained from a new system fall naturally into three categories: direct savings, measurable benefits and intangible benefits.

(a) Direct savings

These are the costs which are reduced or eliminated as a **direct result** of the new system. Historically, they were the main

Fig 16.1 *Distribution of costs of a typical system during development and operation*

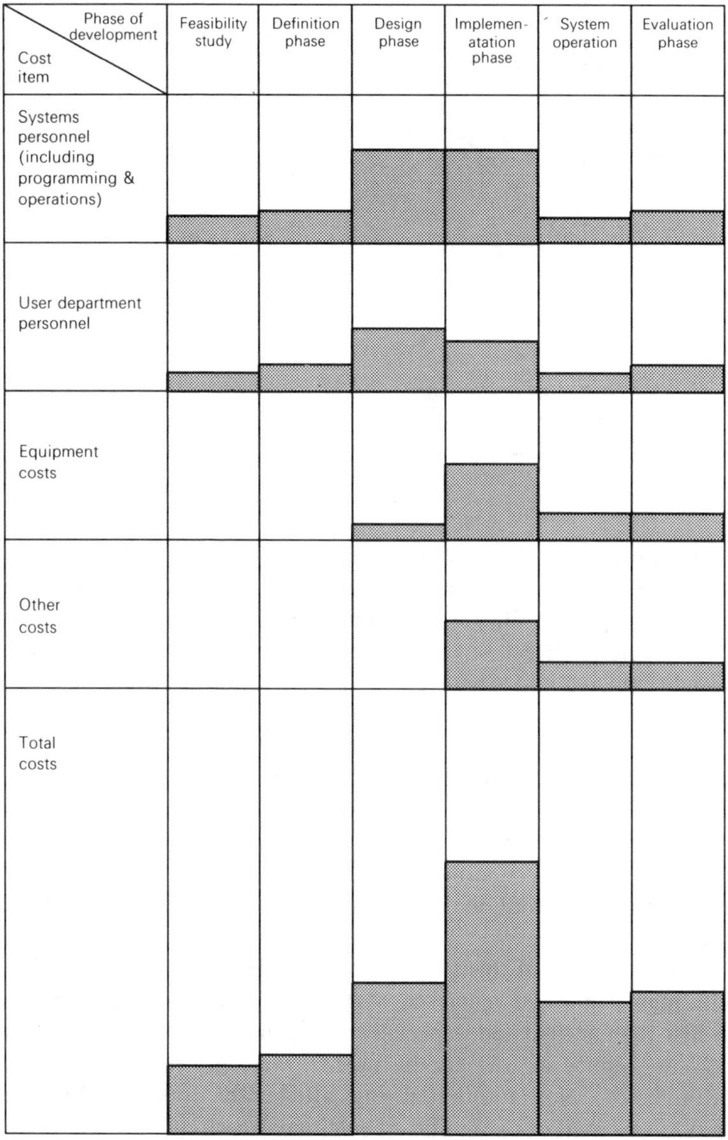

Phase of development / Cost item	Feasibility study	Definition phase	Design phase	Implemen-atation phase	System operation	Evaluation phase
Systems personnel (including programming & operations)						
User department personnel						
Equipment costs						
Other costs						
Total costs						

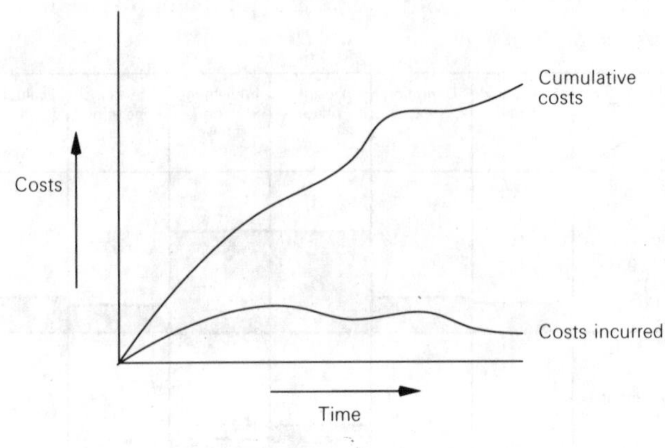

Fig 16.2 *Cumulative cost curve for the development and operation of a typical system*

justification for the introduction of computers, although as noted above the emphasis has now shifted towards the opportunities for improved profitability rather than direct cost savings *per se*. Nevertheless, direct savings remain important and should be sought and realised wherever possible. Typical examples of direct savings are:

1 Reduction in clerical personnel
2 Elimination of direct costs e.g. postage, telephone charges
3 Elimination of work (e.g. the installation of point-of-sale (POS) terminals in a supermarket chain) may eliminate the whole process of conventional data capture and data entry/validation.

Direct savings of this type are readily identified and quantified, although it may be remarked that they frequently take **longer to realise** than anticipated, especially where they involve the reduction of staff numbers (whether by normal wastage, redeployment or redundancy). Note too that savings attributable to staff reductions may also entail very significant **additional costs** if they are to be achieved (e.g. redundancy payments).

(b) Measurable benefits

These are the benefits which provide a **definite improvement** in the organisation's **cash flow** as a result of the use of the new system. An example would be a reduction in inventory levels due to improved stock control and computerised reorder calculation leading to the deferment of purchasing and a reduction in the capital employed.

* Many benefits which at first sight seem intangible are capable of being **quantified**. A good example is the improvement of invoicing procedures which reduces the time between the delivery of goods and the despatch of the invoice. Every day gained will produce a measurable benefit which may be regarded as either a one time cash gain equal to the average billing rate multiplied by the number of days gained, or as the interest accruing to the same sum for each period the system is in operation.

The point here is that by sending out the invoices at an earlier time the money is also obtained more quickly (assuming that paying patterns and credit terms remain the same). The introduction of a new system to send out the invoices earlier therefore results in a direct and measurable benefit to the organisation.

* A further common example of a benefit which, while not producing immediate savings is nonetheless relatively easily quantified, is where a system enables an expansion in **business** without a commensurate increase in some measurable factor such as **staff** or **stock**. In these cases it is merely necessary to compute the costs that would have been incurred by extrapolating the costs of the present system and deducting the costs of the new system to estimate the benefits attributable to the change.
* Many other applications which have been justified on the basis of direct savings or intangible benefits can be shown to have measurable benefits of the type indicated above.

(c) Intangible benefits

(i) What is meant by 'intangible' benefits?

* In almost every application there are clearly desirable effects which are difficult to evaluate in monetary terms. In fact, it is

probably true to say that such benefits are the *raison d'être* of the majority of systems developed today.

* Very often the benefit seems best described as 'better information', which may mean more accurate, more timely, better collated, better presented, more rigorously analysed or more comprehensive information. It is nevertheless sometimes possible to analyse in any particular case what is meant by 'better information', and to ascribe a monetary value to it. It is always worth the effort, because the benefits are often very significant.
* In fact, it is normally because the benefits are expected to be substantial that the system is under consideration at all. Why, then, bother to try and quantify them? The answer is quite simply that quantification is the best way of securing management approval for the often substantial investment involved, and remains the only **objective way** of comparing the relative merits of different possible uses of the scarce **systems development resource**.
* The order of magnitude of potential benefits for intangible benefits is often known intuitively to the user management concerned which can frequently indicate, at least in general terms, how its decisions will be improved by the new system. This already provides a first opening for analysis of the benefit – how can we measure better decisions?

(ii) Quantifying intangible benefits

The approach to follow is to examine each decision in turn and to study in **quantitative terms** the effect of improved information. An improvement in the accuracy can be stated as an increase in the probability that the information is correct.

1 *Credit policy management*

For example, a manager who has to decide whether credit should be granted to a customer depends very much on the payment record of that customer. If the facts are rather uncertain (say a probability of accuracy of 0.5 – that is, it is a fifty-fifty chance whether or not the information is accurate and complete), then it may be the manager's decision not to award credit because the risk is too great. On the other hand, if the accuracy was known to be 0.9

then the decision can be taken on the basis of fact and the company has the potential both to increase sales and reduce the absolute and percentage levels of bad debts.

The two are obviously closely related to the company's previous performance in this area. If they have had an 'easy' credit policy, then the immediate impact of an improved credit information system may well be a decrease in sales but this should be accompanied by a reduction in bad debts which will more than compensate for the loss of 'profits' on sales to customers who subsequently fail to pay. Conversely, if the company has previously had a restrictive credit policy which resulted in the denial of credit to potential customers who were, in fact, credit worthy, then the impact of an improved system will probably be an increase in sales without a commensurate increase in bad debts.

Self-check

What types of intangible benefits other than improved assessment of credit-worthiness might accrue from improved information systems for credit management?

In practice, the application of information systems to credit management goes way beyond the provision of accurate historical data to include the analysis of good and bad payers to establish 'profiles' or patterns against which new applicants may be matched and their creditworthiness forecast. Information systems support to the assessment of credit risks also includes the maintenance of **inter-company data bases** which record the experience of many suppliers of goods and services so that each may benefit from the experience of others in assessing the credit risk of existing or potential customers. Moreover, information systems can track the varying commercial fortunes of customers and recommend an increase or decrease of credit facilities accordingly. In these ways, suppliers of goods and services may maximise bottom line profitability by pursuing an aggressive sales policy without incurring a high level of bad debts – all by courtesy of imaginative information systems! Assessing the financial impact of systems of this nature is not easy but monetary estimates of their value can be derived.

2 *Cash management systems*
Other examples of the value of improved information which can be quantified include cash management systems which maintain accurate and up-to-date records of cash balances, expenditure commitments, income forecasts, exchange and interest rates enabling cash balances to be put to the most profitable use whilst maintaining liquidity to meet outstanding liabilities. In this case historic records may be analysed to ascertain the interest which would have been earned had the system been in use and this can be compared with the interest **actually earned**.

(iii) Unquantifiable intangible benefits
Although many apparently intangible benefits can be quantified by inference as indicated above, there remains a category of clearly recognisable benefits which are not susceptible to this approach.

Self-check

How do you think intangible benefits might be assessed when there seems no way to quantify them by inference along the lines described?

---

1 *'Bracketing'*
In such cases there are a number of approaches that the analyst may adopt. The first approach is to use the 'bracketing' technique.

* This approach, which was introduced in Chapter 4, takes its name from the artillery practice of bracketing a target by noting whether the first round is short or over the target then firing the next round at a greater or reduced range as appropriate. Once the target has been bracketed (i.e. a round has fallen either side of it) the gunner can home in on it by progressively reducing the range producing the overshoot and/or increasing the range producing the undershoot.
* As applied to the evaluation of benefits in a systems development context, the technique requires the analyst to make an **initial estimate**. A knowledgeable user can then either agree with the estimate or, more likely, indicate whether it is, in the user's opinion, too high or too low. In the light of this opinion the analyst can make further estimates until he or she has bracketed the range in which the user believes the benefit

lies, then progressively refine the estimate until a reasonable estimate (or range of estimates) has been established. A simplified form of the type of dialogue involved is included in Chapter 4.

2 *Delphi technique*

The second approach, based on the Delphi technique (which takes its name from the story of the Delphic Oracle who combined subjective judgements with the analysis of birds' entrails to make forecasts), also uses **progressive approximations**. In this approach, the analyst gets a number of users to estimate the likely benefits independently. The individual estimates are then revealed to all the participants who, in the light of their colleagues' opinions, revise their own estimates. Within a few iterations a consensus will usually emerge.

3 *Points weighting scheme*

The third approach is to adopt a points weighting scheme of the type introduced in Chapter 8. This approach is particularly useful in comparing a proposed system or a series of alternatives with the existing system.

* As applied to the estimation of benefits the approach works in the following way. A list of the intangible benefits is drawn up. Each is then allocated a **relative value** by assigning points, with a maximum of, say, 10 points for each benefit. By calculating the total of these and by comparing benefit to benefit, an evaluation between alternatives can be made. Furthermore, in some cases a criterion may be set which equates an intangible benefit score of x points with a monetary value of y units. Hence this approach may be used as a basis for justification of systems which have many and/or significant intangible benefits, even if in strict financial terms no direct return on the money invested is generated.
* Let us take an example comparing two order entry systems (Figure 16.3). This comparison would indicate that both alternatives A and B are very much preferable to the present system and that alternative A is preferable to alternative B. This then acts as part of the economic justification of alternative A. System A is so much more beneficial than the present system (by a factor of 2) that it may well be decided

Intangible benefit \ System	System A	System B	Present system
Errors in resultant reports	2	6	1
Flexibility for adding new products	4	2	4
Ease of inserting urgent orders	5	5	6
Possibility to link with production planning system	8	1	0
Ease of answering customer enquiries	6	5	1
Total	25	19	12

Fig 16.3 *Sample points weighting analysis of intangible benefits*

that it is well worth the extra cost of installing it. At the very least it gives an indication of the relative values of the systems.

* With each of the methods which are based in essence on judgement it is important to recognise that they cannot provide an accurate assessment of the benefits that will be realised but they are, nonetheless, an essential part of the process of systems justification and prioritisation. When any of these techniques are used, it is good discipline to get the originators of the estimates to confirm them in writing. In this way there can be no misunderstanding about the basis upon which the system was justified.

(d) Realisation of benefits

The point has already been made that costs start being incurred as soon as the investigation of the proposed system commences, but benefits, of course, are not realised until **after implementation**. Indeed, benefits are often not realised for a considerable time.

For example, where the benefits of a system include a reduction in the level of spare parts held for plant and machinery, the value of the inventory will fall only slowly as the 'surplus' items are used. In

Figure 16.4 a typical time versus value of benefits graph has been superimposed on the graph of costs over time. Note that although the break-even condition is reached fairly soon after implementation (i.e. the benefits outweigh the costs in each time period), the actual break-even point (i.e., that point in time when the cumulative benefits exceed the cumulative costs) does not occur until significantly later. As Figure 16.4 is a generalised picture, the timescale has not been quantified.

For a relatively modest system, which takes six months to conceive and implement it would not be unusual for the break even point to occur well into the second year of operational use.

16.4 The Time Phased Analysis of Cash Flows

Once the analysis of costs and benefits has been completed, the crucial test then arises of whether the combination of the two factors makes the system a worthwhile proposition to the organis-

Fig 16.4 *Cost-benefit curves for a typical system*

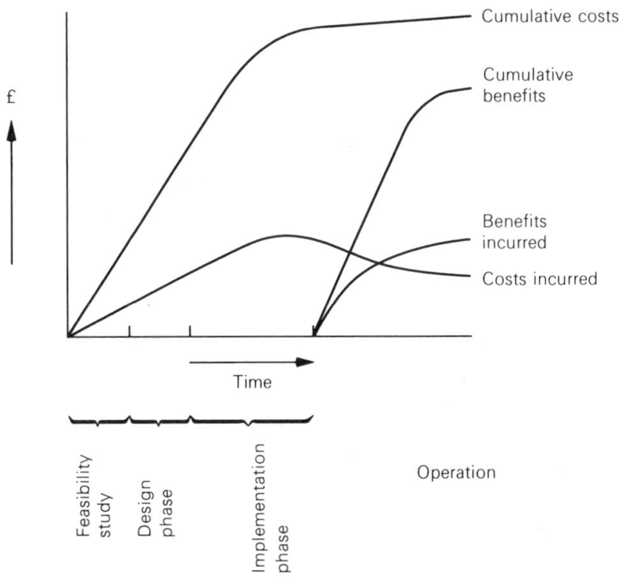

ation. The term 'worthwhile' has, of course, to be defined. If the criteria are to be strictly **financial**, then a clear basis for decision can be established. One way to do this is to state the required **payback period**.

(a) The payback period

The payback period is simply the span of time which elapses from the time the first part of the new system goes operational to the point where development and cumulative running costs to date have been **recovered** through the benefits of the new system. Policy may require that potential systems have to meet a maximum payback period of say, 2 years or, alternatively, systems development may be prioritised on the basis of the payback period.

Whilst the payback period is a useful indicator and simple to calculate, it does not, as usually applied, recognise the **changing value of money over time**. Since systems development may extend over several years and the benefits may not be realised until well after implementation, it is important to recognise that a unit of money today is worth more than the same nominal value at some future time. Whilst this is always true, it assumes even greater importance during periods of high inflation and/or high interest rates.

(b) DCF techniques

The time value effects of money have long been recognised and techniques have been developed to evaluate their effect. The method known as Discounted Cash Flow (DCF) should belong to the repertoire of techniques of every analyst.

* The most straightforward way of using the DCF technique is to apply a **standard interest rate** to the **net cash flows** (i.e., benefits **less** costs) for each period of the system life-cycle from the commencement of development and extending over the projected life of the system. (System life is usually estimated at a conservative figure of, say, 7 years.)
* These cash flows, which normally start with negative values and become positive only some time after systems implementation, make no distinction between capital and revenue items. Neither do they take into account book keeping transactions

such as depreciation which do not cause any change in the cash flows into or out of the business, but it is important that they include taxes and, where relevant, investment or other grants.

* It is usually sufficient to use quarterly periods for evaluating cash flows.
* The discount rate chosen should reflect not only the cost of money in the economy but also the degree of **risk** (i.e. of overrunning costs or failing to realise benefits associated with the proposed system – a higher rate being used for 'risky' projects).

(c) NPV

When all the cash flows have been discounted to reflect their present worth, the Net Present Value (NPV) of the system can be calculated. The NPV is the sum of **all the cash flows** over the life of the system discounted to allow for the time effect of money. Only if the NPV is **positive** is the system economically viable. Generally systems with a high NPV are preferred for the obvious reason that they have a higher projected bottom line impact – i.e., they are more 'profitable'.

(d) IRR

Alternatively, using the same cash flow data the Internal Rate of Return (IRR) may be calculated. The IRR is the calculated discount rate at which the **present value of the costs** is equal to the **present value of the benefits** (i.e. the discount rate at which the NPV equals zero). Obviously the higher the IRR the more attractive the investment.

Self-check

What techniques can you use to estimate the main financial benefits estimated to be obtainable from a new information system?

Financial analyses of the type outlined above are readily performed using a PC and any one of the spreadsheet packages available. Figure 16.5 shows a typical example of a cash flow analysis and DCF calculation prepared in this way.

Fig 16.5 *Proposed system life cycle cost-benefit analysis*

SYSTEM EVALUATED: New Accounting package
DISCOUNT RATE = 15%

	1st QTR YEAR 1	2nd QTR YEAR 2	3rd QTR YEAR 3	4th QTR YEAR 4
COSTS:				
ONE TIME COSTS:				
HARDWARE PURCHASE				40000
HARDWARE RENTAL				
HARDWARE MAINTENANCE				
OPERATING SYSTEM LICENCE				
SYSTEMS SOFTWARE LICENCE				
COMMUNICATIONS SOFTWARE LICENCE				
COMMUNICATIONS CHARGES				
APPLICATIONS SOFTWARE PURCHASE				100000
APPLICATIONS SOFTWARE MAINTENANCE				
APPLICATIONS MODIFICATION				
APPLICATIONS NEW RELEASE CHARGES				
APPLICATIONS DEVELOPMENT	8000	16000	16000	24000
TRAINING FEES	1000	1000	500	500
TRAINING TRAVEL & SUBSISTENCE	3000	3000	1500	1500
COMPUTER RUNNING COSTS				3000
OTHER ONE TIME COSTS (Redundancy costs)				
TOTAL COSTS	12000	20000	18000	169000
BENEFITS:				
DIRECT SAVINGS (Reduction in staff costs)				
DIRECT SAVINGS (Stationery/ communications)				
INTANGIBLE BENEFITS (Faster information)				
TOTAL BENEFITS	0	0	0	0
TOTAL BENEFITS MINUS TOTAL COSTS	–12000	–20000	–18000	–169000

NPV OF BENEFITS = %

This illustration of the first two years of hypothetical cost-benefit analysis for a new accounting system through the purchase of a software package shows the typical picture of high front end costs with benefits only starting to become apparent well into the second year of the project.

1st QTR YEAR 2	2nd QTR YEAR 2	3rd QTR YEAR 2	4th QTR YEAR 2	CONTINUED BY QUARTER FOR ESTIMATED LIFE OF SYSTEM	TOTAL
					40000
5000	5000	5000	5000		20000
1200	1200	1200	1200		4800
					0
					0
					0
					0
					100000
			10000		10000
25000	25000				50000
					0
32000	32000	32000	16000		176000
					3000
					9000
3000	3000	3000	3000		15000
	10000				10000
66200	76200	41200	35200		437800
	22500	22500	22500		67500
	2500	2500	2500		7500
	5000	10000			15000
0	30000	35000	25000		90000
–66200	–46200	–6200	–10200		–347800

(Calculated using a formula embedded in the spreadsheet)

A positive NPV would not be expected until after the new system had been in use for a considerable period of time.

(All figures in pounds sterling)

It cannot be overstated that the results of any analysis of this nature are as good only as the **data upon which they are based** – the expression GIGO (Garbage In Garbage Out) applies just as much to the techniques we use as it does to the systems we develop!

In practice, many of the computer systems currently in operation would be found uneconomic if subjected to a rigorous cost-benefit analysis of the type advocated in this chapter. This reinforces rather than undermines the case for such analysis. The logic is that if an organisation is to make investments without economic justification, it being an act of faith that they will improve the organisation's competitive edge, then it becomes particularly important that the portion of the total investment which is not covered by direct or measurable benefits must be clearly identified and accepted by management **before development proceeds**.

Activity

Develop a pro-forma cost-benefit analysis for any computer system with which you are familiar. Identify the one time costs, on-going costs, one time benefits and ongoing benefits. Check to ensure that you are not double counting (e.g. including a benefit in both 'one-off' and 'ongoing' categories). This can easily occur, for instance when a reduction in inventory (stock) is involved.

Part III

General Systems Considerations

17 Data Capture and Output

17.1 General Design Objectives

The data capture and output aspects of a system are often neglected, because the analyst tends to concentrate on the computer processing part of the job. Yet this ignores the fact that more time can be wasted in a system through poor data capture techniques and through excessive output than can ever be saved by the most elegant programming.

In Step 5 (Chapter 7), the main activities related to data capture and output were identified. These are expanded below in order to give detailed guidelines to the systems analyst in this extremely important part of systems design. What, then, are the objectives of the systems analyst with regard to data capture and output?

(a) To minimise the amount of data that needs to be captured

The purpose here is not only to minimise the amount of human and machine work necessary to input the data, but also to minimise the number of **errors** introduced into the system. How can the volume of input be reduced?

* The first general rule is that only **variable data** should be entered, accompanied by the minimum of constant data. Thus, in a payroll system, the input giving the hours worked needs to be accompanied only by the paynumber of the employee working those hours, not the individual's name as well.
* The second general rule is that repetitive data should be entered into the system only **once**. For example, in a payroll system the week number and date need be entered only once for all persons covered by the period in question.
* The third general rule is that only **exception data** need be entered into the system. An example of this in a payroll system would be the number of working hours in a normal working week: the number 40 (say) could be stored as a constant and the hours worked entered only for those persons who depart from this norm.

* The fourth general rule is to exclude **editing** operations from input to be keyed in. Editing should be built as far as possible into the predetermined format and validation controls of the computer system.

(b) To design the input in such a way as to ease the task of any person engaged in the preparation of that input

There are two reasons underlying this objective.

* First, on the grounds of job satisfaction and efficiency it is clearly desirable that the work should be made as easy and interesting as possible for the people operating the system. This point is discussed in more detail in the discussion on ergonomic and other human factors in section **17.3** below.
* Secondly, the more complex the input, the more errors it will in general contain. A major aim of the systems analyst must therefore be the simplification of the **human procedures** in data capture.
* For the person creating the source data, the natural order for it to be recorded will normally be that which follows the chronological sequence in which it **arrives** or is **extracted** from other sources, or some other 'natural' order. For example, in recording personal data, name, address, telephone number would be a natural sequence, whereas address, name, telephone number would not, although the latter order may be preferred where it is anticipated that many individuals will share a single address (as in the case of families and students).

(c) To apply appropriate error control to the original data and to the data capture process

* Capturing data in a **natural sequence** is a significant step in reducing input errors, as the requirements of the system are reinforced by an already conditioned pattern of thought. Similarly, the layout for data input should also be **natural** (i.e. left to right and top to bottom). Again, if the data is captured from documents by keying in, the operator should be allowed to follow the sequence on the **source documents**. The volume of errors will rise considerably if the screen input implies jumping around to pick up data elements on the source document.

* In addition to reducing errors by improvements in the way in which data is presented for capture, much can also be done in making the data **self-checking** or **verifiable** at data input time. Fixed data (e.g. part numbers) can be constructed with self-checking digits, quantity fields may be subject to reasonableness checks, etc.
* Ideally, data should be captured at source in **machine readable** form (e.g. diskette) as a product of the basic procedure or to combine the data entry function with a routine operational task. In travel bureaux, for example, information is sifted through and then transaction data is input as part of the natural process of making a reservation.

(d) To design the final output of the system in a way that facilitates the use of the data in achieving the aims of the system

* The volume of data produced in most systems is usually beyond the ability of the user to assimilate. So the first point for the analyst to consider is that every effort should be made to reduce the level of output to the **minimum** necessary.
* One approach that is useful in this regard is **exception reporting**, whereby only information which departs from the norm is output from the system in human-readable form. For example, a stores manager would receive notification only of those items where the stock levels were unusually high or low. Exception reporting has two advantages: firstly, it reduces the **overall volume** of output and, secondly, it helps the user focus on that information which needs **most attention**. However, to be successful, exception reporting depends on the full confidence of the user in the system, and gaining this confidence is an important goal for the analyst.
* Other approaches for minimising the volume of data include the provision of information on an 'as required' basis, rather than regular circulation of the available information. Here the systems analyst must monitor the operational system to ensure that user needs continue to be met as the **environment changes**.
* Finally, the major design consideration for output should be the **convenience** of the form in which information is presented to the user. Unfortunately, every experienced analyst comes to know numerous examples where users are forced to undertake extensive processing of the data provided to them, including

manual copying and recalculation and other such tasks which should have been built into the system. That is not to say that the analyst should slavishly provide all that the user states as requirements; distinguishing the users real needs from the range of requirements initially stated is at the heart of the systems analyst's work.

(e) To provide the output to those who need it

One aspect of meeting user needs is often neglected, namely that the provision of output should be linked to its 'advisory' or 'operational' role with regard to individual users.

* **Advisory information** is aimed at keeping people informed, without implying action (e.g. the catering department may be informed of new staff members).
* **Operational information** is that which may cause action (e.g. deviations from foreseen expenditure would initiate an investigation of the causes).
* The requirements for detail contained in the output will vary considerably between the two classes of user and often with the **seniority** of the recipient. In general, senior staff have less requirement for detailed information and need information of a summarised nature.

Activity

For any system with which you are familiar, identify the inputs and outputs and evaluate the extent to which they meet the criteria identified in the text. Where these criteria are not met, what alternative approaches can be adopted?

17.2 Work Stations

The concepts of data capture and output are essential to systems design. Later sections in this chapter describe a range of ways in which these may be achieved using different technical means. Before examining these, however, it is important to set them in the broader context of the **work environment of the user**. Technical advances change the physical characteristics of data capture and output devices, but there are major elements which remain common to the systems design process.

(a) The concept of the 'work station'

For both the user and the systems analyst, the 'work station' has become a key concept in defining the physical interface for the human being when using computerised information systems. The term is applied to the combined set of input, processing and output facilities in the immediate physical area of the user for the purposes of accomplishing the tasks related to his or her information systems work. The importance of this concept is that it focuses attention on the practical world of the **end-user**, recognising the constraints of the individual work place.

(b) Meeting 'local' needs

Technical, human and organisational factors need to be taken together in designing the system most suited to the end-user. Often it is the ability of an information system to take into account quite 'local' needs that determines its success.

(c) Office automation

A major reason why the concept of the work station has become essential in systems analysis is the increasing common ground between office automation and data processing. A range of office functions – such as facsimile, telex, indexing of documents, planning meetings, monitoring of expenditure, word processing, electronic mail, etc. – are now all available via personal computers (PCs), which themselves may well have been installed in the first place for purposes more related to traditional data processing, such as retrieval of data from mainframe data bases. Office automation and development of information systems can hence, no longer be seen as **separate activities**. This implies awareness on the part of the systems analyst with regard to:

* **technological trends** in relevant areas, notably local area networks (LANs), electronic mail facilities, facsimile

* **user needs** in a broader context, for example calculator functions, single keyboard, automatic dialling to a range of services
* **local applications** which tend to develop around office automation facilities, such as text preparation leading to small documentary data bases.

(d) Multi-functional work station

Organisationally, office automation is frequently separated from systems development and this leads to difficulties concerning **user support**. Even equipment installation, including cabling, can be complicated and inconvenient for the user if office equipment and data processing devices are treated separately from each other. However, the trend towards multi-function work stations and the use of universal cabling within office blocks is gradually reducing this problem.

17.3 Ergonomic and other Human Factors

No matter how well designed an information system is, its effectiveness in the end depends on the way the end-users are able to adapt their individual styles of working to the new system. This places a heavy burden on any systems design and indeed no unique solution – by definition – can be found. Hence the guiding principle for the ergonomics of information systems is: give maximum flexibility to the user to organise his or her work in relation to the needs of the system.

This principle is translated into practice in three main areas.

(a) Physical facilities

Much study and practical experience has gone into trying to achieve the optimal physical arrangements for a human being in relation to a work station (for a full understanding of this subject, the reader is referred to the many texts published on ergonomics). The systems analyst should at least be familiar with the accepted requirements for the environment around work stations with screens, such as the recommendations of the International Labour Office in Geneva (see Bibliography). Figure 17.1 presents some of the most important recommendations of this and other authorities.

1 The top line on the screen should never be higher than the operator's eyes. The whole screen should be readable within the span of 5 to 35 degrees below the horizontal.

2 The distance from the eyes to the screen should be in the range 45 to 70 cm.

3 The screen should be at 90 degrees to the window or other major light source. It should never be positioned so that the light falls directly on to the screen or is directly behind the screen.

4 The height of the surface on which the keyboard rests should be in the range 62 to 80 cm and adjustable by the individual operator, where possible. If the height of the table top is not adjustable, 72 cm is the most widely acceptable height.

5 The working surface of the table top, including the area occupied by the screen and keyboard (but not printer), should be 120 to 160 cm wide and 90 cm deep for most applications. Adequate legroom beneath the working top is essential. The seat should be adjustable for the operator.

Fig 17.1 *Key recommendations for ergonomic conditions for work stations with visual display units.*

(b) Software ergonomics

In Chapter 4 on design, the importance of the man-machine interface was stressed.

* Software ergonomics is one of the key aspects affecting the success of the design of the man-machine interface. The term 'user-friendliness' is often used in this context, though some systems have been described as 'user-hostile' or even 'user-vindictive'!
* Awareness of the principles of user-friendliness is strongest when **interactive systems** are being designed, but the concept is of course fundamental to all systems design. The process of meeting user needs in a way that adapts best to human requirements starts at the **definition phase** and continues throughout system design and implementation.
* The experienced systems analyst recognises the realities of human behaviour and is willing to make compromises between what is technically possible and what is likely to obtain best results with the user in practice.
* The design should aim to minimise irritations of the following types:

- re-inputting of data when errors are found
- ambiguous commands and error messages
- overcrowded or confusing screen layouts
- lengthy procedures helpful for the occasional user, but unnecessary for the experienced one
- difficulties in re-establishing former positions when problems are met.

* **Prototyping** can play an important role here in gaining user feedback on how the system can best match the users' needs. Although software ergonomics is technical in nature, it is in fact fundamental to good systems design and deserves close attention by the systems analyst.

Activity

Observe an employee whose job involves the use of a screen work station (e.g. airline check-in clerk, bank teller, travel agent, etc.). Write a commentary on the way in which the work station is integrated into the employee's general work pattern (e.g. how often does the employee have to note details from a screen display on to paper and/or rekey data into the system? If data has to be obtained from multiple systems, how easy is it to transfer from one system to the other?)

(c) Other human factors

Examination of the factors affecting the way human beings behave with information systems is beyond the scope of this book. However, the systems analyst should be aware of certain major concerns that users have and should know when specialised expertise is required. Those factors which are now recognised as playing a critical role in working with information systems are:

* **Stress**: Certain types of screen work can cause higher than usual levels of stress. Such work is not (as frequently believed) of the repetitive kind. On the contrary, the most exhausting work – mentally and physically – is the process of correcting data, looking for errors, etc. because these require **continuous concentration**, often under time pressure.

  The other factor, unique to computerised information systems, is that the machine is almost always **faster** than the human being. So the person working on the screen is constantly in the situation of being required to make the next step. To the user, the computer appears to be waiting impatiently for the next input. This can lead to a feeling of continuous pressure and subsequent stress.

Although the occurrence of stress will depend on many other factors, such as the individual's personality and the organisation's attitude towards individual performance, the systems analyst should do everything possible in systems design to minimise the potential stress factor. This implies giving considerable attention at the design phase to such aspects as **error messages**, **user help facilities**, etc.

* **Work organisation**: This is a key aspect in enabling individual users to gain maximum job satisfaction. Every person has minor differences of approach to the way he or she handles a given task and a well-designed system will allow some flexibility to the individual. This is achieved in quite simple ways, for example by not fixing rigidly such aspects as when hardcopy may be printed, time to correct errors, layout of the work station, etc.
* **Safety and health considerations**: Most experts agree that continuous work with work stations in excess of around 5 hours a day can affect human beings' health in two areas: visual strain and musculo-skeletal strain. It is now law throughout the European Community countries that people working with screens should have an eye test at intervals not later than every 2 years. Musculo-skeletal disorders depend heavily on the way the immediate environment is designed: many disorders arise simply because of poor layout and physical facilities. The systems analyst should be aware of such factors and call in specialist advice (ergonomic or medical as appropriate).

17.4 Data Capture

The term 'data capture' as used in this chapter covers all the stages that can be involved from initial recording of basic data to the input processing by computer. The four steps in this process are:

* Recording
* Transport and collection
* Inputting
* Validation and control

In any particular application these functions may not all exist or they may take place in a different sequence from that shown above, according to data volume, time constraints, acceptable error rates and cost. The technical means by which the data is captured may be classified under three headings.

(a) Off-line data capture devices

* In many situations it is advantageous to collect data in **machine-readable** form without proceeding to immediate processing. This applies, for example, to applications where high mobility of the person collecting the data is essential, as in checking contents of shelves in supermarkets or when it is more cost-efficient to accumulate data and process it in batch later.
* **Hand-held microcomputers** are now used for a wide range of data capture purposes. Examples are: salespeople filling in order 'forms', nurses recording patient data, and drivers confirming the delivery of goods to shops. Usually, the user enters the data via a simple keyboard, but there are some systems which work via other means for conveying alphabetic or numeric characters, such as electronic 'pens'. Indeed some devices have been designed to look as much like a paper document as possible in order to increase acceptance by users.

  After input has been collected, the data is either transmitted using a **modem** and a telecommunications line to a central computer system or is processed locally along with other local data, before being forwarded for central processing.
* Where source data has been collected in documentary form, it may also be input to a local system, which does little else but assemble and store the data ready for sending for processing elsewhere. The data may be transmitted by use of telecommunications facilities but may also be physically transported via diskettes or other similar media. If large volumes of data are involved, the choice of **remote batch terminals** should be considered.

(b) On-line data capture

* This category of data capture is concerned with direct input to a computer system which carries out at least some processing

functions, such as validation of the data, guidance when errors occur, specification of formats, storage and organisation of the data ready for further processing. As explained in more detail in Chapter 19, on-line working of this type does not imply real-time processing, such as that required in on-line transaction processing (OLTP) systems.

* Although data is validated and the user works interactively with the system, the data base is not updated constantly so that other users always have access to the latest information. Such real-time working makes heavy demands of the system in terms of performance, security guarantees, etc. which is not normally necessary for the data capture process in most applications. On-line input with periodic updating (in batch mode) of the main data base is usually adequate for most applications.
* The device most used for on-line updating is a screen (visual display unit) terminal or PC, often with a printer attached. The system to which the device is attached may itself be linked to other systems; for example, in the case of retail stores it is common for the local point-of-sale terminals to be linked to a local processor, which at the end of the day sends sales data to a central computer for amalgamation and processing with the data from other retail outlets.

(c) Character recognition devices

This group of data entry devices includes optical mark readers (OMR), optical character recognition (OCR), magnetic ink character recognition (MICR) and bar code reading devices. Such devices may be either off-line or on-line to a computer.

(i) Optical mark readers (OMR)

These read, by optical methods, specific marks made on a special source document. The marks are made either by hand or machine in preprinted positions and the machine then interprets the value by the **physical position** of the mark (or combination of marks) on the document. Forms up to A4 size can be handled, though for many applications smaller sizes are used. Basically, optical mark readers are suitable for capturing fairly simple numeric data. Applications are often in areas such as grocery stores stock reorder systems, personnel application forms for vacations, etc.

(ii) Optical character recognition (OCR)

This is in principle functionally similar to OMR. Technically, it is much more complex as whole characters have to be read optically instead of simply marks. Also the physical positioning of the characters on the source document is usually less precise than that of OMR.

* For these reasons OCR technology uses lasers and considerable software to enable the recognition process. Nevertheless, its main successes are still in tightly controlled applications where the source documents are prepared by well-trained personnel using a fount fixed for the application.
* Two of the most used founts, OCR-A and OCR-B, are shown in Figure 17.2. Some machines can read handwritten characters provided these conform to fairly stringent shape and size requirements, again illustrating the need to have trained personnel for applications using this type of data capture. One type of approach to aid OCR applications is the development of hand-held 'wand readers', namely a small piece of equipment resembling a large pen which contains a scanning device.
* The main problem faced by the analyst in considering the use of OCR is the potential **error rate**. The two common causes of errors are **ambiguous characters** and **documents in poor physical condition**, both of which may cause false readings or rejection of the document. Keeping error rates within acceptable limits requires strict control over document preparation and handling as well as the use of such approaches as check digits and repeated data fields.

(iii) Magnetic ink character recognition (MICR)

These devices read data printed in special magnetisable ink using a special type fount.

* Reading is a two-stage process. The first stage is to **magnetise the ink**. The second stage is then to use the electromagnetic properties of this magnetised ink to enable the characters to be **identified**.
* The most widely known application of MICR is for the identification of cheques and other banking documents. Reading speeds for MICR tend to be faster than for OCR

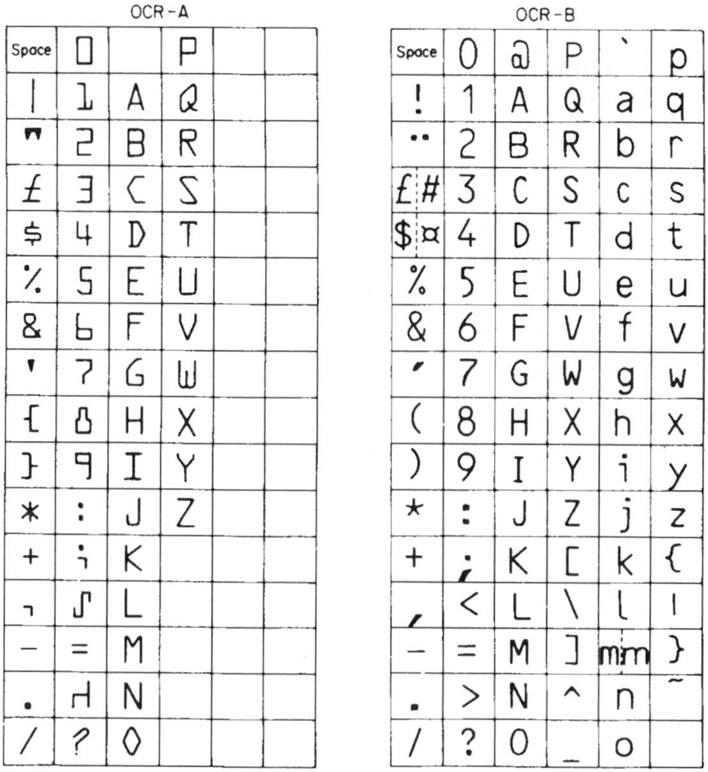

OCR-A

Space	0		P		
|	1	A	Q		
"	2	B	R		
£	3	C	S		
$	4	D	T		
%	5	E	U		
&	6	F	V		
'	7	G	W		
{	8	H	X		
}	9	I	Y		
*	:	J	Z		
+	;	K			
¬	⑁	L			
-	=	M			
.	⑂	N			
/	?	O			

OCR-B

Space	0	@	P	`	p
!	1	A	Q	a	q
"	2	B	R	b	r
£ #	3	C	S	c	s
$ ¤	4	D	T	d	t
%	5	E	U	e	u
&	6	F	V	f	v
'	7	G	W	g	w
(	8	H	X	h	x
)	9	I	Y	i	y
*	:	J	Z	j	z
+	;	K	[	k	{
,	<	L	\	l	|
-	=	M	]	m m	}
.	>	N	^	n	~
/	?	O	_	o	

Fig 17.2 *OCR founts*

but the highly stylised founts and the high accuracy of the printing required has severely limited the applications of this technology.

(iv) Bar code reading devices

These are a specialised type of character reader for data coded in a series of lines or bars. Most of these codes can neither be written nor readily interpreted by humans.

* Reading of the codes is done either by feeding the document into a reading device or by passing a light pen over the coded information. This latter approach has led to widespread applications in supermarkets and other retail stores. **Bar codes** are printed on the packaging of a wide variety of goods and are read at the cashier's work station. The light pen is connected to the point-of-sale terminal or microcomputer, which records and often processes details of the sale.
* Such a system obviates the need to price each item individually (to avoid negative customer reaction, the price is often printed alongside the bar code) or capture stock and sales data at source and improves the productivity of the cashier.

Self-check

What devices are available for data capture? How do their applications differ?

17.5 **Output**

The term 'output' covers all the stages between the production of the results in machine-encoded form and their presentation to the user in a form that he or she can understand. Five major types of device are used to present the output.

(a) Visual display units (VDUs)

These serve both as input and output devices and are used in the interactive mode.

* Although the principal means of interaction is via the keyboard, there are various alternatives available, such as a 'mouse', a light pen or just a touch of the finger, all of which provide a simple way of positioning the cursor on the screen.
* Visual display units increasingly have local programmable memory and may well be PCs in their own right.
* Units with high definition and powerful memories allow extensive graphics facilities; many PCs fall into the 'desk top

publishing' class, on which high quality documents comprising both text and graphics may be produced.

(b) Printers

This group of devices includes line printers, character printers and non-impact printers.

* Line printers still account for a major part of total computer output, being used to produce invoices, payroll listings and other high volume output.
* Character printers are widespread, normally being a output device for PCs and other local facilities.
* However, non-impact printers using laser technology are increasingly used as local high-quality printers and have the advantages of quietness and flexibility of operation (variety of founts, etc.).

(c) Plotters

For some applications, large complex and often multi-coloured graphics output is needed, beyond the capabilities of normal laser printers. Examples are engineering drawings, meteorological analyses and cartography. In such cases, plotters may be used, either off-line or on-line.

Technologically, plotters can be classified into flatbed, drum and electrostatic types.

* Flatbed plotters utilise a flat sheet of paper mounted on a suitable base, while the drawing head is moved in two directions to create a two-dimensional graphical representation of the data provided by the computer.
* Drum plotters use the movement of the paper to provide one dimension of the drawing, thus requiring the drawing head to move in only one direction.
* Electrostatic plotters are similar to drum plotters in general layout, but use the electrostatic printing principle to replace the conventional pen(s).

The software to support devices of this type is complex and their use should not be taken lightly, but for applications of the kind mentioned above they are invaluable for producing high quality output.

(d) Voice output

The technology for voice output basically falls into two categories: synthesised speech and prerecorded standard messages. The former has in principle far greater potential and will eventually be a feasible form of output for many applications involving a great number of possible outcomes to each enquiry. However, the technology is not yet mature enough for widespread user acceptability for synthesised speech, though specialised applications exist.

For **enquiry systems** having only a limited number of outcomes to an enquiry (for example, train timetable enquiries, currency rates, etc.) pre-recorded messages are well accepted, especially since the arrival of compact disks as a fast and high-quality medium for storing and retrieving the messages.

(e) Other output devices

Two additional forms of output device are of particular interest:

* **Computer output microfilm (COM)**, which converts the computer's digital output into analogue form and stores it on film. This form of storage has advantages which make it attractive for certain types of application, such as archiving of documents. These advantages are first, the reduced bulk (less than 5% of that of paper) and, secondly, the faster retrieval and handling possibilities. However, a special reader is required and the indexing techniques are not flexible, once established. COM is therefore not suitable for every application, but can be very economic for some types of high volume but relatively low reference applications.
* **Electromagnetic media storage devices**. Although these are not strictly output devices, they must be mentioned in this context, since electromagnetic media of various kinds (such as floppy disks, compact disks, etc.) are extremely important as a means of storing output ready for subsequent reading by the end-user via the appropriate reading device. The advantages are significant: convenience, portability and low cost. Incompatibility between devices, formats and software used is the major problem, but such media are nevertheless an integral part of the means of preparing and presenting output to the user.

Self-check

What are the main forms of output method that need to be considered by the systems analyst?

18 Data Management

18.1 **Data Concepts**

(a) Data and data storage

Data is the raw material with which the systems analyst works, developing procedures (which may be thought of as analogous to processing machinery) to forge the data into the end product - **information**. Traditionally, each analyst was responsible for the collection and storage of the data for 'his' or 'her' applications; this approach was inherently wasteful because it led to **duplication** in collection and storage when the same data was required for different applications. More seriously, it caused **inconsistencies** between what was ostensibly the same data collected for different applications. Data collected in this way was difficult to use for any purpose other than that for which it was originally intended.

(b) The data base concept

It was to overcome these objections that the data base concept was developed.

* The data base approach aims to make the storage and processing of data as far as possible **independent** considerations.
* In essence the approach is to regard data as a **resource** which is maintained independently of the immediate concerns of its use, so that the data is available to the analyst or user with a business problem to solve in just the same way as the computer itself – i.e. data becomes a corporate resource or 'utility' for use by any member of the organisation with 'a need to know'.
* Of course, in practice, it would be uneconomic to store all data without any regard to its potential use and there is a delicate set of trade offs between present need, efficiency and potential need. These trade offs are, moreover, constantly changing as the real cost of data storage falls and more technologies are

developed to capture data at source or as a by-product of other processes (see also Chapter 17).

(c) Data management

Typically, data management in most modern EDP environments is the responsibility of a specialist (usually called a Data Administrator or Data Base Administrator) and it is necessary and desirable for the analyst to work in close collaboration with such specialists on the data aspects of each application.

Even in the most sophisticated data processing environments, however, not all data will be available within the established data bases and the analyst must have the capability to specify data requirements and the ability to define data.

18.2 Data Terminology

In a discipline bedevilled by the use and misuse of jargon, data management does perhaps suffer more than any other facet of the subject from the looseness with which the terminology is used. The basic terms and the concepts they represent are, however, simple.

(a) Data element (also called data item and elementary item)

A data element is the **lowest level logical** unit in any data structure. It is the only level of the data structure with which a value may be associated. Examples of data elements might be: payroll number, part number, department number or surname. The term data element is analogous to 'field' but is to be preferred because it does not imply association with any **physical media**.

(b) Group (also called data structure and data aggregate)

The term 'group' may be used to denote two or more data elements which are **logically related** but do not of themselves form a complete unit of information. Examples might be: the data elements surname and Christian name together form the group 'name'; the data elements number, street, town and postcode together form the group 'address'.

(c) Record

The term 'record' is used to denote a collection of data elements (which may or may not be associated into groups) which are all related to a common identifier or key. This definition refers to a logical record. A record may be composed of a fixed and constant number of data elements each of a fixed format (a fixed length record) or contain a variable number and/or size of data elements (a variable length record).

(d) File (also called data set)

Related records on a common theme are often organised into files. Files are the usual way in which data is **physically stored** in a computer.

(e) Data base

The classic definition of a data base is: 'a collection of data on a common theme or themes which is conceived as a coherent whole to satisfy a variety of users and/or processing requirements'.

(f) Data base management system (DBMS)

A DBMS is a software package supplied by a computer manufacturer or software house to 'manage' collections of data (usually organised in files). Functions include data update and security as well as access methods. DBMSs usually include a **data description** and **manipulation language**.

(g) Data description language (DDL)

The descriptive syntax (usually embedded in the DBMS) used to define the **physical structure** of a data base.

(h) Data manipulation language (DML)

An extension to a programming language (e.g. COBOL), for supporting access to a data base by applications written in that language. A DML may include a **query language** or **facility**.

(i) Data dictionary

A data dictionary is a repository in which data is **described** and its **usage** recorded. Data dictionaries may, conceptually, be implemented using manual records but software packages are normally used for this purpose. A data dictionary may be stand alone, be linked to a DBMS or (at the design level) be incorporated into a Computer Aided Systems Engineering (CASE) tool (see Chapter 2).

(j) Key

A key is that part (or those parts) of a record which are used for **identification** purposes. A key may be part of the data or a separately allocated reference number.

(k) Logical organisation

The logical organisation structure of a file is the way that the file appears to be organised to the **user or users**.

(l) Physical organisation

The physical organisation of a file is the way it is **actually stored** on the storage device being used. The physical organisation may be (but is usually not) the same as the logical organisation.

(m) Schema

The representation of the logical organisation of the data contained in a data base.

(n) Sub Schema

The representation of the logical organisation of a part of a data base oriented towards the needs of one or more users or application programs.

(o) Entity

An entity is something about which an organisation **maintains information**. For most organisations, employees, customers, suppliers and products will be among the entities which may be identified. In data base theory, entities are stable while processes are relatively less stable: that is to say that the things about which the organisation keeps data (as distinct from their values at any given time) are subject to little change, whereas the data processing performed on those entities is relatively changeable.

(p) Attribute

An attribute is a property **associated with an entity**. For example, the entity customer is likely to have attributes such as name, shipping address, invoice address, payment terms, credit limit – etc. while the entity employee is likely to have attributes such as name, address, date-of-birth, qualifications etc.

(q) Value

Value is the actual **alpha or numerical data held** for a particular attribute of a given entity at any particular point of time. Thus the value of date-of-birth for A.N. Other will be a date in a range from, say, 1 January 1925 to 31 December 1974 (reasonable values for the oldest and youngest employee respectively at the time of writing).

Activity

Identify the likely data groups and data elements in a typical accounting application, e.g. accounts payable.

18.3 File Organisation Methods

When data is stored in a computer system, its physical organisation has to reflect the capabilities and limitations of the storage devices in use. The most widespread **storage device** is, almost certainly, the disk drive which exists in a wide variety of sizes and capacities and is widely used in conjunction with mainframe, mini and personal computers. Historically, the various types of magnetic tape drives have also been extensively used for data storage, and they remain important in many areas.

The characteristics of these devices are such that physical organisation is effectively limited to a small number of file organisation methods. The most important of these are:

* Sequential
* Indexed sequential
* Random

(a) Sequential

(i) Organisation principle

The sequential organisation (which was mandatory when magnetic tape was the principal means of computer data storage) arranges the records in a file in sequence on the basis of a **common attribute or key**. Thus a simple file of sales data containing only area code and value of sales could be organised sequentially on either data element (Figures 18.1 and 18.2.)

Fig 18.1 *Sales data file organised sequentially by area code field*

Record 1		Record 2		Record 3		Record4		Record 5	
Area	Value	Area	Value	Area	Value	Area	Value	Area	Value
1	£1250	7	£3750	9	£2876	11	£950	38	£1256

Fig 18.2 *Sales data file organised sequentially by value of sales field*

Record 1		Record 2		Record 3		Record4		Record 5	
Area	Value	Area	Value	Area	Value	Area	Value	Area	Value
11	£950	1	£1250	9	£2876	7	£3700	38	£4256

Note **1** The key field is not necessarily the first in the record

2 Records may also be stored sequentially in descending order

* Although the sequential organisation method was, in a sense, born from the limitations of the early forms of data storage devices, it nevertheless represents a data structure widely found in the real world, and for this reason it remains in widespread use.
* On magnetic tape and similar media, the **physical** organisation of a sequential file is the same as the **logical** organisation (i.e. each individual record follows the previous record in the sequence in which the file is organised). It follows that to read a particular record the file has to be read from the beginning up to the point where the required record is found. Similarly, to insert a new record into the file, the file must be read up to the point where the record is to be inserted, the new record added and the remainder of the file rewritten in its new location (this is usually achieved by copying the first part of the file onto a new tape, adding the new record then copying the remainder of the old file onto the new file in its new position - a procedure which means that the old file remains unamended and a new file with the addition is created.
* Although these somewhat cumbersome procedures may be acceptable for files to which new records are infrequently added and which are always used in the same sequence, they are neither desirable nor necessary where these conditions are absent and more modern data storage devices available.

(ii) Direct access storage devices

With the advent of direct access storage devices (DASDs) such as magnetic disks it became possible to divorce the logical and physical organisation of data. This meant, *inter alia*, that a sequential organisation could be preserved as far as the user was concerned although the physical layout on the disk was quite different. This was achieved by adding a **pointer** to each record which indicated the physical address of the next logical record in the sequence.

* The initial application of this approach was to permit the addition of records to a sequential file without the need to copy all the data. All that was necessary was to insert a pointer in the record before the insertion which gave the physical address of the inserted record and to add to the inserted record a

pointer which gave the physical address of the next record in the sequence.

* Other applications of the same concept enabled multiple sequential files to be created with only one physical set of data. This is achieved by adding pointers to each of the fields within the data which is to be used as a key. Each pointer indicates the physical address of the next sequential record on the basis of that particular key. Figure 18.3 shows what are, to the user, effectively two sequential files using a single set of physical records. Files organised in this manner are often called **list structures**. When multiple lists are used it is, of course, necessary to maintain a table of the initial record in each list.

(iii) Closed loop or ring files

The next extension of the basic sequential organisation method was to close the loop for each list – i.e. for a pointer in the last record of a sequence or list to point back to the **first record**. Such closed loop or ring files obviated the need to read a file from the beginning each time and opened the possibility for lists to be read in either direction with the certainty that the required record would always be found. A schematic of a simple ring structure is shown in Figure 18.4.

(b) Indexed sequential

The basic concept of the indexed sequential file organisation method is somewhat akin to the indexing method adopted in a conventional dictionary. A **primary index** (often a thumb tab) enables the user to find the correct initial letter; a **secondary index** (the words in bold type at the head of each column) enable the correct column to be found and this column is then searched sequentially to locate the required word. In other words the hierarchy of indices is used to find the relatively short sequential sub-file containing the information required.

* The indexed sequential file organisation method applies this basic approach to files held on DASDs and, in theory, any number of levels of index may be used. Searches always commence at the highest level of index which gives the last key entry in the next lowest level physical sub-divisions of the file,

Fig 18.3 *Multiple list structure*

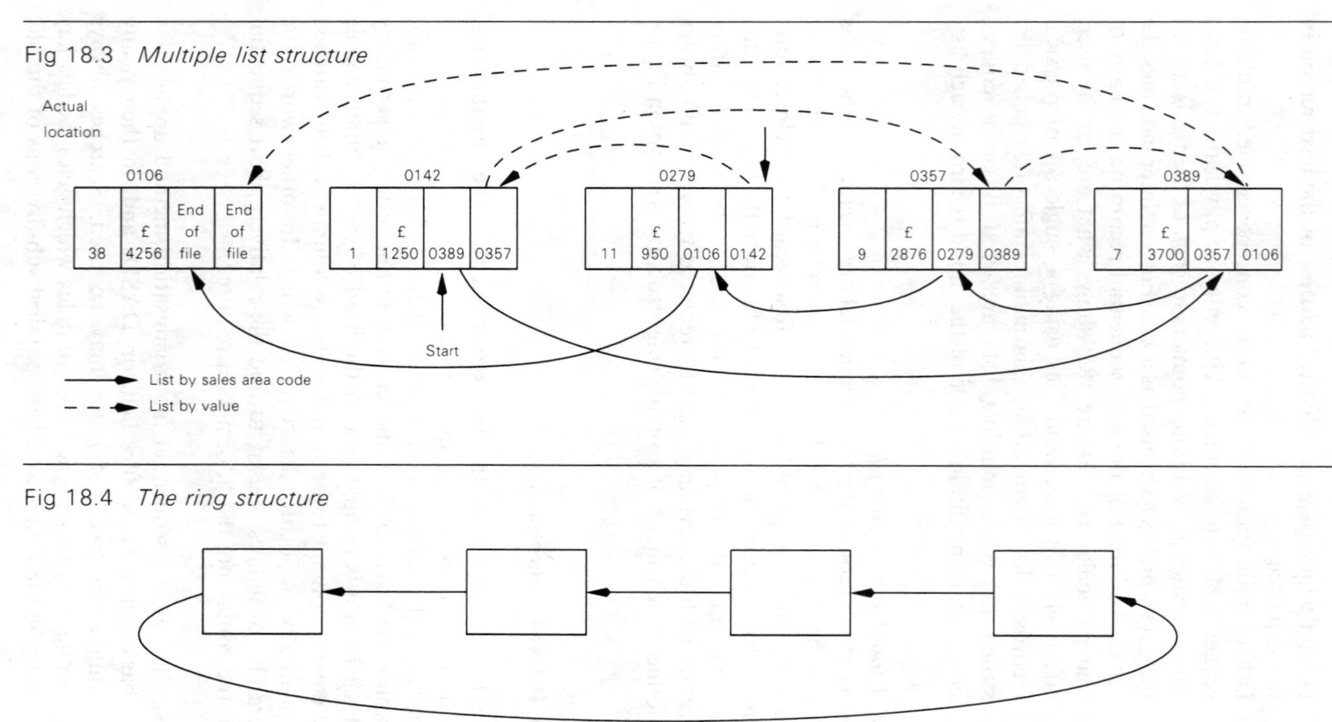

Fig 18.4 *The ring structure*

and this approach is followed to the lowest level of index within the file. At each level the index is searched sequentially until a value above the required value is found. The schematic in Figure 18.5 illustrates this process. The most efficient indexed sequential files are those in which the hierarchy of indices is related to the **physical organisation** of data on the DASD, since this will provide the best access times.

* Space may be left within each sequential sub-file for the insertion of records and, when this is full, additional records may be added in special **overflow areas**.
* The indexed sequential file organisation method's principal advantage is that it enables both sequential and quasi-random access with reasonable efficiency. It is for this reason that this approach has been widely used for applications which combine **batch and on-line data processing**.

Fig 18.5 *An indexed sequential file structure: the search to find record 13487 will follow the dotted line*

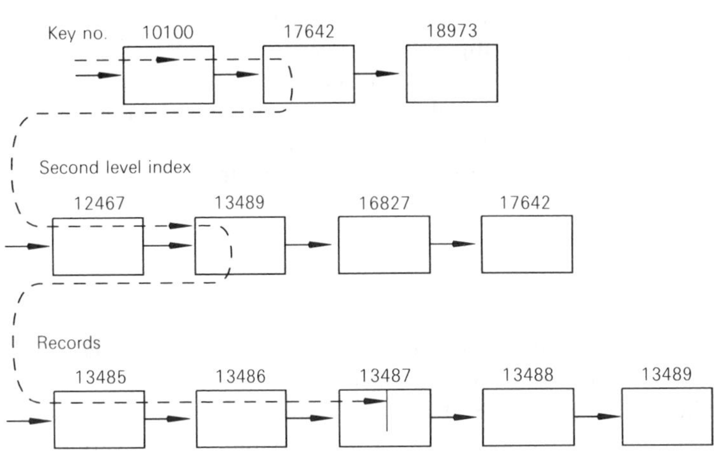

(c) Random

Strictly speaking it is incorrect to call the random approach a file organisation method since, by definition, the data in the file is dispersed in a random manner throughout the physical area of the DASD allocated for that file. But although this dispersion is random there must, of course, be some manner for the data to be retrieved if the system is to be of any practical use. Three methods have been advanced to provide this control.

(i) Relative addressing
The first method is for the programmer to retain all the information about where each individual record has been located. The most usual approach is called **relative addressing**, in which the programmer maintains a table which records the location of each record relative to the beginning of the physical file (e.g. record 123 is the nth record in the file). There are, however, significant programming overheads in using this approach and its use is limited to a few specialised applications.

(ii) Sequential dictionary
The second method relies on the use of a dictionary. Using this approach (see Figure 18.6) a sequential dictionary is maintained showing the key and location for each record. It is, of course, possible to have multiple dictionaries for the same file, providing an alternative approach to realising the same objective as with multiple lists in sequential files. The disadvantage of this approach is that the time taken to **search the dictionary** may erode a significant part of the time saving sought from direct access and it is useful only where the key is a very small part of the total data stored.

(iii) Algorithms
The third method of organising a random file so that retrieval is possible is to use an algorithm to convert the key into a **hardware address** (see Figure 18.7). This system, which obviates the need to maintain dictionaries – does, however, require special care because of the possibility that the algorithm chosen will not always produce unique results. This problem can be overcome by the use of more sophisticated algorithms and the use of overflow techniques.

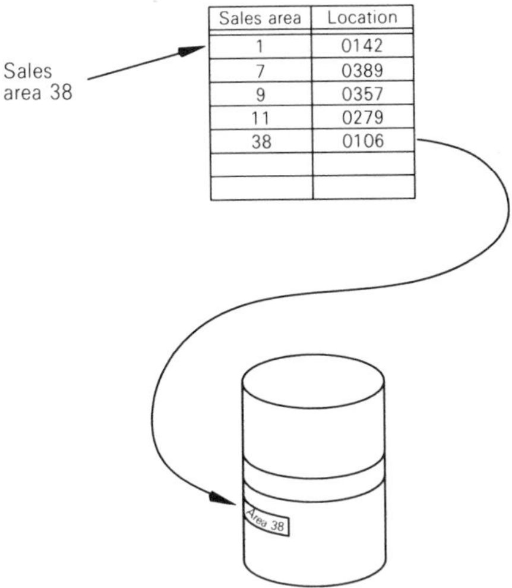

Fig 18.6 *Dictionary look-up of a random file*

Whenever a record needs to be retrieved, the same calculation as was originally used to create a storage address is performed and the result is the address of the record.

Activity

State whether an accounts payable data base/file should be organised according to a sequential, indexed sequential or random method. Give your reasons, and the criteria upon which you make your choice.

Activity

Write a list of the applications most likely to require sequential/indexed sequential/random data organisation. State the reasons for your choices. Does the availability of efficient relational data base software affect your choice?

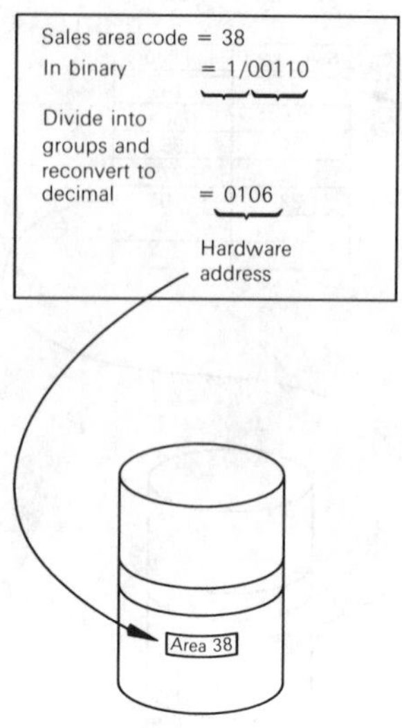

Fig 18.7 *A calculation method for detemining the location of a record in a random file*

18.4 Data Models

A data model is a representation of the data used within an organisation. As such it may be regarded as being an intermediate between the specific user views recorded using the bubble charting technique described in Chapter 13 and the physical organisations described above. Three data models are commonly used:

* The hierarchical model
* The network model, and
* The relational model

(a) The hierarchical model

The hierarchical, inverted tree or bill of material (BOM) structure is one that is frequently encountered.

* Perhaps the most obvious occurrence is that of the lists of parts commonly used in manufacturing industry to show not only

the components which are used in an assembled product but also the way in which they are combined into sub-assemblies. These lists (bills of material), resemble an inverted tree when drawn, see Figure 18.8. This representation is, of course, a logical model of the data structure which is actually implemented (the physical model) on a DASD using pointers to provide to the data user the apparent structure shown in Figure 18.8.

* In addition to bills of material, the hierarchical data model is a good approximation of many other naturally occurring relationships and it is, therefore, a model which is readily understood.
* Not all hierarchies are as straightforward as that shown in Figure 18.8. Returning to the bill of material example, for instance, a real world iteration would typically show a number of anomalies.

Consider the assembly of a motor car, for example. The box at the apex of the hierarchy would represent the complete vehicle; the boxes at the next level down would represent the

Fig 18.8 *A hierarchical (or tree) structure: at each level of the hierarchy data elements are maintained with pointers to (theoretically) unlimited subordinate elements*

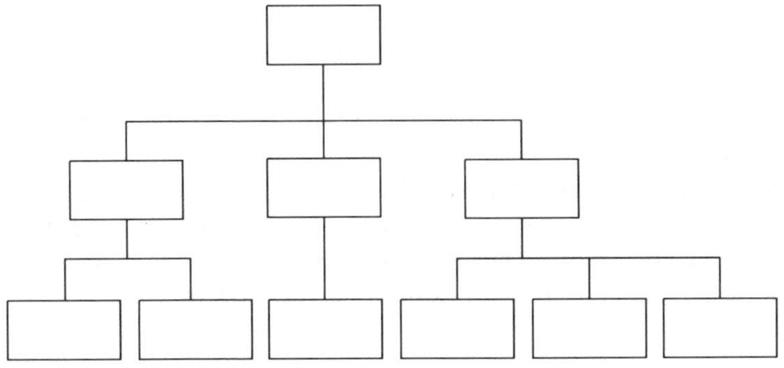

major sub-assemblies (say, body, drive train and axles). These sub-assemblies are assembled using a variety of nuts, bolts, screws, etc. (collectively called 'fasteners'). The sub-assemblies are themselves composed of further sub-assemblies (in the case of the drive train these might include: engine, clutch, gearbox, transmission, etc.). These sub-sub-assemblies might be assembled using many of the same fasteners as are used during the final assembly process. Moreover, this pattern might be repeated at several levels. Although this situation may be represented pictorially (the parts used at multiple levels may be included each time they are used or additional linking lines may be drawn), it will be appreciated that there is a rapid increase in the complexity of the physical implementation and, frequently, a significant amount of duplication of data.

* Although the hierarchical model is a reasonable approximation to many naturally occurring data structures and, for that reason, is the basis of a number of the most widely used DBMSs, the complexity which results when the real data diverts from the model means a loss of flexibility in the ways in which the stored data may be **retrieved**.

(b) The network model

The network (see Figure 18.9) is another data model which is readily understandable and reflects some of the data structures encountered in the real world. In practice, most of the DBMSs which implement so-called network structures provide only a subset of the full, conceptual network structure shown in Figure 18.9. Two main families of implementations are in widespread use: the limited network and Conference of Data System Language (CODASYL) Data Base Task Group implementations. To model many types of data in the partial implementations of the theoretical network data mode, it is necessary to introduce additional (intersection) records. The introduction of such records does again limit the flexibility of data **association and retrieval**.

(c) The relational model

The relational model, which was first postulated by E. F. Codd in 1970, has become perhaps the key data model in recent years.

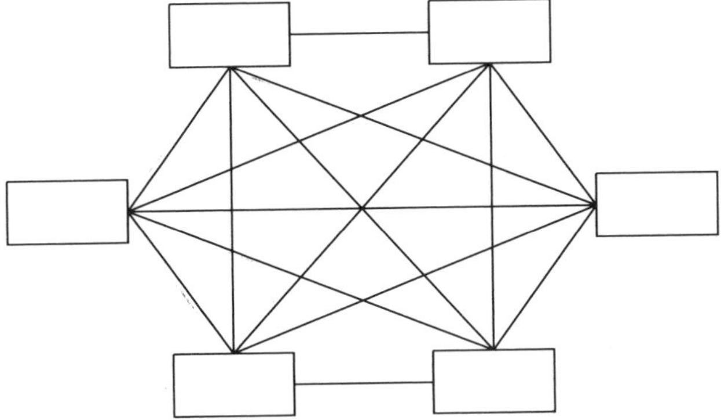

Fig 18.9 *A network structure: note that data elements may (theoretically) be related via pointers to $<(N-1)$ other elements (where N is the total number of elements)*

(i) Important features

The two most important features of the relational model are:

* First, that it must support relational algebra without any reference to physical structure (i.e. all relationships are implicit, so that without reference to the internal data structure there is no way of knowing which associations are physically present).
* Secondly, the resultant data base must be viewed as a series of tables with no user visible navigation links between them.

In the relational model, all data is included in relations which are simply two-dimensional tables with some special characteristics. Within a relation, the columns are called 'domains' and the rows 'tuples'. A typical relation is shown in Figure 18.10.

The special characteristics of a relation are that:

* Each domain contains values for the **same attribute** – i.e. all the entries in each column are measures of the same thing (e.g. each one is a part number or a stock quantity).

EMPLOYEE NAME	DATE OF BIRTH	SALARY	DEPARTMENT
SMITH	10-10-67	£15000	ADMIN
JONES	14-9-40	£35000	ENGINEERING
BROWN	6-2-41	£28000	MARKETING
WILLIAMS	1-6-47	£22000	SALES
FOSTER	1-6-68	£15000	ADMIN
JAMES	22-6-40	£33000	ENGINEERING

A TUPLE

A DOMAIN

Fig 18.10 *A relation*

* The **order** of the tuples and domains has no significance.
* Each **cell** (the intersection of tuple and domain) has only a **single value** (this means that each tuple is in first normal form (1NF) – see Figure 15.3).
* Each tuple is **unique**.

(iii) Tabular presentation of a relation

Tuples are, by definition, in first normal form (1NF) (see Chapter 15), and the column heading of a key attribute which is not duplicated (or the column headings of key attributes which are not duplicated) is the primary key for the relation.Although the tabular presentation of relations shown in Figure 18.10 is a good representation of a relation, it quickly becomes somewhat unwieldy and, in practice, can be used to illustrate only a small fragment of a few relations.

In Figure 18.11, the relation shown in Figure 18.10 has been redrawn using a vertical format. Note that Figure 18.11 does not attempt to show even specimen values but concentrates on providing a compact representation of the domains contained in a relation.

(iv) Relational data base

A relational data base consists of multiple relations, which may be visualised as a stack – reminiscent of the pile of index cards used in

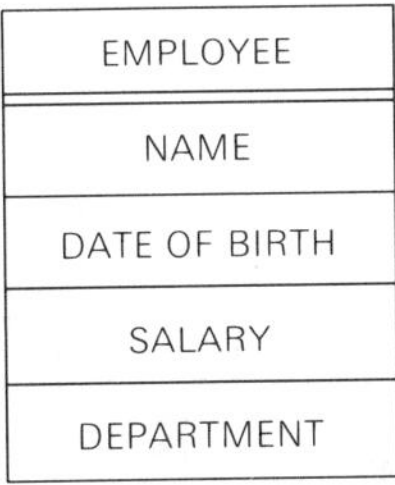

Fig 18.11 *A relation: Fig 18.10 redrawn showing the vertical format*

conventional, hardcopy, filing systems. A schematic of a relational data base using the pile or stack analogy is shown in Figure 18.12. Again, although this analogy is powerful in representing the concept of a relational data base, it is not especially useful in helping to understand how the data may be used.

Using the vertical format shown in Figure 18.11 for the multiple relations in a data base is both practical and enables a good understanding of the data. Figure 18.13 shows a number of relations – a relational data base – drawn using the vertical format. Charts drawn in this way may have symbols added to the domain headings to indicate the primary keys or have common domains linked graphically. In Figure 18.14, Figure 18.13 is redrawn with such additional data added.

(v) Relational algebra

The relations in a relational data base may be manipulated using relational algebra. Relational algebra defines a set of eight operations: union, intersection, difference, product, select, project, join and divide. These eight operations together with commands to insert and delete tuples and update cells provide a powerful set of tools to combine, analyse, cross-reference and manage data contained in a relational data base to present information in a form which replicates a wide range of user views and enables many, previously unanticipated, queries to be answered with reasonable efficiency from the data contained in the data base.

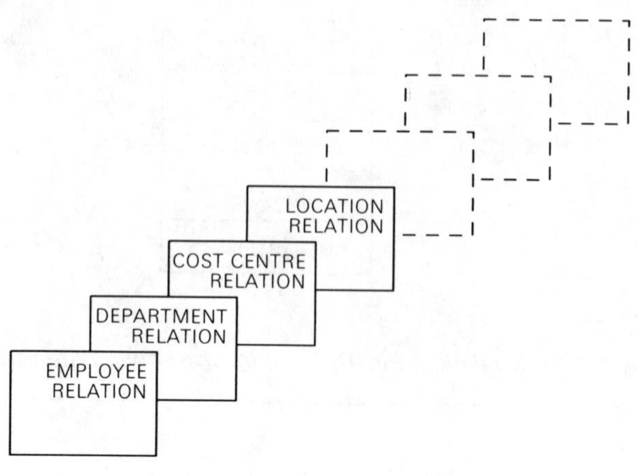

Fig 18.12 *A representation of a relational data base*

Fig 18.13 *Four relations – a relational data base – drawn using the vertical format*

EMPLOYEE RELATION
NAME
DATE OF BIRTH
SALARY
DEPARTMENT
COST CENTRE

DEPARTMENT RELATION
DEPARTMENT
LOCATION
MANAGER
PRODUCT

COST CENTRE RELATION
COST CENTRE
DEPARTMENT

LOCATION RELATION
LOCATION
ADDRESS

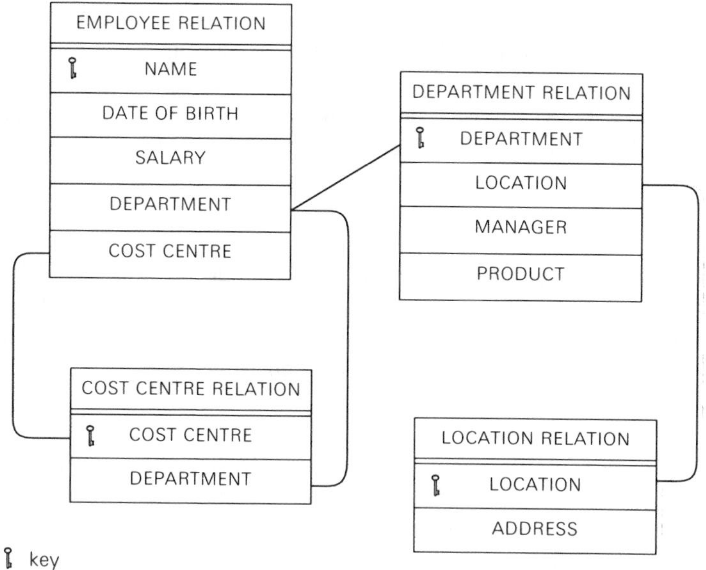

Fig 18.14 *Fig 18.13 redrawn with primary key data added*

Self-check

What are the distinctive characteristics of the three main types of data model?

18.5 **Object-oriented Systems**

As noted in the first part of this chapter, a key design consideration is the separation of **data** from the procedures which **process** it. In practice, this implies storage and updating of a data base independently of the various applications which depend on it for the various end-users.

(a) Object-oriented design procedures

With the aim of moving systems design as close as possible to the user, this separation of data and procedures is dropped in the approach known as 'object-oriented design methods', (OODM). The general approach has given rise to a number of related subjects, notable among which are object-oriented programming systems (OOPS), object-oriented technology (OOT) and object-oriented data base management systems (OODBMS).

(b) Object

The basic concept of the object-oriented design method is to define with the user self-contained modules each of which fulfils a complete set of functions, such as drawing a histogram of sales or calculation of the balance of a customer's account. These modules are called '**objects**'.

The advantage of the OODM approach is that it relates closely to the users' natural way of thinking. The systems analyst can readily define objects in discussion with users. The refinement of objects and the ways in which they interrelate can be explored further by prototyping.

(i) Implementation

The implementation of object-oriented systems, however, depends – as in all systems design approaches – on very carefully defined **boundaries** for each systems unit – in this case, the object. Especially important is the reconciliation between partly conflicting design aspects, namely the self-standing nature of each object and the need to update the data within it by calling on other objects. For this reason, object-oriented data base management systems represent a compromise between 'traditional' data base management systems, whereby central control is maintained over the main source of data, and objects, which operate their own data structures.

(ii) Programming languages

Certain programming languages are particularly suitable for the object-oriented approach. The essential feature that such languages must have is the 'class' construct. In the example cited earlier, a class called 'histogram' could be defined, characterised by a set of parameters for specifying the divisions and frequency distributions. Hence a class construct consists of a **data structure** and a set of **procedures**: the concept of an object in software terms. The class construct first appeared in the SIMULA language (otherwise similar to ALGOL) and subsequently in others, notably in the C++ language.

Self-check

In what way does the object-oriented approach differ from other design methods?

18.6 Data Dictionaries

As defined above, a data dictionary is a repository of information about the definition, structure and usage of data. That is to say it is a **data base of data about data**. As such, the data dictionary is a valuable tool throughout the entire system's life-cycle from project selection to the ongoing maintenance of the installed application system.

* In the early part of the system's life-cycle the data dictionary is valuable in identifying **what** data to be used in the proposed system is currently available in computer-readable form, **how** the data is defined, captured and validated, and the various **uses** to which the data is put. As the new system is defined, the role of the data dictionary (at this stage often as an element of a CASE tool, see Chapter 2) changes to one which defines and documents the data for the system.
* In the later stages of the system's life-cycle, the data dictionary becomes an essential part of the systems documentation supporting both routine operation and, especially, **maintenance**.
* In practice, data dictionaries tend to exist at two distinct levels.

- The first, which may be termed the 'departmental (or corporate) data dictionary' is usually a single package or system, often resident on a mainframe computer and frequently an adjunct of the main DBMS in use. Departmental data dictionaries normally focus on the data contained in existing operational systems.
- The second type of data dictionary, which may be termed a 'system data dictionary', often forms part of an analyst's workbench or CASE tool and is used by the systems analyst

and/or project team throughout the systems development process; it therefore focuses on a single system (although several such system data dictionaries may exist in the same organisation at any time). In is essential that adequate cross-reference exists between the various data dictionaries – and, especially, that an orderly transfer of data occurs from the system data dictionaries to the departmental data dictionary as part of the system **handover process**.

18.7 Data Administration

Data is, as we have seen, a major element of the complete systems development process and one which, moreover, impacts not just a single system but (through the interconnections of a data base used for multiple applications) a whole range of systems and users. Because of its importance and the wide-ranging ramifications of its use, most medium to large scale data processing installations appoint specialist data administrators to oversee the organisation's data resource. Three sub-specialties may be distinguished in this area, those of data strategist, data administrator and data base designer, although there may not be three separate job titles in any but the largest installations.

(a) Data strategist

The data strategist is responsible for the long-term evolution of data management within the organisation and liaises with the analysts in regular contact with system users on **future data base requirements**. The data strategist is also responsible for integrating the data base plans with the installation's application, hardware, software and personnel development plans.

(b) Data administrator

The data administrator **defines and models data** using the techniques of data analysis which were introduced in Chapter 15. He or she works in close cooperation with the systems analyst in preparing logical data base designs and in resolving **conflicts of data definition** which often arise within an organisation with a comprehensive data base environment. The data administrator is directly responsible for the maintenance of the **data dictionary**.

(c) Data base designers

The data base designer is concerned with the building, performance and fine tuning of physical data bases using the facilities of the available DBMS. Whereas the data strategist and data administrator are often from a systems analysis background, data base designers will have skills more akin to those of systems programmers.

Clearly, to achieve the objective of effective and efficient systems, the systems analyst has to work closely with each of the disciplines of data administration (and especially those of data strategist and data administrator) and know enough of their tools and techniques to be able to play a meaningful role in data management as it pertains to the projects on which he or she is employed.

Self-check

Distinguish between the differing roles of data strategist, data administrator and data base designer in the data processing installation.

---

19 Data Communications

19.1 Role of Data Communications in Systems Analysis

Every information system depends to some extent on **data communications**. Any process which forwards data from place to place is a form of data communications; this process may include such varying means as postal services or wired connections between parts of a central processor and its peripherals. It is, however, the exploitation of telecommunications facilities for transmitting data which is the normal meaning of the term 'data communications' today.

(a) What do data communications offer the system designer?

To the systems analyst, data communications are much more than a transportation mechanism. Many concepts in information system design become possible only through the use of data communications facilities. Examples are: on-line updating from geographically separate locations, interactive searching of remote data bases and electronic mail. Data communications offers the systems designer:

* **Speed**. Data is routinely transmitted today at rates of between 100 and 1000 characters per second and on high speed links can reach ten times that figure. This means that several sales orders of typical size can be transmitted in less than one second.
* **Accuracy and security**. The fact that data is captured in machine-readable form at or near its source has major advantages with regard to its subsequent accuracy and security. First, no further transcription processes are necessary to transfer data from one medium to another. Secondly, the risk of damage or loss to source data (otherwise usually in document form) during transit is avoided. Thirdly, the detection of most errors is immediate and the correction process can take place without delay.
* **Involvement of the user**. When direct contact between the user and the information system takes place, he or she has a greater

feeling of involvement. Rapid feedback, even when errors are signalled, enhances the role of the end-user and generally increases user satisfaction.

(b) Trade offs involved

The above advantages are not, of course, gained without some penalties, the primary ones of which are cost and the need for technical expertise. Careful balancing of the factors involved has to be undertaken in any systems design in which it is planned to use data communications facilities. These are discussed in section **19.2**.

19.2 **Design Factors**

There five main elements which the systems analyst has to examine when studying a system with regard to data communications.

(a) Traffic analysis

The **quantities** and **geographical distribution** of data are key factors in the design of a data communications system. Data flows can easily be measured for operational systems, but for new systems traffic estimates are often difficult to produce with any confidence. There is no easy solution to this estimation process and many assumptions will have to be made. A reasonable approach is as follows:

* For each location acting as a source or as a destination for data, estimate the number of basic **inputs** or **outputs** per day (or whatever time base is the most convenient). These basic inputs or outputs may be measured in the unit most suitable to the application concerned (e.g. order forms, enquiries, production report, financial statement, etc.).
* Estimate the **average volume of data** associated with each basic input or output.
* Calculate for each potential link (i.e. potential flow of data) the **average volume of traffic**.
* Estimate the **peak volumes of traffic** (e.g. that flowing in the busiest hour of the day or busiest week of the year). If no information at all is available, assume a peak volume of 3–4 times the average.

The figures derived from an estimation procedure such as this are needed for design decisions on the basic **configuration** of network facilities and for **loads** on the computer(s) handling the data.

(b) Response time

'Response time' is the delay between the last input from the user and the receipt of the first output again at the user end. In the context of data communications systems, this may cover a range of factors, such as efficiency of the local work station, transfer rates used in the network, computer time for processing the data, etc. and is subject to the peak load performance problems that the various components may be exposed to individually. Hence, response times are notoriously difficult to forecast at the design stage, and during implementation it is frequently necessary to make adjustments to the network facilities in order to meet user requirements.

As described in Chapter 5, **benchmark** tests can be very useful in indicating performance before the final design is implemented. It may be necessary to use **simulation techniques**, whereby a model of the system is subjected to different conditions (such as peak load) in order to assess the likely performance.

Activity

For any system with which you are familiar, measure the response time at the end-user work station. Compare this (empirically obtained) response time with the 'official' statistics of the EDP department. Calculate the standard deviation for the response time so observed. Ascertain whether your results are statistically valid. Why will deviation influence user reaction?

(c) Reliability and security

In addition to the general policies and techniques applicable to information systems design relating to reliability and security (see Chapter 7), two aspects are of particular importance in the context of data communications systems:

* **Backup**: Breakdown of equipment can cause very serious problems in data communications based systems. Front-end

processors, concentrators, switching nodes – malfunction in any of these can cause one or more links in a network to fail and, frequently, overloads to occur elsewhere in the network. Users may be cut off or at least suffer degradation of performance.

For this reason, backup hardware for key components is almost always part of network design. Alternative routeing also belongs to such design, and this is becoming more economical through the use of higher quality public facilities. The main design decisions in this area arise through trading costs of back-up hardware against the probability of failure in the different parts of the system, and the consequent costs to the organisation.

* **Access control**: The decentralised nature of most data communications systems increases the problem of access control. Physical control of access to work stations is sometimes difficult to ensure, and this places a greater burden on the basic system and applications controls for authorising access.

(d) Network components and configuration

The definition of what components are, and how they are arranged, is possible only after the preceding factors (traffic, response time, security) have been analysed in depth. There are five main building blocks:

* **Host processor**: This is the name commonly given to the computer system which **handles the applications**. When a user carries out data processing work via a terminal (e.g. retrieving data, updating a file, requesting a job to be run), he or she is therefore dealing with the host processor. There may well be a considerable amount of other equipment between the terminal and the host (such as control units, concentrators, front-end processors), but the user should not be aware of them. There may be more than one host accessible from the user's terminal and one of the functions of the system will be to help guide the user to the host he or she needs.
* **Servers**: Some hosts may be dedicated to particular functions (such as helping the user **select** a host or data base). These are commonly called servers and may be relatively small, a PC

often fulfilling the purpose. Other examples of servers are data base processors, communications servers on local area networks (LANs) and password management servers.

* **Work stations**: These are the devices with which the user **interfaces** with the network. Increasingly, they are usable as stand alone devices (such as a PC) and the connection to a network is initiated only when necessary. Work stations may include a range of other devices, such as printers, plotters, data capture equipment and controllers for allowing all the devices to function via the network. The role of the work station in systems design was discussed further in Chapter 17.
* **Network equipment**: Of major importance here are modems, control units, multiplexers, concentrators, nodes and front-end processors.

Modems are the hardware interfaces between data processing equipment and the telecommunications link over which the data is transmitted. They are often integrated with the equipment itself. An acoustic coupler can substitute for a modem when telephone lines are used by allowing a direct connection between a terminal and the (telephone) network.

Control units are pieces of telecommunications equipment which need not concern the systems analyst, except for their cost, number needed and data transfer rates. They are needed to match the various speeds of transmission of work stations and the telecommunications links used.

Multiplexers and **concentrators** are placed within a network at points where telecommunications links converge in order to allow sharing of links of relatively high data transfer rates. Traffic can be interleaved to minimise the cost of the telecommunications links.

A multiplexer is a simple hard-wired device with predetermined functions, whereas a concentrator has a programmable memory which allows it to carry out a number of operations when it concentrates or deconcentrates the data traffic, performing additional functions such as error control.

Nodes are intelligent switching devices which route the traffic, usually also performing concentrator functions, as well as management tasks, such as collection of statistics.

Front-end processors are computers dedicated to data communications functions and which control the traffic into and out from a host processor. Logically they are associated with a particular host, but physically they may be situated far away at the end of a long telecommunications link.

* **Communications links**: The term 'link' is used to describe the actual data communications path between two points (such as a work station and a computer).

  The medium used may be a digital, telephone or microwave connection. The major sources of communications links are the standard services of the telecommunications authorities. Dedicated links may also be rented or leased from the same sources. There is a major trend to offer more and more powerful dedicated data communications facilities and Integrated Services Digital Networks (ISDNs) are being built up in most industrialised countries.

  For the systems analyst, it is important to know that these networks primarily offer services using the 'X' series of packet-switched data communications standards (as defined by the international telecommunications body, the CCITT). However, other possibilities exist, notably the **videotex** services now offered nationally (and in some cases internationally) by the public telecommunications authorities. Within enclosed geographical sites, **local area networks** (LANs) are normally used; these do not operate using standardised communications protocols, though in practice the field is dominated by just a few well-known proprietary products (e.g. Ethernet). The connection of a LAN to a wide area network (WAN) therefore requires a special interface, which must be provided for in the overall design.

Activity

Ascertain the current cost structure for data communications within your own country. Compare data communications costs between two adjacent countries (e.g. the UK and France) and two widely separated countries (e.g. the UK and Australia). What, if any, restrictions apply to the transfer of data across the national boundaries involved?

---

* **Communications software**: The whole structure of a data communications system is held together through the data

communications software. This comprises many components held at different places in the system. A typical structure is shown in Figure 19.1.

- The host processor software is essentially an extension or part of the operating system supplied by the manufacturer, having the following functions:

  to prepare messages generated by the applications software for transmission and to initiate the transmission process
  to receive and acknowledge incoming messages and pass them to the applications software via the operating system
  to provide queueing facilities for incoming and outgoing messages
  to apply line control procedures
  to apply terminal control procedures (e.g. 'polling' – the systematic calling of terminals to invite them to send messages, if ready to transmit)
  to provide facilities for recovery from breakdowns, mainly to protect the data within its immediate control.

  These functions may be partially incorporated into a physically-separate front-end processor, dedicated for the purpose.
- The network software is likely to be outside the domain of the systems analyst. The wide area network facilities will be provided by the telecommunications authorities and the local area network software will be an integral part of the specific network chosen. In both cases (wide and local area networks), the main factors concerning the systems analyst will be **cost** and **technical standards** with which the facilties operate, since these determine the way the applications data must be presented to and received from the networks.
- The work station software is available only when programmable memory is present, as with PCs. The data communications control functions of such devices will normally be part of the proprietary software, but programmable memory in a work station connected to a data communications network is very important to the systems analyst, because it offers design options as to what tasks may be done locally and what can be carried out elsewhere – options which can have a major impact on **response times** and **system economics**.

Fig 19.1 *Typical structure of data communications software*

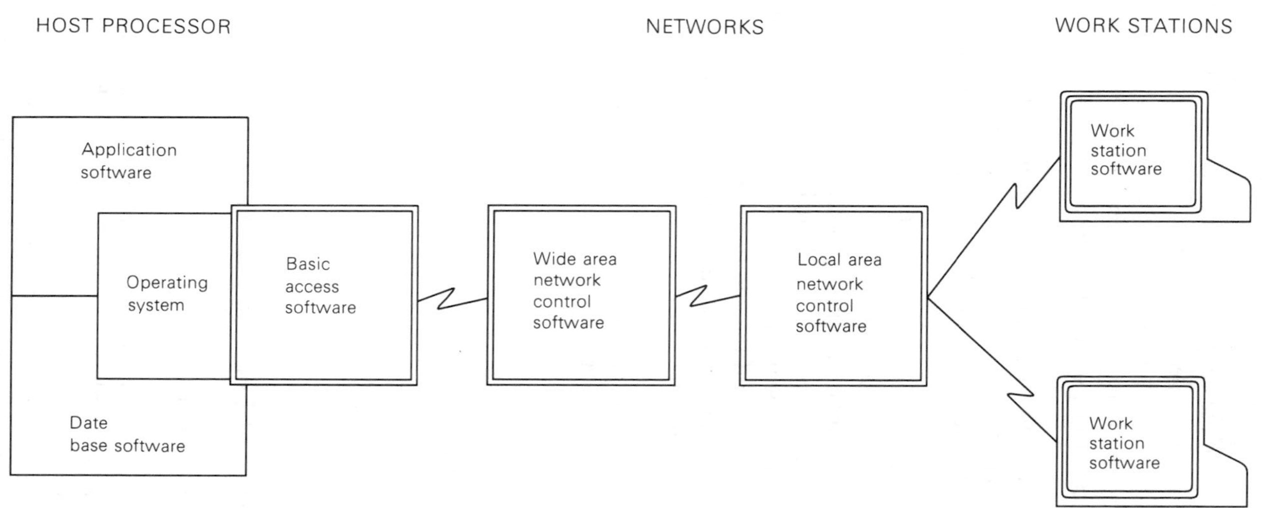

(e) Cost

The analysis of the design options and cost implications of the data communications aspects of a proposed system is just part of the overall cost-benefit treatment described in Chapter 16. It is, however, important to note certain cost elements which arise in most systems using data communications:

* Costs due to the **physical separation** of many of the systems components. Maintenance costs will be higher than systems on a single site, as will user support costs where visits are necessary.
* The **multiple vendor** effect. In most data communications systems, multiple vendors are involved: the telecommunications authority, suppliers of network hardware and software, modems, terminals, etc. Though there may well be a price advantage in acquisition costs, the cost calculation should also take into account the additional work needed by development and operations staff to deal with the multiple contracts and their interactions.

These costs, which are often **underestimated**, are important input to the decisions arising in the design, implementation and operation of data communications systems.

Self-check

What main design factors will be specifically associated with data communications systems?

19.3 Types of Function and Application

(a) General-purpose functions

Data communications networks can be used simply as a **transport mechanism** for applications which reside on host computers and which have users geographically remote from the host itself. The types of application commonly found are described in the last part of this section. However, there are some important functions of a general nature which are frequently offered as part of a network service. These have given rise to the term 'value-added networks' (VANs) to indicate that the network itself provides a service **beyond that of the simple transfer of data**. Notable among these network services are:

* **Electronic mail**: This is one of the most common and one of the most useful services offered by networks or hosts connected to networks. It enables users to send messages to each other with quite sophisticated possibilities for ensuring that the message has been received, read and/or acknowledged. Incoming messages are stored until dealt with and outgoing ones may be archived in various ways. It is possible to build entire applications around an electronic mail system, especially when there is a mix of user requirements with regard to standard and personal information.
* **Document delivery**: Although electronic mail is a form of document delivery, it generally falls short of file transfer. The bulk transmission of potentially lengthy texts requires **file transfer protocols**, which may not be part of an electronic mail facility. Hence some value-added networks offer document delivery as a special service.
* **Access to services in other networks**: An increasingly important function of networks is to provide gateways to other networks and information services. Although such access could be arranged on a user by user basis, there are advantages of simplicity, convenience and cost if the connection and billing process is handled by the user's 'own' network. Examples of the types of service where access to external networks can be very useful are electronic mail (to communicate with persons connected to other networks) and on-line data base services (such as those offering financial, news or techical information, which would be prohibitively costly to maintain in-house).
* **Directory, news and help services**: Most value-added networks provide their own information service to help users' awareness of the latest situation on what is available and what is planned. In addition, some help facilities are normally available for the user.
* **Accounting functions**: Monitoring and billing facilities give certain information to users of the network on their particular usage of the various facilities.

(b) Types of application

Some very simple uses of data communications are among the most effective systems to be found. In other cases, substantial benefits arise only when complete and sophisticated facilities have been created. The following classification is intended to indicate the types of application which have been developed using different types of data communications.

* **Off-line data transmission**: This is the simplest use of data transmission. Data is sent from one terminal to another without involving any computer. An example would be the daily collection of sales statistics from regional outlets.
* **Remote batch transmission**: This type of transmission allows the submission of batch data processing directly to a central computer from a remote location using a terminal. As in off-line transmission, immediate turnaround is not a prime requirement, though generally the delay between job entry and receiving results is at most a matter of hours. This makes it suitable for many kinds of application, varying from salary processing to scientific computing. Furthermore, a work station used primarily for local processing can act as a remote batch terminal for those jobs where greater computing capacity is required.
* **On-line data collection**: In many applications it is useful to collect data as events occur and then update the main file(s) from time to time as needed. This approach does not imply real-time updating (see below) and is much less costly to implement. The data collection process is on-line, but the updating takes place in batch mode at high priority.

  An example of this type of application is in a retail store chain, which might collect data constantly from its point-of-sale terminals located in the branches and then process the data at head office at certain defined intervals (e.g. close of business for the day, staff shift change, etc.). This type of application uses local network facilities constantly, but makes relatively low use of long-distance facilities.
* **Enquiry-response applications**: These applications are probably the most common of those making use of data communications. Although the data volumes exchanged are normally low (very low for input, with bursts of medium-volume output), the

essence of their usefulness lies in the speed of the system. This does not depend only on the data communications facilities, of course, but also on the efficiency of the host processor in handling the user's requests. Typically, the user will initiate a request for information from the system via a terminal by keying in commands and being guided by the system itself until the desired information is presented. Figure 19.2 takes the example an information system on the capital assets of a company, showing how an exchange might go:

Fig 19.2 *Enquiry–response dialogue: information system on the capital assets of a company*

(System) WHAT CAPITAL ASSETS ARE YOU INTERESTED IN? THE FOLLOWING AREAS ARE ON FILE:
1 PRODUCTION MACHINERY
2 OFFICE FURNITURE
3 BUILDINGS
4 VEHICLES
5 MISCELLANEOUS

(User) 3

(System) AT WHAT LOCATIONS ARE THE BUILDINGS? THE FOLLOWING LOCATIONS ARE ON FILE:
1 LONDON
2 BIRMINGHAM
3 PARIS
4 NEW YORK
5 OTHER

(User) 2

(System) THE FOLLOWING BUILDING IN BIRMINGHAM IS ON FILE:
1 WAREHOUSE AT 147 KIDSBURY AVENUE
DO YOU WISH FULL INFORMATION?

(User) Y

(System) WAREHOUSE AT 147 KIDSBURY AVENUE, BIRMINGHAM

	£
PURCHASE VALUE	258,000
DEPRECIATION	180,000
INSURED FOR	300,000

etc.

Figure 19.2 illustrates a dialogue approach, but a frequent user of such a system would probably want to ask directly for information on buildings in Birmingham. As discussed in Chapter 7, options should be provided for a direct enquiry by an experienced user and for a system-guided approach for the less sure. Undoubtedly, enquiry-response systems are among the most attractive uses of data communications. The benefits are usually well-recognised by the user, even if they are not directly measurable. Frequently there is willingness on the part of users to experiment with the system, which sometimes leads to additional unforeseen benefits.

* **Real-time systems**: All the applications discussed so far in this section have had the common feature of not involving immediate updating of a data base each time a new piece of data arrives. This action of on-line updating is, however, the characteristic of the last major class of applications: real-time systems.

Such systems are needed whenever the information has to be completely **up-to-date** in order to take action or decisions. Familiar examples are to be found in banking, production control, reservation systems of all types, etc. but increasingly also in administrative systems where the operational effectiveness of the organisation is improved through the certainty that the information held does indeed reflect the exact current situation. Hence, personnel management, budgetary control and sales planning are all examples of where real-time systems are providing effective solutions to ordinary operational needs.

The hardware, software and network demands are correspondingly high, particularly with regard to ensuring the integrity of data under all operational conditions and maintaining performance levels while handling highly variable numbers of users.

Furthermore, the management of real-time systems involves certain problems not experienced in other types of system, such as the phasing-in of modifications to the applications software. Real-time systems represent a big opportunity for systems developers, but involve commensurately higher costs and expertise. The decision to implement such a system should therefore be taken only after a very thorough analysis of the

needs of the organisation balanced against the **commitment** required for development.

Self-check

What is the key factor which distinguishes a real-time system from other types of data communications system?

---

20 Management Considerations

There are many aspects of systems analysis which are **strategic** in nature and which relate to the management of systems development rather than to any one particular initiative. This chapter considers some of the most important issues which influence the successful management of systems development.

20.1 End-user Computing

The widespread use of personal computers has enabled many end-users to develop information systems themselves. The benefits to an organisation of such systems are great, though extremely difficult to measure. The systems analyst's role in end-user systems is limited by the size of the task, but there are certain areas where guidance is essential if the organisation is to protect its investments.

(a) Data definition and strategy

Although systems developed at end-user level are in principle based mainly on 'local' data (i.e. data originating within the department concerned), this data may be of interest to other departments and it is rare that a department uses no data at all from external sources. It is the responsibility of the systems analyst to ensure that there is a minimum degree of **consistency** and **coherence** between departmental systems in terms of data definitions, duplication, data base design, etc.

(b) Security

The systems analyst should ensure that end-users are aware of the security precautions appropriate for their own situation. In particular, this implies consideration of the **confidentiality** of data and procedures relating to **damaged** data (backup, recovery, etc.). Further aspects of security are examined later in this chapter.

(c) Standards

Standards save time in development and maintenance, as well as assuring minimum levels of **quality** and **consistency**. It is therefore particularly important that standards are used in end-user computing. The problem is that many end-users are not aware of the existence of standards relevant to their own situation and so the systems analyst has again a vital role to play. An example which serves to prove the point with users is the adoption of a common system for the naming of data elements and labelling of files. Standards and documentation are discussed in more detail in section **20.3** below.

(d) Conformity with systems development strategy

Although the end-user may have considerable freedom in the specifics of systems development, the main systems principles applied must – for the sake of the organisation as a whole – fall within the overall systems development strategy. If not, major long-term problems gradually set in, such as incompatibility between data, hardware and software, dependence on individuals, difficulty of maintenance, problems arising from having too many different suppliers, etc. The systems development department should therefore define and disseminate an **overall systems development strategy**, including hardware and software choice and acquisition, to end-users, and **monitor** its application.

(e) Responsibility for maintenance

Most systems developed by end-users need to be modified in the course of time, as needs evolve. If the individuals or suppliers responsible for the original system are still available, then such modifications are normally possible. The difficulty arises when the current user has 'inherited' the system and there exists little or no documentation to aid the maintenance process. It is therefore essential that the systems analyst makes end-users aware of the demands of possible **future maintenance** at the time when the systems are created.

(f) Ergonomic and human factors

A frequently overlooked aspect of systems design and implementation is that of matching the **system** to the physical and psychological needs at the **work place**. Familiarity with ergonomic principles concerning such factors as physical layout is essential knowledge for the systems analyst, but so are aspects related to work organisation, avoidance of stress, and software ergonomics, which are very important in ensuring the best conditions for working with the new system. This knowledge rarely exists at the end-user level and it is a further key function of the systems analyst to give advice on these aspects, or at least to draw attention to them.

(g) The information centre

In order to support end-user computing, many organisations have implemented the concept of the information centre, with the key functions of:

* help-desk availability
* consultancy role on a wide range of end-user questions
* support in analysing user needs and implementing systems
* training
* market monitoring of available products and services which could be useful to end-users
* dissemination of general information of the guidelines and newsletter type.

The information centre approach is a powerful way of enhancing the usefulness of new information technology and is a valuable source of information for the systems analyst on end-user feedback, evolving needs and on the impact of information systems on the organisation.

Activity

Make contact with an information centre in an organisation you know and ascertain its main tasks, with estimates of the proportions of time spent by its staff on fulfilling the different tasks (help-desk, training, etc.).

(h) Organisation needs

Finally, with regard to the expanding use of end-user computing, the systems analyst has the responsibility to ensure that all parts of the organisation, with or without personal computers and with or without the local skills to develop systems on them, are taken fully into account when the information needs and priorities of the existing or potential user departments are assessed. This implies alertness to the broad needs of the organisation, rather than commitment to lines of development determined primarily by local needs.

20.2 Quality Control

For systems management, quality objectives are some of the most difficult to define. For users, it is a matter of wanting totally **reliable** systems that fully meet their **operational needs**. This is much too broad an objective for systems management, and that is why the objectives for quality have to be specified in a more practical form.

Self-check

How do you think quality control objectives can be set?

(a) Overall and specific goals

It is essential to distinguish between the overall goals for quality and those specific to each new system.

* The overall goals for quality should form an integral part of systems strategy and should include statements of the following type:

  quality is a major objective in all services provided by the systems department
  service availability during working hours should be (say) 99.5%
  requests for urgent help will be initially responded to within (say) 5 minutes of the user support personnel (e.g. the Infocentre) being contacted, during normal working hours
  no system will be installed without adequate training and documentation being provided to the users

user involvement and responsibility is an integral part of systems development and should follow agreed steps (as described in Part I)
the enhancement and maintenance process will be carefully controlled to ensure that installed systems continue to meet the quality objectives.

* The specific goals for quality in individual systems should include:

acceptable error rates
security, confidentiality and recovery characteristics
provable correctness of data and traceability of any data movement or modification (audit trail)
performance characteristics
documentation requirements
level of training required for the various tasks involved.

(b) Quality control

Quality control embraces most aspects of systems development. The means for achieving quality assurance are therefore an integral part of systems analysis. This gives rise to the danger that quality control is so all-pervasive that it is accepted as a principle without practical steps being taken to assure its realisation. The main tools for achieving quality in practical terms are through an effective systems development methodology, through good standards and documentation and through good training. Each of these areas is complementary to the other two and all three are essential for successful quality assurance. For larger systems development departments, it is strongly recommended that the functions of quality control be specifically allocated to one or more individuals. Only in this way can the different elements of quality assurance be effectively brought together. Furthermore, on major projects the responsibility for quality assurance should be allocated to a specific individual.

Activity

Examine any operational information system known to you and assess the measures applied to assure and monitor its quality.

20.3 Standards and Documentation

Standards and documentation are one of the key means by which management are assured of levels of quality, maintaining project schedules and security.

(a) Standards

Well-defined working methods, procedures and technical standards are essential for a professional approach to systems development. Particularly important are:

* the methodologies used for systems analysis, design and implementation
* project management and control
* performance standards
* security
* operational procedures
* data interchange standards.

(i) Sources of standards
A great body of knowledge is available on standards, and this should be drawn upon in building up the relevant set for a particular organisation. Among the sources of standards are:

* standards organisations
* user groups and other individual users
* informal standards already in use.

(ii) Standards manual
The most practical way of applying standards is through a standards manual. This manual should cover all areas of systems development and and must be available to every member of the staff. The manual should clearly indicate which standards are mandatory and which are of the 'guideline' type. It is often best to introduce a standard first as a guideline and then move it to 'mandatory' after sufficient experience and confidence has been gained with it in practice.

Activity

Examine a standards manual and note its contents. How is it kept up-to-date?

For ease of updating and expansion, the standards manual should obey the rules of good documentation, described below.

(b) Documentation

Only through the physical presence of documentation do standards come alive. Indeed, there is much truth in the saying 'Standards through documentation'.

A number of basic principles are common to all good documentation systems and care should be taken to comply with these when introducing standards:

* All documentation must be clearly **identified** and **dated**. This identification should include a title, reference number, the name of the author or source, sheet number and date of preparation or issue.
* To facilitate easy referencing, it is advisable for this information to be contained in one designated area of each document, applied if possible to all internal documentation. For filing purposes, this identification box should be on the right-hand edge of the page, and because most people refer to documents by turning over the upper edges of the form, the top right-hand corner is preferable. An example of a simple report form, which is universally applicable and which meets the criteria described above, is shown in Figure 20.1.
* Each document should deal with **one topic only**. In the short run, this requirement may mean the creation of more documents than may seem necessary, but the justification will quickly be realised when amendments are made. Furthermore, this approach enables specific documents (especially those related to the specification of data elements) to be used in the documentation of other systems. This concept of **unit documents** being assembled to form total systems documentation is essentially similar to the concept of modular programs.

* Documentation must be prepared with the specific intention of its use by **other persons**. This means that all documents must be readily understandable for training and other purposes, such as maintenance by new personnel.
* There should be clear procedures for the **handling** and **storage** of documents. Among the points to be stressed here are: the maintenance of a full set of documentation for each system in a central point from which they may not be taken away, and a duplicate set of documentation stored in a different place to guard against the effects of fire or other potential damage or loss. The use of software tools in systems development greatly aids the process of documentation. Much of the documentation can be created, stored and maintained in electronic form.
* All documents should follow the principles of **good forms design**. The following points are of particular importance:

  1 An adequate **filing margin** should be included on each page
  2 Standard sizes of **paper** should be used; this not only eases problems of handling, but also greatly facilitates reproduction
  3 Adequate space should be available for any area where **new data or text** may be required
  4 Each document should be designed specifically with **reproduction** in view: colours, lines, etc. should therefore be selected with suitablility for reproduction in mind
  5 For revisions or updates of previously issued documents, the changes should be clearly indicated, for example by the use of **side bars** in the margins.

* Finally, documentation should be a **natural by-product of systems analysis and design**. As far as possible, systems documentation should be based on documents which need to be created anyway as part of the systems development process. This also makes documentation more acceptable both to those who create it, and to those who use it. Many of the documents forming part of the systems analysis and design process can be produced through the use of CASE tools. As an example of the type of document that is an integral part of the systems analysis and design process, as well as part of the permanent record, Figure 20.2 shows a form for specifying a data element; the completed form is presented in Figure 20.3 for a sample data element 'Part Number'.

REPORT FORM

Reference number	
Title	
Sheet number	
Author	
Date	

Fig 20.1 *Report form*

20.4 Physical Security

In Chapter 7, the need to address security aspects during systems design was stressed. In addition to considerations specific to each application, however, it is management's responsibility to ensure that there are adequate **generic controls** to ensure the overall physical security of the information systems resource.

Self-check

What are the main areas with which management should be concerned with regard to the physical security of information systems?

(a) Controls required

There are seven main controls necessary for ensuring physical security of information systems:

* **Access to facilities**
  Control over access to computer facilities and the means of acquiring sensitive data is an essential part of maintaining adqeuate security. This control should include not only restrictions on **access** to computer **rooms**, **PCs** and **terminals**, but also to **systems documentation**. A frequently overlooked aspect is that of **output control** – much sensitive data is highly protected within the computer system, only to end up in printed form lying on people's desks and, eventually, in wastepaper bins!
* **Natural hazard protection**
  This area of security covers fire, flood, storm and riot protection and should, of course, be provided as standard for all systems. Prior to implementation, however, the analyst should check that adequate safeguards in the form of **duplicate software** and **data bases** will be created and maintained in a location remote from the data processing centre.
* **Backup, recovery and contingency planning**
  Procedures for recovery from security incidents should be **defined** and **rehearsed**, including transfer of critical applications to a backup facility (which may be another user with whom a reciprocal arrangement has been signed). Included in contingency planning is the need for appropriate **insurance** to cover some or all of the costs of loss and recovery.
* **Control of documentation, system releases, etc**
  There is need for close control over the library of documentation and software. The purpose is to ensure absolutely that in

Fig 20.2 *Data element description form*

	DATA ELEMENT DESCRIPTION		
		Reference number	
		Title	
		Sheet number	
		Author	
		Date	
Description	Data type:	Basic	
		Constant	
		Variable	
		Resultant	
	Justification	Left	
		Right	
	No. of characters:	Fixed – Actual	
		Variable – minimum	
		– maximum	
	Value range:	Constant	
		Variable – minimum	
		– maximum	
	Picture:		

Use	Input				Data base				Output			
	Ref.	Fre-quency	Use per frequency	Total p.a.	Ref.	Fre-quency	Items/file	Total p.a.	Ref	Fre-quency	Use per frequency	Total p.a

Program use			

Fig 20.3 *Completed data element description form*

DATA ELEMENT DESCRIPTION		
	Reference number	*04167*
	Title	*Part number data definition (part no.)*
	Sheet number	*1 of 1*
	Author	*A. N. Analyst*
	Date	*3rd January 1991*

Description

	Basic	√
Data type:	Constant	
	Variable	
	Resultant	
Justification	Left	√
	Right	
No. of characters:	Fixed – Actual	7
	Variable – minimum	
	– maximum	
Value range:	Constant	
	Variable – minimum	*A001400*
	– maximum	*G876500*
Picture:	*X 999999*	

Use

Input				Data base				Output			
Ref.	Fre-quency	Use per frequency	Totalp.a.	Ref.	Fre-quency	Items/ file	Totalp.a.	Ref.	Fre-quency	Use per frequency	Total p.a.
STOR 7	*Daily*	÷ *100*	*25,000*	*O4M*	*Daily*	*10,000*	*2,500,000*	*STOR 40*	*Daily*	÷ *110*	*27,500*
STOR 4	*Daily*	÷ *10*	*2500*					*STOR 41*	*Weekly*	÷ *10,000*	*500,000*
STOR 77	*Week*	÷ *1000*	*50,000*					*STOR 42*	*Monthy*	÷ *10,000*	*12,000*

Program use

ST 4 1 A		
ST 4 6 A		
ST 4 8 C		
ST 1 1 B		

a given situation the correct version of the software is used with the right data. This is greatly aided by the use of specialised software available for controlling system releases. In addition, routine **housekeeping procedures** of the computer centre with regard to labelling of output, preventative maintenance, etc. form part of the overall controls to assure the security of the information resource.

* **Use of external resources**
  Specific attention should be given to security aspects where the use of outside resources is concerned, including:

  network services, because of the risk of unauthorised access to internal systems via an external network connection
  service bureaux, because of the risk that third parties may accidentally or deliberately gain access to confidential information or software
  personnel, because of the risk that they may take, amend or use data or software on leaving
  software, because of the risk of viruses.

* **Statistics and monitoring**
  One of the most important management tools for assuring security is the analysis of routine statistics on **incidents**. The frequency and nature of attempted breaches of security are key indicators to the security requirements of the informations systems concerned.
* **Privacy legislation**
  Many countries have legislation concerning the protection of personal data and it is management's duty to ensure that the information systems in their organisation conform to these legal requirements. In the United Kingdom, the Data Protection Act of 1984 provides for all computerised records falling within the scope of the Act (primarily all personnel files maintained by commercial and public administrations) to be registered with the publically appointed Data Registrar and for the use of such files to be confined to the designated users and purposes stated. In 1991 the European Commission proposed similar measures to be applied throughout the European Community, with the notable addition that the legislation is to apply not only to computerised files but also manually maintained files.

(b) Security strategy

The security strategy for information resources should include generic controls of the type described, which complement those specific measures built into the design of each application. Finally, it is essential to build into the **overall budget** adequate means for meeting the requirements identified above.

20.5 Organisation

The task faced by systems management is how to encourage development and growth of information systems while at the same time being able to plan and control accurately the use of resources. This responsibility is made more difficult by the fact that much of the development work is user driven and not completely within the sphere of control of systems management. Furthermore, every project breaks new ground to some extent and planning is subject to the classical problems of uncertainty associated with any development activity. Various organisational approaches have been applied to meet this challenge of managing systems development. The three key concepts are as follows:

(a) Steering committee

Whatever name it is given, a group having the function of a steering committee is a useful way of providing general guidance for the development of systems within the organisation. Its role should be strictly limited to matters of **policy and priorities**: involvement in short-term or operational matters will dilute the effectiveness of the systems department. The main aims of such a steering committee are to:

* strengthen the links to top management
* ensure that systems development contributes to the goals of the organisation as a whole
* provide a monitoring and reporting mechanism on the main lines of progress
* give guidance to the systems department on priorities and resource planning.

The steering committee should be chaired by a member of senior management and should include the heads of major user departments and the head of the systems department. If possible, the **internal auditor** should also be a member of the steering committee. Meetings should take place about once every 2 months for half a day or less and should be triggered by milestones, such as preparation of the annual budget, a consultant's report, year-end report, a proposal for a new security policy, etc.

(b) User involvement

A major benefit arising from the work of a steering committee is the involvement of **user management** in the systems development process. Such involvement helps to ensure that user requirements are properly formulated and that the resulting systems are fully accepted. Furthermore, the steering committee is a good forum for review of **experience**, both benefits and problems, arising from the use of well run-in information systems. However, user involvement is a concept that applies not only to the steering committee, but throughout user departments. A good systems analyst will spend much of his or her time in close interaction with staff in the user departments – end-users and line management. For large projects, a project steering committee comprising the parties involved is a helpful way of gaining collaboration and consensus on all policy issues.

(c) Budgetary planning and control

All development work involves **uncertainty**. This makes budgetary planning and control all the more important, difficult though it may be. Experience shows that systems development is frequently subject to escalating costs and that only through strong management control of budgetary (and other) resources can project objectives be met. It is therefore important that adequate manpower and skills are allocated to this important function, both for overall planning and control and for individual projects.

Activity

In an organisation with which you are familiar, describe the management procedures applied to deal with: (i) proposals for new data processing projects; (ii) coordination among user departments; (iii) security of the information resource; (iv) preparation of the annual budget for data processing; (v) reporting to top management on progress with information systems.

Bibliography

Part I The Nine Steps of Systems Analysis

Boar, B. H., *Application Prototyping*, New York, Wiley, 1984.

Boardman, J., *Systems Engineering: An Introduction*, Englewood Cliffs, NJ, Prentice-Hall, 1990.

Davis, G. B. and Olson, M. H., *Management Information Systems: Conceptual Foundations, Structure and Development*, 2nd edn, New York, McGraw-Hill, 1985.

Holloway, S., *Methodology Handbook for Information Managers*, Aldershot, Gower, 1989.

Martin, J., *Strategic Data-Planning Methodologies*, Englewood Cliffs, NJ, Prentice-Hall, 1982

Yourdon, E. and Constantine, L. L., *Structured Design*, 2nd edn, New York, Yourdon, 1978.

Part II Techniques

Ball, R., *Management Techniques and Quantitative Methods*, London, Heinemann, 1984.

De Marco, T., *Structured Analysis and System Specification*, New York, Yourdon, 1978.

Gane, C. and Sarson, T., *Structured Systems Analysis: Tools and Techniques*, Englewood Cliffs, NJ, Prentice-Hall, 1979.

Martin, J. and McClure, C., *Diagramming Techniques for Analysts and Programmers*, Englewood Cliffs, NJ, Prentice-Hall, 1985.

Martin, J. and McClure, C., *Structured Techniques for Computing*, Englewood Cliffs, NJ, Prentice-Hall, 1985.

Peters, L., *Advanced Structured Analysis and Design*, London, Prentice-Hall International, 1988.

Rock-Evans, R., *A Simple Introduction to Data and Activity Analysis*, Sutton, Computer Weekly, 1989.

Roetzheim, W. H., *Structured Design Using HIPO II*, Englewood Cliffs, NJ, Prentice-Hill, 1990.

Stanton, N., *Communication* (Professional Masters Series), London, Macmillan, 1990.

Part III General Systems Considerations

Bull, M., *Students' Guide to Databases*, London, Heinemann, 1990.

Deen, S. M., *Principles and Practice of Data Base Systems*, London, Macmillan, 1985.

De Marco, T., *Controlling Software Projects: Management Measurement and Estimation*, Englewood Cliffs, NJ, Prentice-Hall, 1982.

Devargas, M., *Introducing the Information Centre*, Oxford, Blackwell, 1991.

Gandoff, M., *Students' Guide to Data Communications*, London, Heinemann, 1990.

Keen, J., *Managing Systems Development*, 2nd edn, Chichester, Wiley, 1987.

Kitihara, Y., *Information Network System: Telecommunications in the Twenty-First Century*, Tokyo, Telecommunications Association Japan, 1982.

Lane, V. P., *Security of Computer Based Systems*, London, Macmillan, 1985.

McFadden, F. R. and Hoffer, J. A., *Data Base Management*, 2nd edn, Menlo Park, Ca., Benjamin Cummings, 1988.

Otway, H. J. and Peltu, M., *New Office Technology: Human and Organizational Considerations*, London, Frances Pinter, 1983.

Shackel, B. and Richardson, S., *Human Factors for Informatics Usability*, Cambridge University Press, 1991.

Stanczyk, S., *Theory and Practice of Relational Databases*, London, Pitman, 1990.

Stamper, D. A., *Business Data Communications*, 2nd edn, Menlo Park, Ca., Benjamin Cummings, 1989.

Working with Visual Display Units, Occupational Safety and Health Series No. 61, Geneva, International Labour Office, 1989.

Glossaries and Background Reading

Anderson, R., *Management, Information Systems and Computers: An Introduction*, London, Macmillan, 1986.

Bingham, R., *Data Processing*, 2nd edn (Professional Masters Series), London, Macmillan, 1989.

Boehm, B., *Software Engineering Economics*, Englewood Cliffs, NJ, Prentice-Hall, 1981.

Cawkell, A. E. (ed.) *Handbook of Information Technology and Office Systems*, Amsterdam, Elsevier, 1986.

Jowett, P. and Rothwell, M., *The Economics of Information Technology*, London, Macmillan, 1986.

Longley, D. and Shain, M., *Macmillan Dictionary of Information Technology*, 2nd edn, London, Macmillan, 1985.

Sippl, C. J., *Macmillan Dictionary of Data Communications*, 2nd edn, London, Macmillan, 1985.

Strassman, P., *Information Payoff*, Aldershot, Gower, 1985.

Thimbleby, H., *User Interface Design*, Reading, Mass., Addison-Wesley, 1990.

Wright, G. G. L., *Mastering Computers*, London, Macmillan, 1982.

Index